THE MARINE CORPS

THE MARINE CORPS

B. L. CRUMLEY

FOREWORD BY
LT. COL. JON T. HOFFMAN, USMCR

THUNDER BAY
P · R · E · S · S
San Diego, California

Thunder Bay Press
An imprint of the Advantage Publishers Group
5880 Oberlin Drive, San Diego, CA 92121–4794
www.advantagebooksonline.com

Editorial and design by
Amber Books Ltd
Bradley's Close
74–77 White Lion Street
London N1 9PF
England

ISBN 1-57145-784-4

Library of Congress Cataloging-in-Publication Data available upon request.

1 2 3 4 5 06 05 04 03 02

Project Editor: Charles Catton
Designer: Zoë Mellors
Editor: Caroline Curtis
Picture Research: Beth Crumley and Lisa Wren

Printed and bound in Italy

Contents

FOREWORD

A corps of American Marines has existed almost since the first days of the Revolutionary War in 1775. With the end of the Continental Navy following that conflict, American Marines also briefly passed from the scene, to reemerge simultaneously with the U.S. Navy in 1794. They have been a fixture of the American military scene ever since, despite numerous attempts—by economy-minded government officials, the Army, and even sometimes the Navy—to do away with them. Marines, in fact, do stand out as an apparent redundancy. They fight on the ground like the Army, in the air like the Air Force, and at sea with the Navy. And yet the American people, with their will expressed on numerous occasions via their representatives in Congress, have kept the Marines in existence.

What has sparked and fanned this affection for the smallest of the U.S. armed forces? One answer might be the simple American penchant for rooting for the underdog, which the Marines often are when they fight with the bigger military branches for personnel and budget dollars. Another may be the resourcefulness of Marines, who seem to always be on correct and cutting edge of innovation. It was the Corps that focused its energy on amphibious operations before World War II and thus played an outsize role in making Allied victory possible. It was the Corps that foresaw the value of the helicopter and first brought it to bear on the battlefield in the Korean War. It was the Corps that developed the concept of maritime pre-positioning of equipment and supplies, which proved so critical in the early days of Operation Desert Shield. But perhaps most important of all, Marines have demonstrated time and again their readiness to fight on a moment's notice and their ability to win, even against the odds.

In this short and stirring account, Beth L. Crumley has brought to life the story of the Corps in peace and war. She has managed to convey not only the facts and deeds but also the emotions that make up the history of one of the world's finest military institutions.

Lt. Col. Jon T. Hoffman, USMCR

Left: Members of the Marine Corps in full dress uniform parade during a ceremony at the Marine Corps Memorial in Washington, D.C.

Chapter One

The Early Years

"Resolved, That two battalions
of marines be raised ... that they be
inlisted and commissioned to serve for
and during the present war between Great
Britain and the colonies, unless dismissed
by order of Congress: that they be
distinguished by the names of the first and
second battalions of American marines."
Thus was the Marine Corps born,
on November 10, 1775.

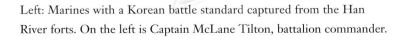

Left: Marines with a Korean battle standard captured from the Han
River forts. On the left is Captain McLane Tilton, battalion commander.

It had been a tumultuous year for the colonies. Seven months before, the American revolution had begun with the battles of Lexington and Concord. Throughout the fall, the Second Continental Congress, meeting in Philadelphia, had debated the subject of a Continental Navy. By February 17, 1776, the debate was over. A contingent of eight ships sailed down the icy Delaware River, bound for the Bahamas. It was the first deployment of the Continental Navy. Under the command of Commodore Esek Hopkins was the flagship *Alfred* with her 24 guns. Beside her sailed the *Columbus*, the *Andrea Doria*, and the *Cabot*. The sloops *Hornet* and *Providence* were nearby, as were the schooners *Wasp* and *Fly*. Sailing with the Continental Navy were 234 enlisted Marines under the command of Captain Samuel Nicholas. Hopkins planned to seize the capital city of Nassau, on the northern side of New Providence Island. The harbor was guarded by Forts Montague and Nassau. A secret report to Congress claimed a large cache of military stores were located there. Hopkins hoped to obtain casks of gunpowder, desperately needed by Washington's Army.

On March 3, 1776, Samuel Nicholas and his Marines executed the first amphibious landing in Marine history when they came ashore on New Providence Island. The landing was unopposed and Fort Montague was secured. At dawn, Captain Nicholas led his men to Fort Nassau, which was surrendered after a few cannon shots. The British colors were taken down and the Marines raised the Grand Union. When the Continental Navy sailed two weeks later, they took with them 3 captured British ships, 24 casks of gunpowder, cannons, and brass mortars. For his role in the New Providence raid, Captain Nicholas was promoted to the rank of major and ordered to raise four more companies of Marines. These men were to man the tops and the great guns of four new frigates.

By December 1776, a series of British attacks had Washington's Army on the run. Told "the Enemy having overrun the Jerseys, & our Army being greatly reduced," Nicholas was

Right: This painting by James Bingham depicts Marine recruiting at Philadelphia's Tun Tavern. According to Marine Corps legend, the proprietor, Robert Mullen, secured recruits by plying them with drink.

ordered to Trenton. He took with him a "battalion" of 131 Marines, and for the first time, Marines joined an American army in a land campaign. On New Year's Day, 1777, Washington dispatched a force to delay any advance of the British Army, under the command of Major-General Charles Cornwallis. Fighting with the Philadelphia brigade, under the command of Colonel John Cadwalader, the Marines took up position along Assunpink Creek. There the British attempted to cross, but were stopped.

The delaying action gave Washington the time he needed. That night, in the bitter cold, the Continental Army left their campfires burning. They slipped around the left flank of Cornwallis' army and marched toward Princeton. In the morning, Washington divided his forces into two columns. One column, to which the Marines were attached, was to cut the main road from Trenton to Princeton. That column, however, ran into three British regiments and was beginning to falter when Washington rode up and rallied the brigade for a charge against Cornwallis's men. As reinforcement arrived, the tide of the battle turned. It was now the British who were on the run, retreating north. For the "soldiers of the sea," their first land campaign was at an end. Washington's forces moved to their winter quarters in Morristown, New Jersey. Nicholas's "battalion" was down to 80 men.

As the Continental Navy grew, so did the Marines. By 1778, there were 11 detachments of Marines afloat. They fought from the rigging, firing muskets or dropping grenades onto British ships. Often, the Marines manned the great guns, serving as artillerymen. It was from the Marine detachments that boarding parties and raiding parties were formed, carrying the battles onto enemy ships or enemy-held shores.

On January 27, a 28-man detachment off the frigate *Providence* made a second amphibious assault on New Providence Island. The objective was the seizure of the British privateer *Mary*, which was being overhauled at Nassau. Led ashore in darkness by Captain John Trevett, the Marines slipped through a gap in Fort Nassau's palisade. Guarded only

Above: Captain Samuel Nicholas examines Marine recruits on Philadelphia's docks. Behind them is one of the new ships of the Continental Navy. By 1778, 11 detachments of the Marines served with the Continental Navy, firing muskets, battling from the rigging, and dropping grenades onto their British enemy.

Above: On the morning of February 3, 1777, General Washington rallied his forces. Marines who were under the command of Samuel Nicholas fighting with the Continental Army engaged three British regiments near Princeton, eventually forcing the British to retreat and head north, and bringing to an end the Marines' first land campaign.

by two watchmen, the Marines quickly secured the fort. Trevett informed Nassau's town council his orders were to seize the *Mary*. The council decided not to intervene, and the Marines held Nassau for four days, then sailed with the *Mary* and four captured American ships they had discovered in the harbor.

Later that year, Continental Marines accompanied John Paul Jones on the raid of Whitehaven in the Solway Firth. Jones, a fiery Scot, commanded the *Ranger*. On the night of April 22, Jones and a landing party of 30 men rowed ashore. It was the first time since 1667 that a foreign enemy had landed on British soil. Scaling the wall of the fort that guarded the southern end of the harbor, they found the gunners asleep at their post. Jones took them prisoner and spiked the guns. After repeating the feat at the northern battery, Jones procured a torch from a public house and set alight the hold of a large ship. However, the townspeople, alerted that Yankee pirates were burning the shipping in the harbor, extinguished the fires, and Jones and his men made their escape back to the *Ranger*.

The Marines who landed at Penobscot Bay, Maine, the following year were not so fortunate. A large British force, including the Argyll Highlanders and three sloops-of-war, had moved down from Halifax to establish a fort at the mouth of the Penobscot River. The fort was to serve as an advanced base from which to strike American privateers and to protect a colony of Loyalists. The Massachusetts State Board of War assembled a large force to expel the British. Commanded by Captain Dudley Saltonstall, three ships of the Continental Navy set sail, along with the four brigs that comprised the Massachusetts navy. With them went a dozen privateers and some 20 merchantmen.

On July 25, the Americans found the bay protected by the three sloops. In addition, a battery had been established and construction of a log fort begun on Banks Island. An interlocking field of fire covered the entrance to the harbor. The following day, Marines led by Captain John Welsh seized Banks Island and captured four light artillery pieces. The British ships began taking fire from the captured battery and withdrew upriver. Brigadier-General Solomon Lovell, commanding the landing force, wanted to put ashore on the southern side of the peninsula. Saltonstall disagreed, not wishing to enter the harbor until the fort was destroyed. Lovell's force would, instead, land on the western shore of the peninsula. On July 28, the Marines came ashore under heavy musket fire and scrambled to the top of a steep cliff defended by British Marines and soldiers of the Hamilton regiment. The British were driven back to Fort George. The British commander stood ready to haul down his colors and surrender, but an attack never came. Brigadier-General Lovell refused to attack until the American ships were brought in close enough to add their firepower to the fray, and Saltonstall refused to bring the ships close to the British sloops-of-war. By August 13, a British fleet comprised of the 64-gun *Raisonable*, four frigates, and three sloops-of-war entered Penobscot Bay. Saltonstall signaled, "All ships fend for yourself."

Nineteen of the American vessels were captured, sunk, or burned. The soldiers and Marines ashore were left to escape into the Maine wilderness.

By 1779, John Paul Jones had a new ship, the *Bonhomme Richard*. A force of 137 Marines, Irish soldiers of the French Army's *Infanterie Irlandaise Regiment de Walsh-Serrant*, manned the fighting tops. On September 23, Jones sighted a British convoy escorted by the *Serapis* and the *Countess of Scarborough*. Closing, Jones fired a starboard broadside into *Serapis*. Within an hour, the Marines had cleared *Serapis*'s tops. Jones had the two ships lashed together, bow to stern. Marine musketry prevented the British from cutting the grappling hooks. Both ships continued to fire at point-blank range, and soon the two ships were ablaze and in danger of sinking. It was the presence of Marines in the tops that turned the epic sea battle, for they kept *Serapis* cleared of defenders. A seaman then dropped a grenade from the yardarm of the *Bonhomme Richard* into an open hatch of the *Serapis*, exploding powder sacks on the deck below. The British captain, his ship ablaze, struck his colors and surrendered.

The last battle of the Continental Marines, however, was a defeat. Four American ships had been dispatched to bolster Charleston's defenses. A large British force landed in February 1780 and put the American ships out of action. The Marine detachments were ordered to the city's five waterfront batteries. There they fought valiantly but were outnumbered and finally surrendered on May 12. In 1783, the Treaty of Paris ended the Revolutionary War and the Continental Marines gradually disappeared. While the exact number of Marines who fought in the revolution is not known, it did not exceed 2,000.

The Official Founding of the Corps

Fifteen years later, on July 11, 1798, President John Adams approved "an Act for establishing and organizing a Marine Corps." The new law established service at sea as the primary duty of the Marines, but also authorized "any other duty ashore, as the President, at his direction, shall direct." The strength of the service was to number 33 officers and 848 men commanded by a major. The following day, Adams selected William Ward Burrows to command the newly formed Corps.

Burrows was adamant that the role of the Marine Corps as a separate service be established and its duties defined. He staunchly supported his officers in that effort, and demonstrated his support in 1799 after an incident aboard the *Ganges*. First Lieutenant Anthony Gale, commanding the Marine detachment, was involved in a verbal altercation over the treatment of a Marine, and was struck by a naval officer. The *Ganges'* captain ignored the incident, but Gale did not. When the ship reached port, Gale challenged the offending officer to a duel and killed him. Burrows approved of Gale's actions: "It is hoped that this may be a lesson to the Navy officers to treat Marines, as well as their officers, with some more Respect."

Gale challenged the offending officer to a duel and killed him. Burrows approved of Gale's actions: "It is hoped that this may be a lesson to the Navy officers to treat Marines, as well as their officers, with some more Respect."

Below: The *Bonhomme Richard*, under the command of John Paul Jones, engages the British frigate *Serapis* off the coast of England. Both ships were in danger of sinking.

In 1798, the Quasi-War with France began. A French policy of seizing any ship which was known to be trading with Britain or to be carrying goods of British manufacture had exacted a high price on American shipping. Over 300 American vessels were seized. In response to this, American warships were instructed to attack armed French vessels. This was a policy which led to the first Marine Corps landings on foreign soil. The first of these would occur on May 12, 1800, when the French privateer *Sandwich* was captured by Marines in Santo Domingo. A few months afterwards, in September, Marines landed in Curacao, a Dutch possession that had been invaded by French troops. Less than a week later, the Quasi-War had ended.

Above: Lieutenant Colonel William Burrows and President Thomas Jefferson look for a proper place on which to fix the Marine Barracks. They eventually chose an area in southwest Washington, bordered by Eight and Eye Streets.

Peace, however, was shortlived. For years, the Barbary States of North Africa had demanded exorbitant tributes and ransoms from American merchantmen sailing the Mediterranean. Nearly a million dollars was paid to the Barbary pirates, but in May 1801, the Pasha of Tripoli declared war on America. In October 1803, the fast frigate *Philadelphia* was dispatched to blockade Tripoli. The ship, however, went aground on an unchartered reef. The captain tried in vain to free the vessel, while the *Philadelphia* was surrounded by gunboats. The captain struck his colors. The ship and her crew, including 43 Marines, were captured and held hostage. In February 1804, eight Marines joined a volunteer raiding party led by Navy Lieutenant Stephen Decatur. They entered Tripoli Harbor, then boarded the *Philadelphia* and set her ablaze. Not a single man was lost. British Admiral Horatio Nelson would later praise the American raid as "the most bold and daring act of the age."

It was, however, another bold assault that would capture the attention of the American public. In the spring of 1805, an overland expedition, led by William H. Eaton, set out to overthrow the Pasha. With Eaton went seven Marines led by a young lieutenant named Presley O'Bannon. Their 600-mile (966-km) trek across the Libyan desert and subsequent attack on the city of Derna became the stuff of Marine Corps legend. On June 3, Yusef Karamanli, Pasha of Tripoli, concluded a treaty with the United States. The captured crew of the *Philadelphia* was released and all claims to tribute were waived for a payment of the sum of $60,000. The Barbary War had finally been brought to an end.

By 1812, the United States was once again at war with Great Britain. The reasons for the conflict were primarily maritime in nature. The U.S. objected to the restriction of "neutral" American trade, and to the impressment of Americans into the Royal Navy. More than 6,000 American sailors had been seized under the pretense that they were British-born subjects of the king. When the war began on June 18, the majority of the Marine Corps' 493 men were serving aboard ship. Great sea battles marked the beginning of the conflict. On August 19, the Marines aboard U.S.S. *Constitution* were the first to see action when the

American warship met the *Guerrière*. Marine musket fire cleared the deck of the British ship. The commander of the Marine detachment, Lieutenant William Bush, was lost when he leapt to the rail, shouting, "Shall I board her, sir?" The British response was musket fire. The battle continued until the *Guerrière*'s masts were shot away. Defeated, the British surrendered and the ship was burned. Four months later, the United States captured the *Macedonian*. In December, Marines played a major role when the *Constitution* met the frigate *Java* in battle off the coast of Brazil. Commanded by First Lieutenant John Contee, the Marine detachment proved their skills as sharpshooters. As the two ships closed, British Captain James Lambert led his boarding party against the *Constitution*. He was mortally wounded by a Marine firing the Model 1808 U.S. musket. In the three-hour battle, Marine musket fire ripped through *Java*'s crew. British casualties numbered 48 killed, another 102 wounded. Finally, her decks awash with blood, the *Java* surrendered. The British, who had described the American Navy as a "handful of firbuilt frigates with bits of striped bunting at their mastheads, manned by bastards and outlaws," had lost three frigates to this fleet.

The next major action brought defeat to the Americans, but even then the Marines fought valiantly. On June 1, 1813, the American frigate *Chesapeake* sailed out of Boston harbor to engage the *Shannon*. Forty-four Marines were aboard, but otherwise her crew was inexperienced and untried. As the two ships closed, they fired broadside to broadside. *Chesapeake* was heavily damaged, her captain mortally wounded. British fire cut through the crew and many of *Chesapeake*'s sailors fled below. The British boarded, facing only the surviving Marines and a few sailors battling with clubbed muskets. In a quarter-hour battle, half of *Chesapeake*'s crew were casualties. Thirty-four Marines went down fighting.

The commander of the Marine detachment, Lieutenant William Bush, was lost when he leapt to the rail, shouting, "Shall I board her, sir?"

Below: Marine Lieutenant Presley O'Bannon leads the attack on the Tripolitan city of Derna. The victory is remembered in the second line of the Marine Hymn.

When the British boarded, only the surviving Marines and a handful of sailors resisted, battling futiley with clubbed muskets. In a battle lasting barely a quarter-hour, half of Chesapeake's crew were casualties. Thirty-four Marines went down fighting.

Below: Marines under the command of Captain Alvin Edson move toward an undefended beach south of Veracruz. The city capitulated on March 29, 1847.

In 1814, Napoleon was defeated in Europe and exiled to the island of Elba. War with France was over and Britain focused her full attention on the United States. On August 3, a British expeditionary force of 4,000 men, led by Major-General Robert Ross, sailed for the Chesapeake Bay. Sixteen days later, Ross made his way up the Patuxent River and landed his force at Benedict, Maryland. Unopposed, the British marched to Marlboro and rendezvoused with the forces of Rear Admiral George Cockburn, which included two battalions of Royal Marines. They then turned north and began to advance on Washington. Defense of the capital was the responsibility of Brigadier-General Henry Winder, U.S.A. At his disposal were some 6,000 militia, and a single Army regiment. As the British swept up the Patuxent River, the naval brigade under the command of Commodore Joshua Barney moved overland to join Winder's force. Captain Samuel Miller, Marine Corps adjutant, added a small force of some 110 Marines and 5 artillery pieces.

On August 24, 1814, the two armies met at Bladensburg. Winder's army had formed a line on the west bank of the Eastern Branch of the Potomac. Commodore Barney moved his sailors and Marines to a piece of high ground about 1 mile (1.6 km) behind the army lines. Late-arriving militia and infantry units formed up on Barney's flanks. As the British moved across the river, Winder's forces scattered. Assuming the road to Washington was undefended, Ross and Cockburn continued to advance. An unpleasant surprise, however, awaited the soldiers and Royal Marines. Barney's artillery pieces commanded the road. Musket fire and an accurate 18-lb. (8-kg) shot decimated the first British company. The British lines quickly re-formed, but the sailors and Marines repulsed a second attack. A third assault met the same fate. Barney's men had inflicted 200 casualties on the enemy.

Ross ordered an attack on the American flanks, which soon gave way. Commodore Barney's force was taking heavy fire from three sides, and short on ammunition. Casualties mounted. Both Barney and Miller were wounded. Overwhelmed, Barney ordered the guns spiked and his forces to retreat. As the battle raged, President James Madison and his cabinet fled the city, as did Lieutenant-Colonel Commandant Wharton. When the Corps records and paychest were loaded onto a wagon, Wharton and the paymaster made their escape to Frederick, Maryland. This scandalized the Marine Corps. By evening, the British were in the capital. Ross and Cockburn ordered much of the city burned, personally putting torch to the White House. The Marine Barracks and the Commandant's House were spared. According to Marine Corps legend, Ross and Cockburn left the buildings unharmed out of respect for the stand made by the Marines at Bladensburg. More likely, they were simply overlooked in the chaos.

The British re-embarked and turned their attention to their next objective: the city of Baltimore. The Americans, distraught at the fate of

Left: Marines disembark from their boats to land on an undefended beach south of Veracruz in 1847. The war with Mexico came about due to the Americans' desire to annex California and Texas, and it ended with the Treaty of Guadalupe Hidalgo.

Washington, defended the city with much greater determination. The British landed before dawn on September 12. They encountered a force 10,000-men strong. Included were Marines who had fought at Bladensburg, as well as detachments from several ships. The American forces were pushed back a distance of nearly 10 miles (16 km), but they refused to break. When Ross went down to a sniper's bullet, the British advance stalled. On the night of September 13, the Royal Navy began a bombardment of Fort McHenry. After a 24-hour-long battering, the Stars and Stripes still flew over the defensive works. Broken down by the Navy's guns, the British invaders withdrew from Baltimore.

After the death of Major-General Ross, command of the British forces was given to Major-General Sir Edward Pakenham. On November 26, 1814, he sailed from Jamaica with a force of 9,000 troops. Their destination was New Orleans. They hoped to seize the city and the lower Mississippi region before any peace treaty could end the war. The British approached the city through Lake Borgne. Major-General Andrew Jackson, who was charged with the defense of New Orleans, needed more time, so Navy Lieutenant Thomas ap Catesby Jones was ordered to delay the British. With 147 sailors, 35 Marines, and 5 gunboats, Jones met a British force numbering over 1,000. One by one, Jones's gunboats fell, but his force fought valiantly: over 300 British soldiers were killed or wounded.

When the British finally came ashore, Jackson had gained time to strengthen the city's defenses. On December 23, he ordered an attack on the British advanced guard, 9 miles (14.5 km) from the city. The attack, however, fell into confusion, and casualties mounted on both sides. Jackson halted the attack and took up defensive positions along the Rodriguez Canal. Twelve gun batteries were posted, and the aid of Jean and Pierre Lafitte's pirates accepted. A total of some 300 Marines, under the command of Captain Daniel Carmick, formed the center of Jackson's lines.

The Treaty of Ghent was signed on Christmas Eve, ending the war. The forces in the field, however, were unaware, and the battle continued. On December 28, two columns of British troops attacked Jackson's line. Artillery shredded the advancing units, and by noon the British were in retreat. Captain Carmick, however, was severely wounded, struck in the head by a rocket fragment. The British attacked in force on January 8. Pakenham marched

Ross and Cockburn ordered much of [Washington] burned, personally putting torch to the White House. The Marine Barracks and the Commandant's House were spared. According to Marine Corps legend, Ross and Cockburn left the buildings unharmed out of respect for the stand made by the Marines at Bladensburg.

Above: American forces, including a Marine battalion, assault Chapultepec Castle. The castle guarded the approaches to Mexico City. The scarlet stripes on the dress trousers of Marine officers and NCOs are said to commemorate the blood shed at Chapultepec.

5,300 men directly toward the American line of defense. Within 20 short minutes, the British commander was dead, and 2,036 of his soldiers had been killed or wounded. Almost six weeks later, in the final battle of the war, the U.S.S. *Constitution* engaged the *Cyane* and the sloop-of-war *Levant*. Musket fire from the Marine detachment under the command of Captain Archibald Henderson contributed to the American victory. After four hours of battle, the British ships were captured. The war had come to an end.

By 1830, a debate raged over the future of the Marine Corps. Many naval officers felt that a Marine presence aboard ship was unnecessary. In the *North American Review*, one proponent of that position stated "we consider the abolition of the Marine corps absolutely necessary to the efficiency and harmony of our ships." In 1831, the Secretary of the Navy recommended the Marine Corps be disbanded or absorbed into the Army or the Navy. Three years later, Congress passed "An Act for the Better organization of the Marine

Right: General John A. Quitman leads his army into Mexico City in 1847. The Marine battalion, shown behind Quitman, sustained heavy casualties in the fighting in Mexico: 11 dead and 47 wounded.

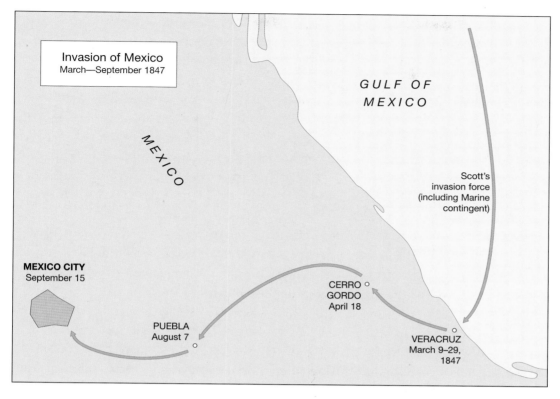

Invasion of Mexico
March—September 1847

GULF OF MEXICO

MEXICO

Scott's invasion force (including Marine contingent)

MEXICO CITY
September 15

CERRO GORDO
April 18

PUEBLA
August 7

VERACRUZ
March 9–29, 1847

Left: A map showing the landing at Veracruz in Mexico and subsequent march on Mexico City during the war of 1846–8. Although outnumbered, and with vulnerable supply lines, Scott's force successfully captured the Mexican capital.

Corps." The legislation decreed the Corps to be part of the Department of the Navy, but a separate service. Under the dictates of the Act, the President could also order the Marines to service with the Army. This was a proviso that would soon be put into use.

By 1836, the Marine Corps was embroiled in the Seminole War. The U.S. Government, under the Indian Removal Act, planned to relocate the Seminoles from Florida to Arkansas. Tribal leaders objected fiercely. The war began on December 28, 1835. Two companies of Army troops were attacked by warriors led by Seminole chief Osceola. A brilliant tactician, Osceola utilized the difficult terrain of the Everglades in a hit-and-run war. The Army pursued the Seminoles, but to little avail. By spring 1836, the Creek staged its own uprising in Georgia and Alabama. Commandant Archibald Henderson volunteered a regiment to fight; in ten days, 400 Marines were ready to take the field. Legend maintains that Commandant Henderson left a note on his office door reading, "Gone to fight the Indians. Will be back when the war is over." Stretching over the next several years, the campaign became an endless guerrilla war. A formal treaty was never signed and although some 4,000 Seminoles were relocated, many escaped into the Everglades. By the time operations were suspended in 1842, 61 Marines had lost their lives.

The Mexican War of 1846–8

By 1846, the American desire to annex California and Texas led to war with Mexico. Marines participated in several battles leading to the conquest of California. By 1847, Commodore Matthew Perry had formed an amphibious task force spearheaded by a battalion of Marines under the command of Captain Alvin Edson. This force successfully executed several landings, culminating in the seizure of San Juan Batista. Commandant Henderson notified President James K. Polk that more Marines were available for service.

Many naval officers felt that a Marine presence aboard ship was unnecessary. In the North American Review, one proponent of that position stated "we consider the abolition of the Marine corps absolutely necessary to the efficiency and harmony of our ships."

Legend maintains that Commandant Henderson left a note on his office door reading, "Gone to fight the Indians. Will be back when the war is over."

A battalion was dispatched to join forces with the Army of Major-General Winfield Scott and was attached to the 4th Division. Its objective was the seizure of Mexico City. On the morning of September 13, 1847, American troops stormed the castle of Chapultepec, the main defensive position before the capital. Marine Major Levi Twiggs was killed in an early volley. Despite heavy casualties, the assault carried to the castle walls. Scaling ladders were put into place and Chapultepec fell to the Americans. General Quitman, commanding the 4th Division, then moved toward Mexico City. Captain George Terrett, on his own initiative, moved his Marine company forward along the causeway approaching the city. Supporting three pieces of horse artillery, Terrett's men successfully scattered a counterattack by Mexican lancers. During the night, the Mexican Army fled. Quitman led his forces into Mexico City, where Marine Lieutenant Nicholson raised the Stars and Stripes. With the Treaty of Guadalupe Hidalgo, the state of war ceased to exist. Marine Corps casualties numbered 11 dead, another 47 wounded. According to legend, the scarlet stripes on the dress trousers of officers and NCOs serve to commemorate the blood which was shed by the Marines during the fight for Chapultepec.

The Civil War

By 1859, political tensions within the United States continued to grow and Civil War loomed on the horizon. On the night of October 16 a group of men, led by abolitionist John Brown, seized the U.S. Arsenal at Harper's Ferry, West Virginia. A number of people had already been killed, and several more taken hostage. As confused reports of the crisis trickled into Washington, a detachment of Marines under the command of Lieutenant Israel Greene was dispatched to Harper's Ferry. Upon arrival, Greene presented his Marines to Lieutenant-Colonel Robert E. Lee, who had been ordered by the Secretary of War to take command of all forces and to put an end to the insurrection.

Early in the morning, Lee ordered Greene to form two squads to storm the armory. Lee's major concern, however, was the safety of the hostages. Ruling out the use of firearms, he ordered the Marines to rely upon bayonets and swords. When Brown refused to surrender, the Leathernecks rushed the door. Sledgehammers proved useless against the armory's double doors, but a ladder was found and used as a battering ram. Greene was the first man through the opening; the two Marines behind him were hit. John Brown kneeled on the ground, reloading his weapon. Greene struck him in the neck, but the light officer's dress sword failed to kill him. Brown's men were quickly killed or captured and the hostages freed without harm.

Below: Marines capture the dedicated abolitionist John Brown. Several people were killed when a group of men, led by Brown, seized the U.S. Arsenal at Harper's Ferry.

Brown survived to stand trial and rally support for the abolition of slavery. Speaking to his captors, Brown declared ominously, "You may dispose of me very easily … but this question is still to be settled … The end is not yet."

Brown was right. On December 20, 1860, South Carolina voted to secede from the United States. Civil war began on April 12, when the forces of the newly formed Confederacy fired on Fort Sumter. With the opening of hostilities, many of the Corps' best men accepted commissions under the Confederacy. Among those were Lieutenant Israel Greene, as well as George Terrett and John Simms, heroes of the Mexican War.

On July 21, 1861, Union troops under the command of Brigadier-General Irvin McDowell approached the rail junction near Manassas, Virginia. With him was a hastily gathered battalion of Marines. Commanded by Major John G. Reynolds, the battalion was largely comprised of raw recruits. Confederate forces waited to the north, across a stream known as Bull Run. Reynolds' Marines were to support the West Point Battery, a Regular Army artillery unit under the command of Captain Charles Griffith. As the battle progressed, the two units advanced to Henry House Hill. An infantry regiment, uniformed in blue, emerged from the woods on the flank. Only too late did the artillerymen and Marines realize it was the 33rd Virginia Infantry, which had not yet adopted Confederate gray uniforms. Taking fire at point-blank range, Griffith's battery and the Marines were decimated. The Union guns were lost, then retaken. Three times the Marines fell back, three times they regained the crest of the hill. Late in the afternoon, fresh Confederate troops hit the Union line, which collapsed in just 40 minutes. Though the disengagement of forces was orderly, a Confederate artillery shell then turned it into a rout, and the Union troops were to be seen fleeing back to the safety of Washington.

Above: The Marine Guard on the deck of the sloop U.S.S. *Kearsarge*, shown in full dress uniform in a photograph taken during the American Civil War. The well-armed sloop carried a crew of 163 sailors and 12 Marines.

*"My station was
first loder & you
never seen a sweep
blacker than me
from powder,
sweat, and smoke
... I had to sight
the guns and do
me own work to ...
the captain of the
ship came along
& looked at my
black figure &
complimented
us on our
good firing."*

Colonel John Harris, Commandant of the Marine Corps reported, "It is the first instance recorded in its history where any portion of its [the Corps'] members turned their back to the enemy." Despite Harris's words, Reynolds rightly felt that his raw battalion had fought well. The First Battle of Bull Run was the only land campaign in which Marines took part. The remainder of the war was spent in naval and amphibious operations that served to blockade the Southern coast. On August 28, 1861, a group of soldiers, reinforced by Marines, landed at Hatteras Inlet, North Carolina. There they succeeded in capturing both Fort Clark and Fort Hatteras. Marine Private Daniel O'Connor was serving with a ships' detachment and described his role in the action against Fort Hatteras:

"My station was first loder & you never seen a sweep blacker than me from powder, sweat, and smoke. ... I had to sight the guns and do me own work to. I had nothing on but an undershirt and pants, no shoes or cap after the first hour & ½ firing. ... the captain of the ship came along & looked at my black figure & complimented us on our good firing."

In September, Flag Officer Samuel F. Dupont requested that a special landing force separate from ships' detachments be formed. Colonel Harris obliged with a battalion of 300 men under the command of Major Reynolds. This battalion was to spearhead a large amphibious operation. The target was Port Royal, South Carolina. The Marines were put aboard the *Governor*, which sank in heavy seas off Hatteras. The majority of the Marines survived, transferred to the *Sabine*. None, however, reached Port Royal to participate in the assault, for on November 7, Army and Navy forces secured Port Royal. In March 1862, the battalion landed in Saint Augustine, Florida. The city had already been abandoned, so the battalion was returned to Washington and eventually disbanded.

On April 29, however, Marines participated in the capture of New Orleans. A naval squadron commanded by Captain David G. Farragut fought its way past the forts that held the lower Mississippi. Private Oscar Smith later recalled, "Both sides fired incessantly and shot and shell fell around like hail. Hotly contested by forts and gunboats, we onward went." Farragut sent a Navy lieutenant and a small party of Marines to demand surrender of the city. It was refused. Some 250 Marines were then ordered ashore; City Hall and the Custom's House were seized, the Union flag raised. The Marines held the city until the arrival of Army troops two days later. New Orleans once again belonged to the Union.

It was Fort Sumter, however, that stood as a symbol of Confederate defiance. Located in Charleston Harbor, it had come under bombardment several times. A battalion of Marines was assembled to attempt an amphibious assault. On the night of September 8, 1863, 500 Marines and sailors set out for the Fort in rowboats. The plan, poorly conceived and poorly executed, quickly turned to chaos. Confederate batteries on nearby James and Sullivan Islands opened up. Rifle fire from Sumter's heights raked the approaching force. Those who made it to shore were showered with intense gunfire, hand grenades, even bricks and debris. Lieutenant Robert L. Meade survived the landing:

> "A heavy fire of musketry poured on us from the whole garrison. Moultrie and Johnson also commenced … a rapid, accurate shelling … the shells falling and exploding all around our boats. I opened fire and kept it up for a short while when I heard a voice ashore … to 'stop firing and land,' which I did as well as possible, my men suffering from the musketry fire and the bricks, hand grenades and fireballs thrown from the parapet. Immediately on striking the beach, I gave orders to land and find cover … A short time later, my boat disappeared. I did not see her anymore …"

The surviving boats withdrew. In 20 minutes, one-third of the assault force had been killed or captured. Fort Sumter still stood.

On January 15, 1865, more Marines lives were lost during an assault on Fort Fisher, North Carolina. A large Army force, under the command of Major-General Alfred Terry, was to land northwest of Fort Fisher. A naval force, comprised of some 1,600 sailors and 400 Marines, was to land to the east. The Marines were to provide covering fire while the naval "boarding party" assaulted the fort. The plan went seriously awry. Before the Marines had reached their firing positions, the sailors were ordered to "Charge! Charge!" Confederate fire from Fort Fisher slaughtered the men, who were, according to one officer, "packed like sheep in a pen." When it was over, 351 men of the naval brigade lay dead or wounded; among them were 57 Marines. While the Navy blamed the rout on the Marines for not being in position, George Dewey, watching from the deck of his ship, stated simply that "Such an attempt was sheer, murderous madness." But while it may have been madness tactically, the plan succeeded. The attack by the naval brigade provided the much-needed diversion for Terry's troops, who assaulted Fort Fisher

Above: On June 10, 1871 Marines stormed the forts guarding the approaches to the Han River near Seoul, Korea. The forts had fired upon five ships of the U.S. Asiatic Fleet.

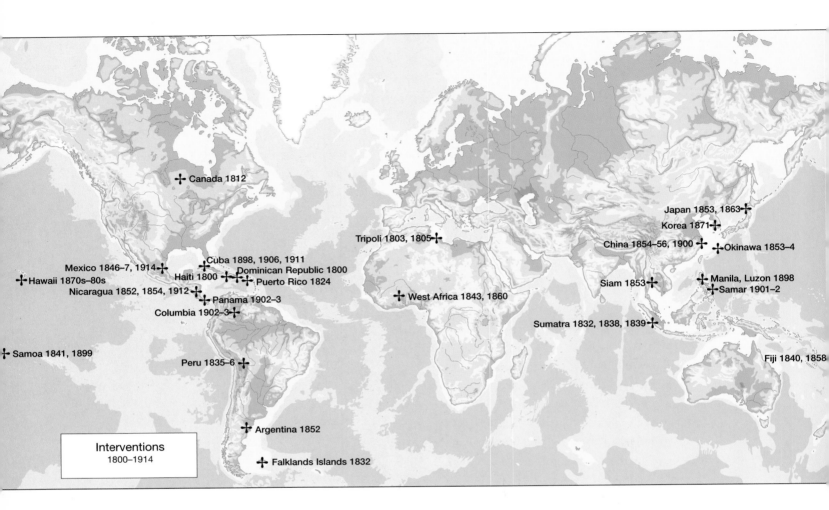

Canada 1812

Japan 1853, 1863

Korea 1871

China 1854–56, 1900

Okinawa 1853–4

Tripoli 1803, 1805

Mexico 1846–7, 1914

Cuba 1898, 1906, 1911

Dominican Republic 1800

Haiti 1800

Puerto Rico 1824

Hawaii 1870s–80s

Nicaragua 1852, 1854, 1912

Panama 1902–3

West Africa 1843, 1860

Siam 1853

Manila, Luzon 1898

Samar 1901–2

Columbia 1902–3

Sumatra 1832, 1838, 1839

Samoa 1841, 1899

Peru 1835–6

Fiji 1840, 1858

Argentina 1852

Interventions
1800–1914

Falklands Islands 1832

Above: The foreign campaigns of the Marine Corps from their foundation to the outbreak of World War I in Europe, showing the global reach of the Corps.

unopposed. Although bitter fighting continued into the night, Fort Fisher's defenses crumbled. Within months after this, the American Civil War was over. Despite the frustrations that the Marine Corps' amphibious operations met throughout the Civil War, Marines served with distinction aboard ship. Corporal John Mackie became the very first Marine to be awarded the Medal of Honor while serving aboard the *Galena*. In addition to this, eight other Marines were awarded the Medal of Honor for their extraordinary heroism during the Battle of Mobile Bay. In all, 17 enlisted Marines were awarded the nation's highest military honor.

Throughout the remainder of the nineteenth century, the Marine Corps wrestled with problems of an aging officer corps, of dwindling numbers, and shrinking budgets. In the words of historian Merrill Bartlett, "it operated in a condition of chronic overstretch." Although there were no major conflicts, the Marines executed no less than 29 landings across the globe. One of the most notable occurred in Korea, then known as the Hermit Kingdom. The American vessel *General Sherman* was shipwrecked in the Han River, her crew subsequently attacked and killed. Frederick Low, Ambassador to China, was ordered to negotiate a peace. On May 30, 1871, five ships under the command of Rear Admiral John Rodgers, one carrying Low, took fire from one of the forts guarding the Han River. When no apology was received, a landing force was put ashore. Numbering 686 men, the force included 109 Marines, who were under the command of Captain McLane Tilton. The force's mission was the capture and destruction of the Han River forts.

Tilton's major concern was the suitability of the .58 (14.7 mm) caliber breech-loading muskets carried by his men. An advocate of the new Remington .50 (12.7 mm) caliber breech-loading repeating rifle, Tilton could only wonder "whatever could Americans do with a blasted old muzzle-fuzzel?" The landing force came ashore, unopposed, in a knee-deep mud flat and struggled toward the forts. The following morning, the two smaller forts were easily seized. The strongest fortification, the Citadel, was heavily defended. Nonetheless, in brief but fierce fighting, much of it hand-to-hand, the fort was secured; some 243 Koreans lay dead. Low was able to continue his journey onto Seoul. No treaty was forthcoming, but hostilities against Americans ceased.

Remember the *Maine*!

By the close of the century, tensions between the U.S. and Spain had grown over the issue of Cuban independence. The armored cruiser *Maine* was dispatched to Havana, to "show the colors" and to protect American lives and interests in the event of trouble. However, on the evening of February 15, 1898, the *Maine* was rocked by two huge explosions. Ablaze, with her bow gone and water rushing in, the ship was reported by Marine Private William Anthony, the Captain's orderly, to be sinking. Among the 266 casualties were 28 Marines. Although no evidence of Spanish sabotage existed, "Remember the *Maine*!" became the national battlecry. In Congress, Cuban independence was recognized and on April 25, war between the United States and Spain was declared.

A battalion of Marines, 647-men strong, was gathered and placed under the command of Lieutenant-Colonel Robert Huntington, a veteran of the First Battle of Bull Run. Organized into five infantry companies and one artillery company, the First Marine Battalion sailed for Key West. By late May, the Spanish fleet was discovered in port at Santiago de Cuba. Rear Admiral William T. Sampson, commander of the U.S. North Atlantic Squadron, hoped to establish a blockade of Santiago. To accomplish that, he needed an advanced base from which to coal and repair his vessels. Huntington's Marines were ordered to seize Guantanamo Bay, defended by a reported 9,000 Spanish troops.

Tilton's major concern was the suitability of the .58 caliber breech-loading muskets carried by his men. An advocate of the new Remington ... rifle, Tilton wondered "whatever could Americans do with a blasted old muzzle-fuzzel?"

Left: The Marine gun crew aboard the U.S.S. *Alliance* in 1888. Marines aboards ships had served with distinction during the Civil War. A total of 17 enlisted Marines received the Medal of Honor, the highest American award, for their heroic actions during that period.

When the Marines came ashore on June 10, they faced no opposition. Cuban insurgents reported the Spaniards were encamped near Cuzco Well, the only source of fresh water in the area. A few days later, on June 14, Huntington dispatched two companies of Marines, which were accompanied by a Cuban guerrilla force, to take the well. The dispatch vessel *Dolphin* was to provide supporting fire. After a difficult march in the Cuban heat, the Marines took cover along the crest of a ridge and opened fire on the Spanish troops. The 6th Barcelona Regiment responded with heavy rifle fire. Captain George Fielding Elliot called for support from the *Dolphin*. The shells she fired began dropping dangerously close to the Marine positions. Elliot shouted for a signalman, and Sergeant John Quick stepped forward. Scrambling to a hilltop in the line of Spanish fire, Quick fashioned a signal flag from his neckerchief. On three separate occasions, Quick relayed corrections to the *Dolphin*. By afternoon, the Spanish troops had been routed, and the well had been destroyed. For his heroic actions in the line of fire, Sergeant John Quick was awarded the Medal of Honor.

On July 3, the Spanish fleet was ordered out of Santiago de Cuba. With cannons blazing, the Spaniards met Commodore Winfield Scott Schley's five battleships and armored cruiser. The Spanish fleet did not survive the encounter; every vessel was sunk. Two weeks later, Santiago surrendered. On August 12, 1898, an armistice went into effect. The Spanish-American war was over, but its consequences were tremendous. The United States, a newly formed nation, emerged from the war as a colonial power. The Philippines, Guam, and Puerto Rico had been claimed as U.S. territory, and the Hawaiian Islands annexed. Indeed, it was in the Philippines that the Marines would be next called to perform their duty.

While the United States was at war with Spain, Commodore George Dewey returned Filipino guerrilla leader Emilio Aguinaldo from exile to fight the Spaniards. At the conclusion of hostilities with Spain, it became apparent that the United States was not going to grant independence to the Philippines, so Aguinaldo turned his guerrilla forces against the Americans. On March 9, 1899, Commodore Dewey sent an urgent request for a battalion of Marines to reinforce Cavite Navy Yard. Within a few weeks, a battalion consisting of 15 officers and 260 enlisted men arrived. Shortly thereafter, a second battalion

was dispatched in response to reports that the Filipino situation was worsening. By the end of 1900, six Marine battalions were in the Philippines. Designated the 1st Marine Brigade, the force numbered a total of nearly 1,600 men.

In March of 1901, Aguinaldo was captured, but insurgents still fought a bitter guerrilla war on the island of Samar. On September 28, C Company of the 9th U.S. Infantry was attacked while eating, and was massacred, the bodies of the men horribly mutilated. A Marine battalion, under the command of Major Littleton Walter Tazewell Waller, was ordered to "pacify" the Samar. Army Brigadier-General "Hell-Roaring" Smith issued the orders: "I want no prisoners. I wish you to kill and burn, the more you kill and burn the better it will please me." On November 15, the Marines assaulted the rebel stronghold, a series of fortified caves in a cliff that overlooked the Sohoton River. Waller had planned a three-pronged assault. He led a flotilla of boats upriver, while two columns of Marines approached the entrenched rebels through the jungle. Surprise favored the Marines, who successfully scaled the cliff face to reach the caves. Covering fire came from the Colt-Browning M-1895 0.24 in. (6 mm) rapid-fire gun, the first true machine gun used by the Marines. The rebels were no match for the Colt-Browning's deadly torrent. The guerrillas were destroyed, and the insurrection on Samar effectively ended.

During the three-year period the Marines sought to quell the insurrection in the Philippines, trouble arose in China. A movement known as the "Righteous Fists of Harmony," called the "Boxers" by Europeans, sought to exterminate foreign influence and presence in China. By the spring of 1900, the movement had swept across the northern regions, and moved ever closer to Peking. The western legations there, concerned for their safety, requested military protection. In late May, a contingent of Marines led by Captain John "Handsome Jack" Myers arrived in Peking. Marching through a mass of sullen, silent

Above: Huntingdon's men at Guantanamo Bay in 1898, the first troops ashore. The bay has been used ever since as a U.S. naval base.

Marines at Samar

After leading his Marines to victory at Sohoton Cliffs, Major Littleton Waller was ordered to survey a telegraph route across Samar. The route was to follow an old Spanish trail, a distance of no more than 35 or 40 miles (56 or 64 km.) Taking four-days rations, the Marine expedition set out on December 28, 1901, from an Army base at Lanang on Samar's eastern coast. The journey quickly turned to disaster. Heavy monsoon rains swelled streams and rivers, and the thick wet jungle soon became impenetrable. Hacking through the dense undergrowth, and crossing the steep ridgelines and ravines of the Sohoton Mountains, Waller's expedition traversed miles of trails. Finally, with his men on the verge of exhaustion and starvation and wracked by fever, Waller divided the force of 54 Marines and 35 Filipino scouts.

On January 3, a small party led by Captain David D. Porter, along with Gunnery Sergeant John Quick, turned back toward Lanang. Waller, with the 13 strongest men, continued to struggle westward. The remaining 33 Marines were left under the command of 1st Lt. Alexander S. Williams. Not until January 6 did Waller finally reach Basey. He gathered help and supplies and re-entered Samar's jungle to search for the remaining Marines, but his search was in vain. Porter's group reached Lanang on January 11. Williams group, comprised of the weakest men, slowly followed behind. The men were sick, starving and, one by one, fell along the trail. Finally, on January 18, a relief column reached the Marines. Eighteen had to be carried from the jungle; another ten had died in the doomed expedition. For years afterward, a Marine entering a room who had survived the disastrous march was greeted by the command to those assembled, "Stand gentlemen! He served on Samar."

Boxers, the Marines took up position inside the Legation Quarter. By June 10, the Boxers had destroyed the railroad linking Peking to Tientsin, and the city was cut off. Demonstrations against the "foreign devils" reached a fever pitch.

A relief column, comprised of 2,500 men from eight nations, set out from Tientsin. Unrelenting fire from Boxer forces, however, forced the expedition to turn back. With heavy casualties, they fought their way to the Hsi-ku arsenal, 6 miles (9.6 km) north of Tientsin. There, they awaited relief. Two days later, an international force, including 138 Marines led by Major Waller, arrived. Waller's pride in his Marines was evident:

> "Our men have marched ninety-seven miles [156 km] in five days, fighting all the way. They have lived on one meal a day for six days, but have been cheerful and willing. They have gained the highest praise from all present, and have earned my love and confidence. They are like Falstaff's army in appearance, but with brave hearts and bright weapons."

In Peking, the fighting had been heavy. On June 20, the Legation Quarter came under siege. The Marines held a portion of the Tartar Wall on the southern side of the Quarter. In the early morning hours of July 3, the Marines slipped over the wall and engaged the Boxers in hand-to-hand combat. On July 15, Dan Daly earned his first Medal of Honor while single-handedly holding the wall until reinforcements arrived. To the south, Tientsin fell beneath the onslaught of a large international force. On August 4, the first elements of a relief force marched toward Peking. As the force approached the ancient city, the Boxers attempted to overwhelm the Legation defenders. On August 14, the assault on Peking began. Marines scaled the walls south of the Tung Pien gate and began firing on the Boxers inside. By nightfall, the city of Peking had been secured.

By 1903, the focus of Marine Corps activities had shifted closer to home. Interest in completing the canal across the Isthmus of Panama, which had been begun by the French, led to the deployment of the Marines. Their mission was to protect American interests while Panama sought independence from Columbia. In Cuba, the Marines intervened, but engaged in little fighting. A clause in Cuba's constitution gave the United States the right to intervene should Cuba's independence be threatened, or if its government failed to protect life, property, and individual liberty. A rigged election in 1906 sparked civil war and threatened American sugar interests. On September 16, a battalion of Marines arrived aboard the transport *Dixie*. Reinforcements soon followed and were organized into a brigade under the command of Colonel Waller. The Marines undertook the task of keeping the peace. By 1909, the Marines departed. Cuban government, however, descended into a mire of inefficiency and corruption. In 1912, the Marines were again deployed when followers of Evaristo Estenoz revolted and began burning sugar plantations and railroads. Marines were given the task of guarding American property. By July, the Cuban Army had crushed the rebellion and the Marines withdrew to Guantanamo. Three years later, rebels once again threatened sugar production. On March 4, 1917, a battalion of Marines, once again, was dispatched to Cuba.

In 1914, it was an incident in Mexico that captured American attention. General Victoriano Huerta had seized power upon the assassination of Mexican President Francisco Madero. Woodrow Wilson received word of a German merchant ship approaching the port of Veracruz. Its cargo was reportedly 200 machine guns and large amounts of ammunition to be delivered to Huerta. The Marines were ordered to "Take Veracruz at once." By April 21, the 2nd Marine Regiment, under the command of Lieutenant-Colonel Wendell C. Neville, was ashore. The landing was unopposed, and the cable office, railroad terminal, and power station were quickly secured. However, by afternoon, the Mexicans were mounting a stiff resistance. Securing Veracruz became a door-to-door battle; hundreds of Mexicans were killed. In July, Huerta was persuaded to leave Mexico.

Over the next several years, Marines would be called to duty to quell violence and revolution throughout the Caribbean. Trouble spots would be Santo Domingo, Nicaragua, and Haiti, where a Marine presence would be required, even as World War I raged across Europe.

Below: Marines encamped in the sand hills near Veracruz, Mexico in 1914. Securing the city required a dangerous house-to-house sweep, punctuated by close street fighting.

CHAPTER TWO

WORLD WAR I

When war erupted in Europe, the Marines were busy fighting brush wars in the Caribbean. They numbered only 511 officers and 13,214 men. The expeditionary doctrine of the Marine Corps was essentially that of a shock troop. The mission of the Corps was to "be the first to set foot on hostile soil in order to seize, fortify, and hold a port from which … the Army would prosecute the campaign."

Left: A Marine delivers mail along the front. Letters from home were highly valued in the trenches of World War I.

The advent of World War I brought significant changes to the Corps. With Congressional approval and a recruiting slogan of "First to Fight," its numbers swelled. Many, including John A. Lejeune, felt that the mission of the Corps was not only to seize bases, but to prosecute a land campaign in conjunction with the Army. Observation of the war in Europe brought a new understanding of the use of machine guns, heavy artillery, and trench warfare. It also spurred on the development of Marine Corps aviation. In 1912, when the first Marine Corps pilots were trained, naval aviation was only two years old. While the military use of aircraft was obvious to some, many others felt it had limited possibilities. This was partly due to the inherent unreliability of early aircraft. However, as aircraft design improved, interest in military aviation grew. The Marine Corps watched the early years of naval aviation with growing interest. The Commandant of the Marine Corps, Major-General William P. Biddle, concluded that the training of Marine aviators would be a benefit to the Corps and an asset to the Advanced Base Force concept. In the spring of 1912, two Marine officers were ordered to flight training.

The first of these was First Lieutenant Alfred A. Cunningham. He strongly believed in the possibilities that aircraft presented for military use. On August 12, after only two-and-a-half hours of flight instruction, he completed his first solo flight. Training continued throughout that year and into 1913. During exercises conducted off the coast of Cuba, the early aviators demonstrated the possibilities of military aviation. The pilots took photographs, demonstrated reconnaissance capabilities, tracked submerged submarines, and scouted for enemy surface vessels. This exercise succeeded in convincing many skeptics that military aviation was a serious matter. The Commandant of the Corps was particularly impressed, and in October 1913, recommended that a Marine Corps flying camp be established. This was initially done, at the Philadelphia Navy Yard.

Over the course of the next few months, the naval aviation flight training camp was relocated from Annapolis to Pensacola. Shortly thereafter, the Marine contingent, including pilots and support personnel, traveled north to Philadelphia and sailed for Puerto Rico. There it joined the Advanced Base Brigade in fleet exercises. It was the first time in history that a Marine Corps aviation force had operated as part of a Marine ground force. The Marines returned to Pensacola, absolutely certain that they had proven the value of Marine aviation. The aviators, however, soon discovered they had been disbanded as a separate force and were, once again, considered as part of Naval aviation.

In August 1914, war broke out in Europe. The German Army marched across Belgium, then entered France before turning toward Paris. By 1916, it was becoming clear that the U.S. would not remain neutral since American shipping had come under submarine attack. With the possibility of war looming on the horizon, Congress passed the Naval Appropriations Act of 1916, which provided a total of $3.5 million for aircraft and equipment, as well as the formation of a Navy Flying Corps.

Below: A World War I recruiting poster. Major-General Barnett, Commandant of the Marine Corps, was determined that Marines be aboard the first convoy to sail for France.

FIRST IN THE FIGHT ~ ALWAYS FAITHFUL ~ BE A U.S. MARINE!

On February 26, 1917, Alfred A. Cunningham was ordered to organize an Aviation Company at the Philadelphia Navy Yard. The total number of Marine pilots stood at five. Cunningham was determined to increase that number, to obtain more planes and equipment, and to fight alongside any Marine ground forces. On April 6, the U.S. Congress issued a declaration of war against Imperial Germany. The newly renamed Marine Aeronautic Company was ordered to fly antisubmarine patrols alongside the Navy. However, the Marine Corps had different plans for its aviators—to fly support for Marines on the ground. The Commandant of the Marine Corps, Major-General George Barnett, was authorized to form a second Marine aviation unit. This unit was to fly reconnaissance missions for the 4th Marine Brigade. Neither the Army nor the Navy was pleased with the idea: the Navy wanted little to do with land-based aircraft in its antisubmarine war; the Army was reluctant to include Marine aviators in a ground war.

By October 1917, the decision was made to restructure the Marine Aeronautic Company into two distinct units. The First Marine Aeronautic Company was equipped and trained for seaplane missions. After limited training, the unit deployed to the Azores, where it flew antisubmarine patrols throughout the war. The First Marine Aviation Squadron was to fly land-based aircraft. In April 1918, the squadron moved to Miami in order to join another Marine aviation unit under the command of Captain Roy S. Geiger. Here, the Marine aviators were given the opportunity to fly the British-designed DH-4, the bomber that they would fly over the battlefields of France.

Too Little, Too Late?

When war was declared, the Germans were sure that any American contribution to the Allied effort would be insignificant. They firmly believed it would be a case of "too little, too late." The Allies, however, were adamant that at least a token force be committed to the battlefields of France. If nothing else, the deployment of American troops would

Major General Barnett was determined that Marines would be aboard the first convoy to sail for France—"First to Fight" would not be simply a recruiting slogan.

Right: Marines bury German dead along the Verdun front on April 4, 1918. It was here the Marines first encountered the grim, unpleasant realities of trench warfare on the Western Front.

Below: German troops advance through a wheat field on Les Mares farm to engage the 55th Company, 5th Marines. It was the closest the German advance came to Paris.

bolster the morale of the battle-weary Allied forces. Major-General Barnett was determined that Marines would be aboard the first convoy to sail for France—"First to Fight" would not be simply a Marine recruiting slogan, but a way of life. The Army had other ideas. Barnett was informed there was no room for Marines aboard the transports. Anticipating this statement, Barnett replied that the Marines would board Navy transport ships. In late May, much to the dismay of General John J. Pershing and the Army, President Woodrow Wilson signed an executive order that approved sending a Marine regiment to France. It was to be attached to the Army, and organized and equipped according to Army regulations. They would trade in their "greens" and "khakis" for Army olive drab. A *New York Times* headline announced the news, "2,600 Marines to go with Pershing."

Pulling manpower from throughout the Corps, companies were brought up to Army strength and organized into battalions. Machine-gun companies were added. On June 14, the 5th Marine Regiment sailed for France. By July, the 6th Marine Regiment was being formed at Quantico. On October 23, 1917, the two regiments, later joined by the 6th Machine Gun Battalion, were brought together as the 4th Marine Brigade. With the Army's 3rd Infantry Brigade and an artillery brigade, they formed the 2nd U.S. Division in France.

Throughout the winter of 1917–1918, the Marines trained and waited for Pershing to send them to the front. They learned to dig trenches, to create barbed wire entanglements, and how to conduct trench warfare. They mastered the use of the gasmask. Weapons practice included bayonet drills, throwing hand grenades, and marksmanship practice with the Springfield 1903 rifle. They traded their beloved Lewis machine guns for French Chauchat automatic rifles and Hotchkiss machine guns. Finally, in March 1918, the Marines were ordered into a sector along the northern edge of the St Mihiel salient, near Verdun. It was the first combat experience for most, and the Marines soon realized that even a "quiet" sector along the Western Front could be deadly. The 4th Marine Brigade suffered its first casualty in April when a private was killed by shellfire. On April 12, the entire 74th Company of the 6th Marines was struck down in a gas barrage. Forty men died.

By March 1918, the U.S. had only six complete divisions in France. The Germans reasoned that a massive attack on the Western Front before the influx of large numbers of American troops could end the war by midsummer. On March 21, the Germans launched a series of major offensives. The first two came against British armies in the Somme. The

Dan Daly

Gunnery Sergeant Dan Daly is a Marine Corps legend. One of only two men to be awarded two Medals of Honor, Daly was described by Major-General John A. Lejeune as "the outstanding marine of all time."

Born on November 11. 1873, Daly enlisted in the Marine Corps at the age of 25, in hope of serving in the Spanish–American War. By the time he finished boot camp, however, the war was over. Daly shipped aboard the U.S.S. *Newark* bound for China, where the Boxer Rebellion was threatening foreign legations and settlements in Peking. While defending the walls of the U.S. Legation, Daly volunteered to hold the wall single-handedly while an officer went for reinforcements. He was awarded his first Medal of Honor.

Fifteen years later, he was in Haiti fighting the *Cacos*. While on patrol, Daly and about 40 other Marines were ambushed by a *Caco* force while fording a river. Twelve horses were killed, but the Marines fought their way to safety. While setting up a defensive perimeter, they discovered that the patrol's only machine gun was lost in the river. Daly slipped back to the river through the *Caco* forces and retrieved the lost machine gun, then returned to the Marine perimeter. For this action, Daly received a second Medal of Honor.

During the course of World War I, Daly fought with distinction. Wounded four times, he was awarded a Distinguished Service Cross for Belleau Wood, a Navy Cross, the French Medaille Militaire, and the Croix de Guerre. It was at Belleau Wood, however, that Dan Daly became a Marine Corps legend. At 17:00 hours on June 6, 1918, the U.S. Marines were about to assault German positions in Belleau Wood. Daly, then a First Sergeant, and the men of the 73rd Machine Gun Company were in position along the edge of the wheat field. Bullets ripped through the trees and shredded the young wheat. When it was time to advance, Daly stepped into the open field. Turning to his men, he shouted, "Come on, you sons of bitches! Do you want to live forever?"

Later, Daly denied using those exact words, but the public accepted no substitutes. Gunnery Sergeant Dan Daly's place in Marine Corps history was secured.

third German attack came on May 27. German General Erich Ludendorff ordered the attack on French lines between Soissons and Reims. The French Sixth Army, comprised of seven battle-weary divisions, crumpled under the onslaught of German artillery and the power of 18 divisions. The Germans crossed the Aisne River, drove past Soissons, and then halted at the Marne River near Chateau Thierry. Paris lay 40 miles (64 km) to the west.

In an effort to stop the German advance, Pershing released his divisions to General Ferdinand Foch, Commander-in-Chief of Allied Forces in France. On May 30, the U.S.

Above: Tom Lovell's painting "U.S. Marines at Belleau Wood" captures the horror of hand-to-hand combat. The 4th Marine Brigade suffered 1,087 casualties on the first day of the battle for Belleau Wood.

2nd Division was ordered to join General Joseph Degoutte's Sixth Army along the Marne. The Division moved forward without supplies and artillery, traveling along the Paris–Metz highway through a scene of chaos. Defeated French soldiers and streams of refugees moved away from the battle. On June 1, Chateau Thierry fell. The Germans seized the towns of Torcy, Vaux, and Bouresches to the north. The 461st German Imperial Infantry occupied a small wooded area, a game preserve known as the Bois de Belleau, or Belleau Wood.

The 9th U.S. Infantry took its position between the Paris–Metz highway and the Marne. Major-General James G. Harbord, commanding officer of the 4th Marine Brigade, ordered the 6th Marines to deploy to the left of the 9th Infantry. The 5th Marines and the 23rd Infantry took positions in support. That evening, the Germans punched a hole in the French lines. The 5th Marines, the 23rd Infantry, and part of the 6th Machine Gun Battalion moved forward in a forced march to plug the gap.

On June 2, the Germans renewed the assault. The French Sixth Army began falling back. A French officer advised Marine Captain Lloyd Williams that the Marines, too, should retreat. Williams response was succinct: "Retreat, hell! We just got here." By the night of June 2, the Marines were dug in, but the line was dangerously thin. On the afternoon of June 3, the Germans attacked Marine positions. They came in lines across the rolling wheat fields, bayonets fixed. The Marines responded with sustained rifle and machine-gun fire. Martin G. Gulberg wrote:

> "They came out of the woods opposite our position in close formation. ... We opened up on them with a slashing barrage of rifles, automatics, and machine guns. ... Three times they tried to break through, but our fire was too accurate and heavy for them. It was terrible in its effectiveness. They fell by the scores, there among the poppies and the wheat."

The offensive was stopped. Over the course of the next two days, the German Army continued to assault the Marine positions. Each time they did, however, they were thrown back by heavy and accurate fire, pounding out of the Marines' weapons.

General Degoutte ordered the U.S. 2nd Division to counterattack German positions. According to Degoutte's plan, the attack was to proceed in two phases. With the 167th French Division to their left, the Marines of the U.S. 2nd Division were ordered to take Hill 142. This task was to fall specifically upon the 1st Battalion, 5th Marines, supported by the 8th and 23rd Machine Gun Companies and a company of engineers. The second phase directed the 2nd Division to capture the ridge above the towns of Torcy and Belleau, to occupy Belleau Wood, and to seize the town of Bouresches. However, elements of the 1st Battalion, 5th Marines, were scattered. Two rifle companies and the 8th Machine Gun Company awaited relief near Les Mares farm. Neither the 23rd Machine Gun Company nor the engineers were close by. Major Julius S. Turrill, commanding officer of the 1st Battalion, 5th Marines was left with only the 67th and 49th Companies for the attack.

Hill 142 was actually an elongated, brush-covered ridge rising above the wheatfields, west of the wood. Two German battalions, reinforced by a company, were well dug in: the wooded areas bristled with deadly machine-gun nests. Artillery fire of the previous evening had alerted the defenders to possible attack. As night slowly turned to day, and the pre-assault barrage intensified, the Germans prepared to meet the Marine onslaught. In the early morning hours of June 6, 1918, the Battle of Belleau Wood began.

The 67th and 49th Companies of the 1st Battalion, 5th Marines, led the assault on Hill 142. Crossing wheatfields splashed with brilliant red poppies, the Marines were met with withering machine-gun fire. The fields were soon splattered with the blood of the dead, the dying, and the wounded. Despite heavy casualties, the Marines continued to advance,

Above: Marines man a 1.46 in. (37 mm) gun, while riflemen advance against German positions.

Crossing wheat fields splashed with brilliant red poppies, the Marines were met with withering machine-gun fire. The fields were soon splattered with the blood of the dead, the dying, and the wounded.

John Thomason

It was a popular story among the enlisted Marines of the 4th Brigade: an officer whose hours free from fighting the war were spent drawing the war. That officer was John W. Thomason, Jr. He sketched continuously, using whatever scraps of material he could find, determined to record his experiences in "the war to end all wars."

Thomason, the grandson of a Confederate officer, was commissioned a Second Lieutenant in the Marine Corps in August 1917. By May 1918, he was in France, serving as a platoon leader in the 49th Company, 1st Battalion, 5th Marines. His first experience under fire came at Belleau Wood. Later, at Soissons, his company took heavy casualties from violent machine-gun fire. Thomason and a Marine under his command advanced on the German position and wiped out the machine-gun nest, killing the crew of 13. For that action, he was awarded both the Navy Cross and the Silver Star for extraordinary heroism under fire.

After the war, Thomason continued to serve in the Corps. He drew upon those experiences for inspiration in both his writing and drawing. In 1924, an exhibit of some of his drawings led to a meeting with Charles Scribner's Sons, Publishers. They were intrigued. Thomason's drawings were stark, powerful images of the war, but the publisher wanted text to accompany these drawings. Thomason had that as well, and the result was *Fix Bayonets!* The critics raved, praising the book's realism, honesty, and powerful description of the horrors of war.

More books followed: *Red Pants; Marines and Others; Salt Winds and Gobi Dust.* Each found its basis in Thomason's life in the Marine Corps. Ostensibly, they were works of fiction. Yet undeniably they were based upon personal experience. The result is a collection of works that describes the "old Corps," and captures the spirit of the Marines of World War I, through the 1920s and 1930s.

determination overcoming German experience and firepower. Once inside the wooded areas around Hill 142, the fighting became even more brutal. The Marines had no trench mortars, and few hand grenades. German machine guns fired at point-blank range. The Marines had the choice of either shooting at the enemy, or crawling into the machine-gun nests and bayoneting the Germans.

First Lieutenant John Thomason described the action:

"Americans fight best with rifles. Men get tired of carrying grenades and chaut-chaut clips; the guns cannot, even under most favorable conditions, keep pace with the advancing infantry. Machine-gun crews have a way of getting killed at the start; trench mortars and one-pounders are not always possible. But the rifle and the bayonet goes anywhere a man can go, and the rifle and bayonet win battles."

"Americans fight best with rifles ... the rifle and the bayonet goes anywhere a man can go, and the rifle and bayonet win battles."

Turrill's two companies were taking very heavy casualties. Some platoons had been decimated, reduced to only a few men. By 05:30 hours, reinforcements had arrived. Turrill's field adjutant notified headquarters that both the 66th Company and the 17th Rifle Company had been deployed. The 8th Machine Gun Company was already in action, moving north down the center of the ridge. By 06:30 hours, the 51st Company of the 2nd Battalion, which had been held in reserve, was thrown into the fray. By noon, the Marines held Hill 142. The main assault on Belleau Wood was launched at 17:00 hours. The 2nd and 3rd Battalions of the 6th Marines attacked from the southwest, while the 2nd Battalion, 5th Marines pushed from the west. Private Bailey, Chauchat gunner of the 9th Infantry, witnessed the assault on Belleau Wood:

> "We saw the long lines of Marines leap up from somewhere and start across the wheatfields toward the woods. Those lines were straight and moved steadily, a few paces in front of each its officer leading, not driving. The attackers went up the gentle slope and, as the first wave disappeared over the crest, we heard the opening clatter of dozens of machine guns that sprayed the advancing lines. Then we heard some shrieks that made our blood run cold."

Lacking adequate artillery support and advancing neatly in line, as per the French instruction, the Marines were almost totally annihilated. Few men of the 2nd Battalion, 5th Marines ever reached the trees. Those who did survive sought cover in the wheat and crawled on through a hail of German machine-gun fire. The 2nd and 3rd Battalions of the 6th Marines faired better, overrunning German machine-gun nests placed at the southern edge of the wood. Major Thomas Holcomb's men took the village of Bouresches, and two-thirds of Belleau Wood were now held by the Marines, but the cost was high. Casualties numbered 1,087. On June 6, 1918, the U.S. Marine Corps had suffered more casualties in one day than it had in its entire history. John Thomason wrote:

> "Night descended over a tortured area of wheat and woodland, lit by flares and gun-flashes, flailed by machine guns, and in too many places pitiful with crying of wounded who had lain all the day untended in the merciless sun. Stretcher-bearers and combat patrols roamed over it in the dark. Water parties and ration parties groped back from forward positions over unknown trails. There were dog-fights all over the place, wild alarms and hysterical outbreaks of rifle fire."

That night, and into the morning of June 7, the Marines consolidated their position, digging a series of shallow pits—"foxholes." On June 8, the battle was renewed. A battalion of the 6th Marines was ordered to drive north. Little was gained, as the German troops were easily reinforced. Artillery raked the wood. The once-beautiful hunting preserve was reduced to wasteland and German resistance remained strong. On June 10, two battalions were ordered to attack. In the early morning hours, the 1st Battalion, 6th Marines and members of the 6th Machine Gun Battalion came from the south. They met heavy German resistance. The 2nd Battalion, 5th Marines once again crossed

Below: Marine Corps artist Charles Waterhouse depicts a U.S. Marine at Belleau Wood. According to Marine Corps legend, the Germans called the Marines *Teufelhunden* ("Devil Dogs") in reference to the ferocity of their fighting.

the wheatfield, many falling under enemy fire. Despite fatigue and heavy casualties, Marines of the two regiments managed to link up and, by June 12, held all but the northern edges of the wood.

The Germans responded on June 13 with fierce artillery fire, clouds of mustard gas, and fresh troops. The Marines suffered horrific casualties. The 1st Battalion, 6th Marines alone lost 450 men, but held their ground. Colonel Wise, commanding officer of the 2nd Battalion, 5th Marines had only 6 officers and 350 men of his battalion remaining. When asked about the condition of his Marines, he responded, "There aren't any more Marines." On June 15, they were relieved by the 7th U.S. Infantry and a French brigade. The exhausted Marines went to the rear to recover form their ordeal.

Ludendorff ordered fresh troops into Belleau Wood. The untried 7th Infantry was unable to remove German resistance and, by June 23, the Marines were again engaged in battle. The Germans were running out of reinforcements, and facing the ferocity of the

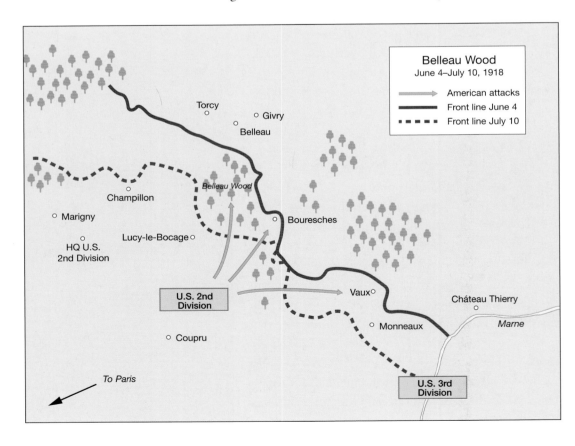

Leathernecks. On June 25, following a massive artillery barrage, the 5th Regiment drove the last German troops from Belleau Wood. In the early morning hours of June 26, Major Maurice Shearer of the 5th Marines sent the message, "Woods now U.S. Marine Corps entirely." Combat in Belleau Wood was savage and brutal, much of it hand-to-hand, and the cost of victory was high: 126 officers and 5,057 enlisted men of the 4th Marine Brigade were dead or wounded. German survivors spoke of the Marines with grudging admiration.

> "The Second American Division must be considered a very good one and may even perhaps be reckoned as a storm troop. The different attacks on Belleau Wood were carried out with bravery and dash. … The qualities of the men individually may be described as remarkable."

Marine Corps legend holds that the German troops described Marine ferocity and determination in one word: *Teufelhunden*—"devil dogs." General Degoutte decreed that "Belleau Wood shall bear the name 'Bois de la Brigade de Marine.' " Marshall Foch would call it "the cradle of victory." Belleau Wood was a proving ground for the Marines—they had met the Germans on the battlefield, had fought well, and had prevailed.

The Chauchat

The Chauchat automatic rifle, named for a French colonel, had its beginnings in 1903. The French Government felt that it had an adequate heavy machine gun in its arsenal, but was searching for a lightweight automatic rifle. After looking at several different weapons, the French Army found what it was looking for in the Chauchat.

Based on a design by Hungarian arms designer Rudolf Frommer, the Chauchat was an extremely lightweight automatic weapon, weighing only 19

lb. (8.6 kg). It could be fired either single shot or fully automatic with a magazine that held 20 8-mm Lebel cartridges. Although very inexpensive to make, and very easy to mass-produce, the Chauchat has long been considered a crude weapon, possibly the worst automatic rifle to be put into the hands of soldiers.

When American forces were deployed to Europe, the U.S. Government contracted the French to equip each division with the Chauchat. The Marines of the 4th Brigade soon discovered that it was difficult to hold on a target and extremely inaccurate. It also created supply problems. Since it required a French cartridge, supply units had to carry two kinds of rifle ammunition. It was soon discovered, however, that with little difficulty the Chauchat could be rechambered to utilize the .30-caliber service cartridge. The magazine was cut from a 20- to 16-cartridge capacity.

On August 17, 1917, some 25,000 of the altered version were ordered for use by American divisions. The altered version proved even more unreliable than the original. It was almost impossible to maintain in the field, suffered from parts breakage, and frequently jammed, as cartridges stuck in the chamber when the barrel heated.

Despite the problems, more than 37,000 Chauchat automatic rifles were purchased from the French and it was issued to nine American divisions. Indeed, throughout the war in Europe, more than twice the number of Chauchats were issued to American troops than anticipated. This is probably due to the American habit of simply discarding the malfunctioning weapons in the field.

A few German shells fell among the men—mustard gas; and there in the wet woods one could see the devilish stuff spreading slowly, like a snaky mist.

One of the greatest casualties of the battle was the relationship between the Army and the Marines—the goodwill that had been built up was now destroyed. The battle was initially referred to as only a minor engagement, and General Pershing's press officers let American newspaper reporters identify the Marines as the attacking force at Belleau Wood. On June 6, a report was filed by Floyd Gibbons, a correspondent with the *Chicago Tribune*. He had been badly wounded while attempting to aid a fallen Marine officer, taking three bullets, including one to the left eye. Rumors of his death were even circulated. Believing Gibbons had filed his last story, it was not altered by censors. It began, "I am up front and entering Belleau Wood with the U.S. Marines." The American public went on to read a laudatory account of Marine skill and bravery, and soon it was widely believed that the Marines had stopped the German advance, saved Paris, and turned the tide of the war. Both the 7th Infantry and the 3rd Division at Chateau Thierry were ignored. Pershing and the Army were furious at the glory heaped upon the Marines and the lack of any mention of Army contribution. Intense resentment surfaced in official correspondence. In a letter written to Major-General James G. Harbord, one army regimental commander referred to the Marines as a "bunch of adventurers, illiterates, and drunkards." That sort of anger against the Marines would continue to simmer for many years afterward.

The Last German Offensive

On July 15, General Ludendorff launched the last German offensive of the war. Eight divisions managed to cross the Marne River between Chateau Thierry and Reims. General Foch ordered a counterattack on the northern side of the German position, near the city of Soissons. The spearhead of the attack was the French Tenth Army, comprised of the 1st Moroccan Division and the U.S. 1st and 2nd Divisions. The 2nd Division Marines joined the French XX Corps in the Forest of Retz. Success of the attack was dependent upon those troops reaching the line of attack by daybreak. Through the night of July 17, the Marines

Right: A lone Marine sentry stands guard over a water cart in a supply area somewhere in France. The Marine wears a gasmask in preparation for a possible attack.

moved through driving rain, mud, and confusion. Some machine-gun units failed to arrive. The battle would be fought with Springfield rifles, bayonets, and the Chauchat automatic rifles. As the preparatory barrage began, the last rifle companies arrived at double time. Battle plans called for the 5th Marines to be part of the initial assault. The 6th Marines would be held in reserve. With little sleep, the 5th Marines fixed bayonets and moved forward. First Lieutenant John Thomason described it thus:

> "The battle roared into the wood. … Here the Foret de Retz was like Dante's wood, so shattered and tortured and horrible it was, and the very trees seemed to writhe in agony. Here the fury of the barrage was spent, and the great trunks, thick as a man's body, were sheared off like weed-stalks; others were uprooted and lay gigantic along the torn earth. … A few German shells fell among the men— mustard gas; and there in the wet woods one could see the devilish stuff spreading slowly, like a snaky mist."

Fighting in that forest was savage, but slowly the Marines advanced against German machine-gun fire. Two Marines would later be awarded the Medal of Honor for their bravery during that advance. Both sergeants in the 66th Company of the 5th Marines, Louis Cukela and Matej Kocak, separately maneuvered behind German machine-gun positions, then single-handedly stormed these nests and destroyed them. The Marines emerged from the forest into the hot, July sun. Ahead of them lay another wheatfield. Accompanied by a squadron of French tanks, the Marines moved forward through the open field. The tanks attracted incessant German fire and the Marines took increasingly heavy casualties. By afternoon, however, Beaurepaire Farm was secured and the Marines were able to turn and proceed to the southeast.

The events of the day's battle left the 5th Marines scattered: attempts to eliminate pockets of resistance and to maintain contact with the 1st Moroccan Division had resulted in confusion in the Marine lines; machine-gun fire and constant shelling added to the chaos.

"We need support, but it is almost suicide to try and get it here as we are swept by machine-gun fire and a constant barrage is on us. I have no one on my left and only a few on my right. I will hold."

Major Julius S. Turrill succeeded in pulling together the remnants of his 1st Battalion, Shearer's 3rd Battalion, and the 8th Machine Gun Company. They joined the 23rd Infantry in the assault on the village of Vierzy, where the Germans had formed a new line. By the evening of July 18, the village was in Allied hands, but the 5th Marines were spent.

On the morning of July 19, the 6th Marines, under the command of Lieutenant-Colonel Harry Lee, resumed the assault. Their objective lay from Bois d'Hartennes to the Bois de Cornois on the road between Chateau Thierry and Soissons. It was a distance of about 2.5 miles (4 km) across open, rolling fields. Crossing those miles would cost many Marine lives. The German lines had been reinforced and machine guns brought forward, and batteries of 77s (77 mm/3 in. guns) could be seen in the distance. The Allied offensive was to be halted at all costs. The 1st Battalion, 6th Marines was deployed on the right, Major Holcomb's 2nd Battalion to the left. The 3rd Battalion was in support. Several hours before the Marine assault began, Allied artillery fired its rolling barrage. With French tanks in the lead, the Marines began to advance. The only artillery fire was incoming from the German lines. It seemed to rain shells. The French tanks were destroyed. Enemy aircraft flew low, guiding the artillery and harassing the Marines with machine-gun fire. Through this hellish maelstrom, the Marines slowly advanced. German shelling and machine-gun fire poured on them incessantly, at almost point-blank range. The 6th Marines were being slaughtered. Lieutenant Clifton B. Cates, who would later become the 19th Commandant of the Corps, was the only functioning officer remaining in the 96th Company, 2nd Battalion. Taking command of the surviving men, he continued the attack. In a message, which had become the stuff of Marine Corps legend, he wrote:

"I have only two men out of my company and 20 out of some other company. We need support, but it is almost suicide to try and get it here as we are swept by machine-gun fire and a constant barrage is on us. I have no one on my left and only a few on my right. I will hold."

At 15:45 hours, Lieutenant-Colonel Lee sent the following message through to his command:

"The Division Commander directs us to dig in and hold our present line at all costs. No further advance will be made for the present. He congratulates the command on its gallant conduct in the face of severe casualties."

Once again, the devastated Marines were replaced by French troops, but the objective had been met. The attack had pushed the Germans back, across the Marne to the Vesle River and into a general retreat. Once again, the cost of victory was high. In two days, the Battle for Soissons had cost the 4th Marine Brigade a total of 2,015 men.

Below: Two Marines behind the front line man a Hotchkiss machine gun that has been mounted for use in an antiaircraft role. One of the Marines uses his binoculars to scan the sky for an enemy airplane.

On July 23, the 2nd U.S. Division received orders to proceed to a rest area in the Marbache sector. Over the next two weeks, the Marines had an opportunity to rest, refit, and absorb replacements, including a battalion from the United States and 2,500 Marines from posts in England and France. During this period, Brigadier-General John A. Lejeune assumed command of the 2nd U.S. Division. Wendall C. Neville, newly promoted to Brigadier-General, took command of the 4th Marine Brigade. On August 5, the Assistant Secretary of the Navy, Franklin D. Roosevelt, inspected the 2nd Division Marines. He had recently visited Belleau Wood and was deeply moved by what he had seen there: "I have seen the blood running from the wounded. I have seen men coughing out their gassed lungs. I have seen two hundred limping, exhausted men come out of the line—the survivors of a regiment of one thousand." As a result, Roosevelt authorized the right of all Marines to wear the Marine Corps emblem, a privilege previously restricted to officers, in recognition of "the splendid work of the Marine Brigade."

In early September, the 2nd U.S. Division marched north to join the newly formed U.S. First Army, then preparing for the St Mihiel offensive. This was to be an operation conducted by an American field army under American command. The objective was the elimination of the St Mihiel salient, the last salient on the Western Front, which spanned the distance between the Meuse and Moselle rivers. This area, 16 miles (25.75 km) deep and 25 miles (40.25 km) wide, had been occupied by the Germans since the beginning of the war. To achieve the objective, and rid St Mihiel of German presence, General Pershing assembled 14 U.S. Divisions, including the 2nd U.S. Division.

Above: Marines move cautiously through the Meuse-Argonne forest. Shelling was often so heavy that forested areas were stripped bare. The Germans held the high ground at the outset of this offensive. Between late September and October 11, half a million Allied troops attacked the German positions.

Right: A map showing the Allied offensives of the summer and fall of 1918. The U.S. Army, of which the Marines were part, were on the right flank of the Allied Front.

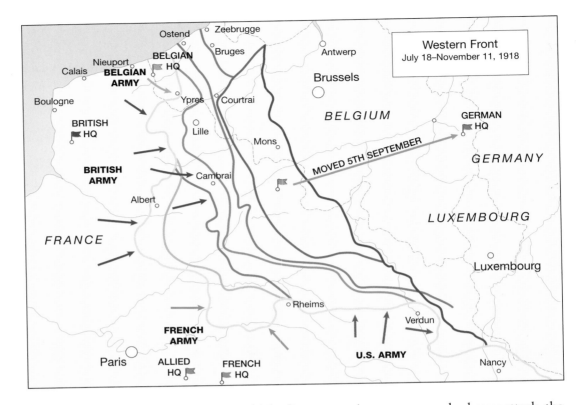

With the realization that the St Mihiel salient was going to come under heavy attack, the Germans began retreating back to the Hindenburg Line. At 01:00 hours on September 12, the bombardment of the German lines began. After a four-hour long barrage, the 2nd U.S. Division went over the top. Through mud and rain, the 3rd Infantry Brigade led the assault, with the 4th Marine Brigade in reserve. German resistance was not heavy, and by early afternoon, the division had reached its day's objectives. The following day, the 4th Marine Brigade took over the attack and advanced through Army lines. The Germans counterattacked several times to slow the Marine advance, but by evening all major objectives planned by General Pershing's headquarters had been reached. The St Mihiel salient ceased to exist. Compared to Belleau Wood and Soissons, Marine casualties at St Mihiel were light. Only the 6th Marines had faced stiff resistance, fighting through thick woods on the division's left flank. They suffered two-thirds of the Brigade's 703 casualties.

On September 26, the great offensive in the Meuse-Argonne region was launched. The British, to the north, pushed east toward Cambrai. The French Fourth Army, west of the Argonne forest, struck across the Aisne. The American sector lay to the south. The 2nd U.S. Division was not committed to opening attacks of the offensive, but rather was loaned to the French Fourth Army.

The Attack on Mont Blanc

What was left was naked, leprous chalk. It was a wilderness of craters, large and small, wherein no yard of earth lay untouched.

After conferring with the commander of the French Fourth Army, General Lejeune was concerned with the obstacles facing the French. Key terrain was the long Mont Blanc ridgeline, where German trenches, concrete bunkers, and machine-gun nests were positioned. This gave the Germans unobstructed observation of the French front and ensured their artillery fire was accurate. French attacks on the German positions were unsuccessful, the better part of three divisions being chewed up. Initially, the French commander, General Gourand, intended to attack using elements of the 2nd U.S. Division separately. General Lejeune assured Gourand that his division, acting as a whole, would take Mont Blanc ridge. Orders from the Fourth French Army, dated October 1, assigned the 2nd U.S. Division to relieve French troops in the front lines along the ridge. On a cold, clear night, the 4th Marine Brigade occupied a 1-mile (1.6-km) section of the front. It was not a promising sight for the Marines. John Thomason wrote:

> "North from the edge of the pines the battalion looked out on desolation where the once grassy, rolling slopes of the Champagne stretched away like a great white sea that had been dead and accursed through all time. ... What was left was naked, leprous chalk. It was a wilderness of craters, large and small, wherein no yard of earth lay untouched."

In the early morning hours of October 3, American and French forces attacked Mont Blanc ridge. The 4th Marine Brigade was positioned to the left, the 3rd Infantry Brigade to the right. They were flanked by two French divisions. A thunderous artillery barrage began at 05:45 hours. At 05:50 hours, the 2nd Battalion, 6th Marines led the attack, supported by a battalion of French tanks. Once again, it was rifles, bayonets, and a few hand grenades against heavy German artillery and machine-gun fire. Even so, by 08:30 hours, the 2nd Battalion had captured its objective. However, the French had been stopped by the "Essen Hook," a German stronghold of machine-gun nests and snipers. The 1st Battalion, 5th Marines succeeded in eliminating that stronghold, but nonetheless the Germans still held the western tip of the Mont Blanc ridge.

On October 4, the battle was resumed. The objective was a line of trenches about 600 yards (584 m) southeast of the town of St Etienne. By the end of the day, the Marine Corps had written one of the bloodiest chapters in their history, for the Germans had reinforced Mont Blanc ridge during the previous night. Without benefit of artillery, the 3rd Battalion,

Left: Members of the Marine 6th Machine Gun Battalion manning a French Hotchkiss machine gun are joined by French Allies somewhere in the Chateau Thierry sector.

5th Marines led the assault, and they were followed by the 1st and 2nd Battalions. As the Marines emerged from cover, they were pummeled on all sides by the incoming artillery and deadly rain of German machine-gun fire. John Thomason remembered the attack:

> "The fight closed upon the battalion with the complete and horrid reality of nightmare. All along the extended line the saffron shrapnel flowered, flinging death and mutilation down. Singing balls and jagged bits of steel spattered on the hard ground like sheets of hail … the high explosive shells came with the shrapnel, and where they fell geysers of torn earth and black smoke roared up to mingle with the devilish yellow in the air. A foul murky cloud of dust and smoke formed and went with the thinning companies, a cloud lit with red flashes and full of howling death … The silent ridge to the left awoke with machine guns and rifles, and sibilant rushing flights of nickel-coated missiles from Maxim and Mauser struck down where the shells spared."

They struggled for about 1 mile (1.6 km) before they were stopped. It was well short of their objective, but the 5th Marines had been decimated. Some companies had only a handful of men left. The 1st Battalion, originally 1,000 men, had been reduced to barely 100. On October 4, the 4th Marine Brigade lost of 1,100 men, and the Germans still held part of Mont Blanc ridge. At 06:00 hours on October 5, the 3rd Battalion, 6th Marines assaulted a crucial German stronghold and silenced 65 enemy machine guns. That afternoon, led by the 2nd Battalion, the 6th Marines attempted to enter St Etienne. The previous days of fighting had reduced the battalion to about 300 men, and they met heavy German resistance. The enemy had positioned machine guns before the town, and troops were moving south toward the Marines. The 6th Marines went no further that day.

October 6 was yet another day of heavy fighting, and the 4th Marine Brigade was relieved that evening by a brigade of the U.S. 36th Division. A battalion of the 6th Marines remained behind. In the early morning hours of October 8, German positions were overrun and the Marines occupied St Etienne. By late afternoon, the Germans countered with fierce artillery fire and attempted to take back the town. They were unsuccessful. On October 10, the 3rd Battalion, 6th Marines was relieved. General Lejeune's promise had been fulfilled: the 2nd U.S. Division had taken Mont Blanc ridge and the Germans were in retreat. Once again, the cost of victory was staggering—2,538 Marines had been killed or wounded. A grateful French Government presented the 5th and 6th Marines, and the men of the 6th Machine Gun Battalion, with their third unit citation for gallantry, the Croix de Guerre. This entitled members of those units to wear the green and red *fourragère* upon their left shoulders in honor of the units' heroism. This practice continues today among members of those units as a reminder of that heroism.

Below: The 5th Marines attack the Essen Hook during the battle for Mont Blanc. The German defensive positions were considered impenetrable.

Left: "The Last Night of the War" by Frederick Yohn depicts the assault across the River Meuse on November 10, 1918. The objective was to sever German lines of communication along the Western Front and compromise the German defenses. The 1st and 2nd Battalions, 5th Marines sustained 179 casualties on the night before the general armistice.

As World War I drew to a close, the 2nd U.S. Division rejoined the American First Army's V Corps to fight what would be the final battle of the war—the Meuse-Argonne offensive. The objective was to sever the German lines of communication along the Western Front and further compromise already crumbling German defenses. This vast battle began on September 26, 1918. Spanning the area between the Argonne Forest and the Meuse River, the Germans had constructed strong defenses along the front. They also held the high ground. Between late September and October 11, half a million Allied troops attacked the German positions, and 75,000 men were killed or wounded. The 2nd U.S. Division was assigned a narrow, 1.25-mile (2-km) front in the center of the American First Army's position. Its mission was to spearhead the attack and drive a wedge deep into German-held territory, through Landres-et-St Georges to the vicinity of Fosse. Unlike previous engagements, heavy artillery was assigned to the division; 300 guns supported the attack.

At 03:30 hours on November 1, Allied artillery commenced firing a

Left: A Marine stands watch along Germany's Rhine River as a member of the Army of Occupation after the armistice. The Marines finally returned home in the summer of 1919, and were honored by a parade before President Wilson at the White House.

thunderous barrage. Explosive and gas shells rained down on German positions for nearly two hours. Gunners of the 6th Machine Gun Battalion fired into the enemy lines. The enemy countered. As the 1st Battalion, 6th Marines formed up for the assault, more than 100 men were killed or wounded by German artillery fire.

The 2nd U.S. Division went over the top at 05:30 hours. The 1st Battalion, 5th Marines was positioned to the right, while the 1st Battalion, 6th Marines was to the left. Under heavy fire, the Marines fought their way forward through a war-torn landscape and tangles of barbed wire. The German Maxim machine guns took a heavy toll. One young Marine distinguished himself that day. With his company taking heavy fire from a German machine-gun nest, Private David T. Depue of the 76th Company took a Chauchat automatic rifle from a dead gunner. Firing all the while as he moved forward, Private Depue was hit twice by German gunfire. By the time he had reached the machine-gun nest, he was out of ammunition as well as being fatally wounded. Using the Chauchat as a club, he silenced the German gun and its crew, before he died.

The Marines smashed through German defenses, gained about 2 miles (3.25 km) and seized the village of Imecourt. At 08:00 hours, the 2nd Battalion, 5th Marines and 3rd Battalion, 6th Marines took the lead. The 3rd Battalion encountered heavy German resistance near the town of Bayonville. Here the Germans had secondary defensive fortifications, the Freya Stellung. French tanks supporting the Marines helped secure the area. By mid-afternoon, the 3rd Battalion, 5th Marines and the 2nd Battalion, 6th Marines leapfrogged to the front of the attack and seized the day's objective—Barricourt Heights

Below: Flying with the British Royal Air Force, three crews of Marine aviators participate in the first aerial resupply in Marine Corps history. Food and supplies were dropped to a surrounded French regiment.

was in Allied hands. The Germans retreated, blowing the bridges as they crossed the Meuse River.

Major General Charles P. Summerall, who was commanding general of the First Army's V Corps, later wrote about that day:

> "The division's brilliant advance of more than 9 kilometers [5.5 miles], destroying the last stronghold on the Hindenburg line, capturing the Freya Stellung, and going more than 9 kilometers against not only the permanent but the relieving forces in their front, may justly be regarded as one of the most remarkable achievements made by any troops in this war."

By November 6, the front lines of the 4th Marine Brigade were along the Meuse. On the evening of November 7, orders were issued from First Army headquarters. The 2nd U.S. Division was to cross the Meuse and seize the ridgeline on the east side. The time set for the attack was the night of November 10, the 143rd birthday of the Marine Corps. Under heavy artillery and machine-gun fire, the Second Engineers threw two footbridges over the Meuse. The 1st and 2nd Battalions of the 5th Marines crossed the river. They took heavy casualties in the process; a total of 31 killed and 148 wounded. Joined by a battalion of the 89th Division, they then advanced eastward toward Moulins. By morning, they had learned of the armistice. The "war to end all wars" was finally over. Thirty-two thousand Marines had served with the Allies in France against the Germans, and the Corps had suffered 11,366 casualties, of whom a total of 2,459 were listed as killed or missing in action.

Six days after the armistice, the 4th Marine Brigade marched toward Germany as part of the U.S. Third Army. They crossed a war-torn landscape, through Belgium and across Luxembourg. The Marines reached the German border on November 23. There, some received fresh uniforms, and new Browning machine guns and automatic rifles replaced old equipment—this was not a time of peace, but rather of truce effected by the armistice. Finally, on December 1, 1918, the 4th Marine Brigade marched into Germany itself. They were to serve as part of the army of occupation. John Thomason commented:

> "There were very few men in the column who remembered the hike to Verdun, in the early spring of 1918; in one company eight, in another eleven; in the whole battalion the barest handful. It had been a long road. The first way-station was the Bois de Belleau; a lot of people stopped there, and were there yet. And there were more, comfortably rotting in the Foret de Retz, south of Soissons. And more yet, well dead around Mont Blanc. And a vast drift of them back in hospitals. Men walked silent, remembering the old dead. ... Twelve hundred men hiking to the Rhine and how many ghosts ..."

The Marines crossed the Rhine on Friday December 13 making their way through in a cold, soaking rain. There, they took up positions in the area of occupation, the 5th Marines in the Wied Valley, the 6th Marines along the Rhine. Some manned the Rhine River

Above: The insignia adopted by the First Marine Aviation Force. Marine aviators flew a total of 57 bombing raids during World War I.

The division's brilliant advance ... destroying the last stronghold on the Hindenburg line ... may justly be regarded as one of the most remarkable achievements made by any troops in this war.

Above: Marine DH-4 Liberty-engined aircraft strike a German-held railroad yard in Thielt, Belgium. The Marine Corps' aviators performed well on a number of occasions during the war, with the British Royal Air Force and on their own.

Patrol. It was an uneventful seven months, before finally, in the summer of 1919, the 4th Marine Brigade returned to Quantico. On August 12, the Marines marched past the White House, reviewed by President Wilson. The next day, the brigade was demobilized. The surviving men of the 4th Marine Brigade either returned home or were assigned to other posts.

The men of the 4th Marine Brigade were not the only Marines to see action in France. On July 10, 1918, the second unit of Marine aviators traveled to New York, where they boarded a Navy transport. Designated the First Marine Aviation Force and operating with four squadrons, the unit deployed to France under the command of Captain Alfred Cunningham. They disembarked on July 30, 1918.

The unit faced problems from the beginning of its deployment. Upon arrival in France, there was no transportation to the base at Calais. After arranging train transportation for his men, Cunningham then discovered that there were no aircraft: the 72 American-built DH-4 bombers had been delivered unassembled. Undaunted, Cunningham approached the British. Fortunately, the Royal Air Force had a shortage of pilots and more aircraft than it could fly. Marine aviators were finally able to go into action.

First Aerial Resupply

On September 28, while flying with RAF Squadron No. 218, the Marines scored their first aerial victory when they were attacked by German fighters over Belgium. One week later, the Marines conducted the first aerial resupply drop in the Marine Corps history. Three crews, who were once again flying with the RAF, dropped food and supplies to a surrounded French regiment. By the middle of October, the unit had received DH-4s and DH-9As, a derivative of the DH-4.

The Marine aviators began to operate on their own. On October 14, the 1st Marine Aviation Force struck German-held railroad yards which were located in Thielt, Belgium. During the return flight, the Marines were intercepted by a dozen German fighters, a force comprised of the highly maneuverable Pfalz D-IIIs and Fokker D-VIIs. The slower, less agile American bombers made the Marines vulnerable. The Germans swarmed the DH-4 which was piloted by Second Lieutenant Ralph Talbot. His gunner, Corporal Robert G. Robinson, shot down one of the Germans, but was severely wounded.

He continued to fire his guns as Talbot attempted to shake off the German attack. Wounded twice more, Robinson collapsed. Talbot turned his aircraft toward the onslaught and shot down one of the Germans with his fixed guns before putting the bomber into a

n

ave

l ear

onr

A lot

nt countries

t

at we

ithout

ne thing

s how

I lliad

steep dive. After swooping low over German trenches, he landed safely at a Belgian airfield. Robinson survived the ordeal, and both he and Talbot were issued with the highest American accolade, the Medal of Honor.

By the armistice of November 11, 1918, Marine aviators had flown a total of 57 flight missions. Of these, 43 had been with the Royal Air Force and 14 were on their own. They had four confirmed victories over German fighters, and claimed eight more. It was an auspicious beginning for Marine Corps aviation.

World War I was undoubtedly a turning point in Marine Corps history. The gallant deeds of the Marines of the 2nd U.S. Division on the battlefield had proven that Marine claims of valor were not simply a recruiting ploy. The Corps had won both military respectability and public approval. Throughout the war years, Marines performed a number of duties. They served on board every naval vessel, as well as in duty stations, from the Caribbean to Siberia. But the glory fell upon those Marines who had served, bled, and died during the "Great War." These men came to symbolize the Marine Corps image of battlefield bravery, comraderie, courage, and ferocity. Brigadier-General Wendell C. Neville, who was commanding officer of the 4th Marine Brigade, published the following tribute to his men:

> "Your display of fortitude, determination, courage and your ability to fight has upon more than one occasion been a determining factor in making history. … Along the fronts of Verdun, the Marne, the Aisne, Lorraine, Champagne, and the Argonne, units of the Fourth Brigade Marines have fought valiantly, bravely, and decisively. They have nobly sustained the sacred traditions and have added glorious pages to the already illustrious history of the United States Marine Corps."

"Units of the Fourth Brigade Marines have fought valiantly, bravely, and decisively. They have nobly sustained the sacred traditions and have added glorious pages to the already illustrious history of the United States Marine Corps."

Left: Marines of the U.S. 2nd Division parade through New York City. They had fought the Germans at Belleau Wood and had enhanced the reputation of the Corps as a fighting unit. News of their deeds was published in a first-hand account in the *Chicago Tribune*.

CHAPTER THREE

BETWEEN THE WARS

The Marine Corps was no stranger to the violence that plagued the nations of the Caribbean. Prior to World War I, the Marines had been involved in the "limited wars" that threatened Haiti and Nicaragua. These were the "Banana Wars," unpopular at home and hated by much of the native populations. As the "great war" raged in Europe, in those small countries, a new era of guerrilla warfare began.

Left: Marines armed with Springfield rifles and a Lewis gun in a stream bed in Haiti in 1918, hunting the *caco* rebels and their leader, Peralte.

Right: U.S. Marines undergo inspections aboard ship. Then, as now, Marines were expected to present a smart and tidy appearance at all times.

American involvement in the Dominican Republic was growing substantially. The United States Government was determined to fight any anti-American activity.

In the spring of 1916, while the United States was drawing ever closer to war with Germany, a situation closer to home demanded attention. The government of the Dominican Republic had fled the country, leaving it in chaos. Throughout the eastern provinces, banditry was rife. President Woodrow Wilson feared for the security of American interests in the small nation. On May 5, as political factions battled in the capital of Santo Domingo, the president ordered 150 Marines into the Dominican Republic, under the command of Captain Frederic M. "Dopey" Wise. They were to guard both the Haitian and American legations. As the political climate grew more unstable, more Marines were ordered into the Caribbean nation. By May 15, a battalion of Marines occupied key points throughout the city of Santo Domingo. Three more companies arrived, and by the end of May more than 750 Marines were ashore. Wise, with a group of sailors and Marines under his command, sailed around the island and secured the town of Monte Cristi. Some 150 rebels launched a counterattack, but were sprayed with fire from Wise's single machine gun. On June 1, fleet Marines landed on the northern coast of the Dominican Republic. They took heavy rifle fire from anti-government rebels. Naval guns were turned on the Dominican positions. The rebels fled and the Americans succeeded in capturing one of the forts overlooking the city of Puerto Plata.

American involvement in the Dominican Republic was growing substantially. The United States Government was determined to fight any anti-American activity, so a larger American presence was required. The 4th Marine Regiment, under the command of Colonel Joseph H. Pendleton, was ordered to New Orleans, where it embarked for the Dominican Republic. On June 18, the 4th Marines landed in Monte Cristi. Pendleton assumed nominal command of the 2nd Marine Brigade, which included all Marine forces on the island. Leaving 235 Marines to garrison the town, Pendleton led 837 men toward Santiago de los Caballeros, where rebel forces had established a government. Twenty-four miles (38.6 km) into the march, they encountered Las Trencheras, two fortified ridges the Dominicans had long thought invulnerable: the Spanish had been defeated there in 1864. This time, though, the Dominicans would not defeat the Marines. At 08:00 hours on June 27, Pendleton ordered his artillery to pound the ridgeline. Machine guns offered covering fire. A bayonet attack led by Major Robert H. Dunlap cleared the first ridge. Rifle fire removed the rebels who were threatening from atop the second.

A week later, the Marines encountered another entrenched rebel force at Guayacanas. Again, machine guns and artillery were used with deadly results. The rebels were routed. Pendleton's Marines reached the town of Navarette, where they joined forces with two companies of Marines from Puerto Plata. Met by a delegation from Santiago, the Marines marched peacefully into the capital city on July 6, and began rounding up rebels. As clashes between Dominicans and U.S. forces became more violent, the State Department took drastic measures. On November 29, 1916, a military government was imposed upon the Caribbean nation. Captain Harry S. Knapp, USN was appointed governor of the Dominican Republic. Dominican officials refused to serve in the government and Americans were appointed to virtually all administrative posts. Knapp's government banned firearms and instituted strict censorship. Northeast of Santiago, in San Francisco de Macoris, the Dominican Governor Juan Perez refused to recognize the military government. Over 150 rebels were held prisoner in the local fortaleza. Fearful that these would be turned loose by Perez, a dozen Marines, under the command of First Lieutenant Ernest C. Williams, seized control of the fort. Perez fled, moving south with over 200 of his well-armed followers.

The military government was widely despised and anti-American sentiment continued to grow. The task of squashing rebel groups and disarming the Dominican populace fell to Pendelton's 2nd Marine Brigade. Hundreds of patrols were sent out in search of rebel forces. The Marines encountered stiff resistance throughout early 1917. In January, they pursued a rebel leader known as "Chacha," whose forces were engaged on a sugar plantation near San Francisco de Macoris. "Chacha" and a few of his men surrendered to the

Below: This painting, by Howard Christy Chandler, was used as a recruiting poster. By the end of World War I, the ranks of Marine aviators had swollen to include a total of 282 officers and 2,180 enlisted Marines.

AVIATION

FLY WITH THE U.S. MARINES.

Marines, but the fight was simply taken up by another rebel leader. To the north, near El Seibo, Vincentico Evangelista held out against the Americans. In March, a Marine patrol was attacked by rebel forces. Fifteen of the rebels were killed and several more, including Evangelista, were wounded. A few months later, the rebel leader surrendered, with some 200 of his men, to Marine Lieutenant-Colonel George Thorpe. Shortly afterward, Evangelista was killed, reportedly while trying to escape. Because of the death of Evangelista, the rebellion was broken.

On the recommendation of the newly promoted Brigadier-General Pendleton, the Dominican Army was disbanded. A native constabulary, the *Guardia Nacional Dominica*, was established. Marine officers and NCOs served as *Guardia* officers. Widely distrusted and considered a puppet of the American oppressors, the *Guardia*'s initial responsibilities were to garrison towns and protect the border with Haiti. However, on April 6, 1917, the United States entered the war against Germany. Much of the 2nd Marine Brigade was sent to France. To the north, the Marines were left with fewer than 500 men to patrol an area covering some 8,400 square miles (21,760 sq km). The situation to the south, including Santo Domingo and the provinces of Macoris and Seibo, was the same. The main rebellion had been broken, but sporadic fighting continued. Marine patrols were ambushed. With insufficient Marines to fight the remaining rebels, the *Guardia* was ordered into the field.

Below: This painting by Colonel D.J. Neary, USMCR shows how Major Smedley Butler, Sergeant Iams, and Private Gross entered Fort Riviere on Haiti in November 1915 via a hole in the old French fort's wall. Major Butler won his second Medal of Honor for capturing the fort.

By 1918, the eastern provinces of the Dominican Republic were a hotbed of vicious guerrilla activity. Marines fought more than 100 skirmishes against the rebels. As the war in Europe ended, the 15th Marines and 1st Marine Air Squadron joined the fighting in the Dominican Republic. In early 1919, with more than 3,000 Marines ashore, the number of patrols in the bandit provinces of Macoris and Seibo increased substantially. The six DH-4s flown by Marine aviators provided invaluable support and reconnaissance, often spotting rebel forces moving through the jungle. Engaging the bandits in one firefight after another, the Marines slowly eroded the strength of the rebel forces.

Above: Native huts in the Dominican Republic are searched for secret arms stores by Springfield-armed Marines. The Marines are being watched by two inhabitants and their dog. Many Nicaraguans suspected of guerrilla activity were arrested during these rural search operations, and most were convicted.

In December 1920, President Wilson announced the withdrawal of Marines from the Dominican Republic, in spite of the fact that the rebels had not been defeated. Marine strength in the Caribbean nation was immediately cut by one-third. In the troublesome eastern provinces, however, the military governor authorized a campaign to eliminate the rebel forces. A series of cordon-and-search operations was planned: entire villages were sealed off and screened for guerrillas. The Marines simply surrounded a village in the early morning hours, and a mounted detail then arrived to question the villagers, often using information provided by local prostitutes. Those suspected of rebel activities were taken into custody. Most were convicted. The remaining bandits either surrendered or were apprehended. By the spring of 1922, the guerrilla war in the Dominican Republic was over. On July 12, 1924, a constitutional government was established and peace reigned. By September of that came year, the Marines had departed the island nation.

Haiti in Turmoil

The Dominican Republic, however, was not the only troublespot in the Caribbean. In neighboring Haiti, a period of relative peace was shattered on October 11, 1917. The *cacos* attacked the home of Colonel John L. Doxey, commander of the *Gendarmerie* district of Hinche. The attack was easily thrown back and the *caco* leader killed. Three brothers were implicated in the plan, and one of them, the European-educated Charlemagne Messena Peralte, was sentenced to five years of hard labor. Humiliated by his punishment, Peralte's hatred of the *Gendarmerie* and the U.S. Marines festered and grew.

In the fall of 1918, Peralte escaped, fleeing into the Haitian hills. At the same time, political unrest grew. The commandant of the *Gendarmerie*, Colonel Alexander S. Williams,

Above: This *Gendarme* was painted by John Thomason. The ranks of the *Gendarmerie d'Haiti* were drawn from the Haitian populace, with U.S. Marines serving as their officers.

ordered the abolishment of the *corvée* (the forced labor system), but rumors ran rampant that slavery was to be re-established. Insurrection spread throughout northern and central Haiti, and the disenchanted found a leader in Charlemagne Peralte. Soon there were thousands of *cacos*, operating in scattered groups. *Gendarmerie* detachments were attacked, weapons and ammunitions stolen. On October 17, a band of 100 *cacos* attacked the *Gendarmerie* post at Hinche. A month later, Peralte and his men raided Maissade, robbing City hall, and burning the town and the *Gendarmerie* barracks. *Caco* activity continued to increase. *Gendarme* patrols were ambushed, officers killed.

Initially, the commandant of the *Gendarmerie* attempted to fight the insurrection with the forces he had available. However, it soon became clear that the *cacos* were too strong, too numerous. In March 1919, Williams requested the assistance of the 1st Marine Brigade. It duly arrived in Haiti, reinforced by seven Curtiss HS-2 flying boats and six Curtiss JN-4b "Jennies" of the 4th Marine Air Squadron. Combat patrols of Marines and *Gendarmes* were sent into the Haitian hills, but the activities of the *cacos* grew bolder and increasingly frequent. An average of 20 firefights a month were fought against Peralte's men, who attacked in force, only to disappear into the jungles. Infantry and aviators began working together to combat the *cacos*. In August, the first coordinated air-ground attack occurred near Mirebalais. A Marine Curtiss Jenny and a DH-4 worked in conjunction with an infantry company to attack a *caco* camp. Ground forces set up an ambush. As bombs were dropped on the rebel stronghold, the *cacos* ran for cover—and into the Marines' trap. More than 200 of Peralte's forces were killed or wounded.

Despite losses in manpower, the *cacos* continued to wage a guerrilla war. On October 7, 1919, Peralte and a *caco* force of over 300 men approached the capital city of Port-au-Prince and demanded that the president surrender. The Marines and *Gendarmes* had been forewarned and, when the *cacos* marched into the city later that night, easily repelled the attack. It was clear, however, that there would be no end to the rebellion until Charlemagne Peralte was confronted. This would not be easy: Peralte was constantly on the move, and heavily guarded. The task fell to Marine Sergeant Herman H. Hannekan, a captain in the *Gendarmerie*. The 26-year-old Hannekan concocted an elaborate plan to ambush the *caco* leader. Two Haitian civilians and a *Gendarme* were to pose as renegades and denounce the American involvement in Haiti; they would then establish themselves as *caco* leaders in the Fort Capois area. Hannekan's three agents attracted a large following, and the notice of Peralte. As a ruse, Hannekan's detachment faked attacks on Fort Capois. He dispatched part of his forces to Cap Haitian, and made it known that his forces were "weakened."

Hannekan's agents convinced Peralte to attack the town of Grande Rivière du Nord. Peralte agreed and arrived at Fort Capois with almost 1,000 of his men. The plan was simple. The *cacos* would attack on October 31. Peralte would wait in nearby Mazare, then enter Grand Rivière in triumph. The night before Peralte's planned attack, the Marines strengthened the garrison at Grand Rivière. Blackening their faces with burned cork, Hannekan and Marine Corporal William R. Button went to Mazare accompanied by some 20 well-armed *Gendarmes*. There was no sign of Peralte. One of Hannekan's agents, *Gendarme* Private Jean Edmond Francois, appeared out of the night. Peralte, he told them, was awaiting the outcome of the *caco* attack in a hilltop encampment located between Fort Capois and Grand Rivière. As soon as Grand Rivière had fallen fallen, the *cacos* were instructed to deliver the news to Peralte, using a coded message.

Hannekan boldly decided that he, Button, and their small group of *Gendarmes* would go to Peralte. The group hiked for several hours before reaching the first *caco* checkpoint. Francois, well known to the *cacos*, easily led them through, but there were several more outposts ahead. One sentry questioned Button about the Browning automatic rifle he carried. Replying that it was a captured weapon, the Marine was allowed to proceed. Before daybreak, Hannekan and his men were escorted to Peralte, who stood by a fire. Drawing his Colt .45, Hannekan fired two shots into the *caco* leader's chest. Button and the *Gendarmes* then opened fire on the rebel forces. Finally, the Marines slung Peralte's body across a mule and returned to Grand Rivière, fighting off sporadic *caco* attacks. To end any speculation on the rebel's demise, photographs were taken and distributed throughout the Haitian countryside. Hannekan's plan had been brilliant, bold, and daring. Charlemagne

Below: Led by a local guide (at the forefront, wearing a straw hat) a section of Marines moves cautiously along a stream bed through the arduous jungle of Haiti, in search of the *caco* guerrillas.

Above: In this 1923 photograph, Marine officers pose for the camera in front of a DH-4B at the Flying Field in Port-au-Prince, Haiti.

Peralte was dead, and not one member of Hannekan's forces had been lost. For their extraordinary heroism, both Button and Hannekan were awarded the Medal of Honor.

Peralte's death, however, did not spell the end of the *cacos*. In central Haiti, Benoit Batraville emerged as the new rebel leader, conducting sporadic raids throughout the countryside. The Marine Brigade, now under the command of Colonel John H. Russell, took steps to crush the rebellion. A system of rotating patrols was established. As one group of *Gendarmes* tired, another would take up the chase in constant pursuit of the *caco* forces. The rebels camped at night, so patrols moved in the dark, seeking the element of surprise. Many days were spent on horseback. It was, according to Marine Private Lewis B. Puller, a Second Lieutenant in the *Gendarmerie*, "a dog's life." On January 14, 1920, the forces of Benoit Batraville attacked Port-au-Prince. The *caco* assault was repelled, more than half of the rebel forces killed or wounded. The fighting, however, continued in the countryside.

It was during this time that Marine aviators began developing better tactics to aid the troops on the ground. In the heavy jungles of the Caribbean, the aviator's role had essentially been one of support, providing reconnaissance, resupply, and medical evacuation. Lieutenant Lawson Sanderson, one of the premier Marine aviators of the era, began experimenting with the technique of "dive-bombing." Sanderson discovered that bombing accuracy could be significantly increased by pushing his aircraft into a 45-degree dive and releasing the ordnance at a low altitude. Pilots of the 4th Marine Air Squadron used this technique with great success. In one instance, the aviators bombed a large *caco* force. The rebels scattered, seeking cover, but were driven into heavy crossfire coming from two converging *Gendarme* patrols. Batraville's forces sustained hundreds of casualties in the attack, and the *caco* leader at once demanded retribution.

On April 4, 1920, Batraville's forces ambushed a patrol and captured Marine Sergeant Lawrence Muth, a lieutenant in the *Gendarmerie*. Muth was badly injured, sustaining several wounds in the initial exchange of gunfire. Three other Marines and a number of *Gendarmes* escaped, but the lieutenant was left for dead. When patrols reached the scene the following day, little was left of the Marine. Indeed, Puller reported, "There wasn't a piece of flesh or bone as large as my hand." Batraville had sliced open the Marine with his machete, then cut out his heart and liver and consumed them. Next, he decapitated Muth and finally smeared the man's brain matter on the rifles carried by his men. As news of the atrocity spread, the Marines were enraged. The hunt for Batraville took on new meaning. On May 18, a Marine patrol led by Captain Jesse L. Perkins and Sergeant William F. Passmore discovered the *caco* leader's camp. Passmore, armed with a Browning automatic rifle, entered the camp and shot Batraville. The rebel struggled to his feet, but Sergeant Albert Taubert calmly shot him again, this time in the head. Batraville died carrying the pistol that had been issued to the butchered Sergeant Muth.

The death of Batraville brought an end to the *caco* revolt. The Marines remained, however, officially to train the *Gendarmes* and preserve the stability that Haiti now enjoyed. There was widespread criticism of their presence on the small island. Rumors insisted that brutality on the part of individual Marines was commonplace, and that atrocities had been committed. Investigations by both a Naval court of inquiry and a U.S. Senate committee

Below: Marines of the 2nd Regiment fire a 1.46 in. (37 mm) gun in February 1926 against the *caco* rebels, who were led by the charismatic Peralte, in Haiti. The gun had given good service to the Marines during the conflicts of World War I.

At dawn, Sandino sent a flag of truce to Captain Hatfield, demanding the surrender of the Marines. Hatfield's response was succinct: "Marines don't know how to surrender."

Below: Marines unload an artillery piece from a armored "Beetle boat." The Marine Corps experimented with the British-designed craft in the early 1920s but found it essentially useless.

largely absolved the Marines, stating that a small number of offenses had been committed by individuals and had resulted in lengthy prison sentences. The 1920s were years of peace in Haiti. Over the course of the decade, the Marine Brigade was reduced to a force of some 500 men, as the *Gendarmerie* gradually improved both its equipment and its training. Finally, on August 15, 1934, the Marines departed Haiti.

The early 1920s seemed to herald a renewed stability in the Caribbean. Peace had come to the Dominican Republic; the *caco* revolt had come to an end in Haiti. In Nicaragua, the Marine Legation Guard had remained throughout World War I. In 1922, the Marines quieted a Liberal revolt, and by 1924 elections had been held and a coalition government had come to power. Carlos Solarzano, a Conservative, was to serve as president. A Liberal candidate, Juan Sacasa, was to be Nicaragua's vice-president. On August 4, 1925, the Marines were withdrawn. Three weeks later, civil war erupted in Nicaragua. By the end of October, both Solarzano and Sacasa had fled the country. Conservative General Emiliano Chamorro Vargas declared himself the new leader of Nicaragua in January 1926. In May, the Marine detachment from the cruiser U.S.S. *Cleveland* came ashore at Bluefields to protect the American colony there. They departed in June, only to return in August when rioting broke out. At that time, the Marines established a neutral zone around the city.

Peace Conference

The opposing factions were persuaded to accept an American-sponsored truce, and to attend a peace conference in Corinto. A Marine detachment from U.S.S. *Denver* landed to secure the city. Chamorro was suspicious and in November, resigned the presidency in favor of another Conservative—General Adolfo Diaz, who had served as President during the American intervention in 1912. He was immediately recognized by the United States, but was unable to end the Liberal rebellion. Liberal General Jose Maria Moncado

commanded an army based in eastern Nicaragua. With Mexico's aid, the former vice-president Juan Sacasa returned to Nicaragua and joined forces with Moncado's army. The rebels began raiding American-held companies. When a U.S. citizen was killed at Puerto Cabeza, President Coolidge authorized the sale of weapons and ammunition to Diaz's government. By March 7, 1927, 2,000 Leathernecks were ashore, including Marine Observation Squadron One with six DeHavilland aircraft. Fourteen towns were garrisoned—the second U.S. intervention in Nicaragua had begun.

President Coolidge sent Henry L. Stimson to Nicaragua to broker a peace treaty. The opposing parties each asked for a greater Marine presence in Nicaragua. It was agreed that the Marines would maintain law and order, and create a national constabulary, the *Guardia Nacional de Nicaragua*. A general amnesty was offered, with both sides required to surrender their weapons. Some 150 Liberals, led by Augusto Cesar Sandino, refused. Sandino, although physically frail, was charismatic: a vicious fighter and a ruthless enemy. With international support, money, and weapons, he fled to Nueva Segovia in northern Nicaragua. A Marine detachment was sent in pursuit. The terrain was wild and untamed, crisscrossed by gorges and rivers, but by July, Marines commanded by Captain Gilbert D. Hatfield, had established a base in Ocotal, capital of Nueva Segovia. These men were soon joined by the First Company of the *Guardia*.

Peking Horse Marines

Duty in China prior to the outbreak of World War II had long been considered very pleasant. To be part of the vaunted Peking Horse Marines was truly an honor. Mounted on sturdy Mongolian ponies, rather than horses, these Marines were the elite of the Peking Legation Guard, the only cavalry unit in the Corps. The unit had been established in 1912 and applicants were required to have clean service records. Their mission was to train as a cavalry unit, to deal with unruly or riotous crowds, and to escort American nationals to the safety of the Legation Quarter in the event of emergency. The duties they performed most often, however, were ceremonial in nature. In Peking, a weekly sunset parade was held for the American colony, followed by a reception. A battalion of infantry as well as the Horse Marines participated. The cavalry unit provided the grande finale, passing in front of the admiring crowd at a walk, a trot and then finally a gallop, their sabers flashing through the air.

Recognized for their "smart appearance, elan in mounted drill and arrogance," the Horse Marines carried Colt Automatic pistols as well as heavy straight-bladed swords. Each year the Marines were required to complete a saber qualification course. Considered a highlight of the year, the course required the mounted Marines to jump several obstacles and to successfully run though ten dummies placed strategically around the course. "Spirit and fighting manner" earned the qualifying Marines extra points. As the Japanese tightened their grip on China, and war with Japan loomed on the horizon, the majority of these Marines were withdrawn from China. Small garrisons remained in Tientsin and in Peking, but war spelled the end of the magnificent era of the Horse Marines.

Above: Marines prepare for a lengthy patrol in Nicaragua. Note their Browning water-cooled machine guns on tripods on the left.

Right: Marines proudly display Sandino's rebel colors, which were captured at Ocotal.

On July 15, Sandino and 500 of his men infiltrated Ocotal. At 01:15 hours, a Marine sentry spotted someone prowling through the dark streets. The first shot was fired. Sandino's men attacked in force. The Marines repelled three charges, but were surrounded. At dawn, Sandino sent a flag of truce to Captain Hatfield, demanding the surrender of the Marines. Hatfield's response was succinct: "Marines don't know how to surrender." Sandino's forces opened up on the Marine garrison. As the bullets flew wildly around him, Hatfield thought they would surely be overrun. However, the sound of aircraft engines overhead brought him renewed hope. Two DeHavilland DH-4s had seen the Marine garrison under attack. While one landed to interrogate a local peasant, the other strafed Sandino's men. Both planes then withdrew, flying to Managua for help.

Aerial Assault

By mid-afternoon, as the Sandinistas were preparing to attack again, five DH-4s and Boeing O2Bs appeared in the sky. Led by Major Ross E. Roswell, the Marine aviators were ready for a fight. The planes were armed with bombs and 600 rounds of machine-gun ammunition per gun. Sandino's men failed to take cover. The Marines dive-bombed the town, dropping bombs from 300 ft. (984 m) and firing curtains of bullets. The sustained attack continued for 45 minutes. Then, low on fuel, the aircraft turned to the south and flew out of sight. Major "Rusty" Roswell became the first Marine to be awarded the Distinguished Flying Cross.

On the ground, it was chaos. Buildings had been demolished. The horses ridden by Sandino's men had stampeded. The streets of Ocotal were filled with the dead and the dying: the Marines estimated that some 300 bandits had been killed in the attack. As the Sandinistas fled from Ocotal to the mountain stronghold of El Chipotle, Major Oliver Floyd was ordered to pursue the rebels. A force of some 225 mounted Marines and *Guardias* moved into Nueva Segovia and began the search for Sandino. They had no luck. When the rainy season began, a garrison force was left at Jicaro and the Marines returned to Managua. Undeterred by the earlier events at Ocotal, Sandino renewed the attack. At 01:00 hours on September 19, 1927, the Sandinistas struck the Marines garrisoned at Telpaneca. They were thrown back, however, and withdrew at daybreak, by which time two Marines had been killed by the rebels.

Sandino began to rethink his tactics. Where he had expected victory, he had instead suffered a humiliating defeat. The rebel leader learned from the mistake he had made at Ocotal: his forces now sought concealment, becoming masters of ambush and evasion; his machine gunners learned how to fight the aircraft that ruled the skies. In early October, those changes in strategy became apparent to the Marines in Nicaragua. Sandino's forces shot down one of two Marine aircraft patrolling Sapotillal Ridge in northern Nueva Segovia. The two fliers, Second Lieutenant Earl A. Thomas and Sergeant Frank E. Dowdwell, survived the crash but were captured by rebels. A Marine reconnaissance plane reported seeing the wreckage on the ridgeline and a 20-man patrol was dispatched to rescue the downed aviators. As the patrol advanced, the enemy opened fire. The Marines had walked into an ambush set up by several hundred Sandinistas. The Marine patrol was forced to withdraw, leaving behind three men dead.

Several days later, two larger patrols converged on the ridge, but the Marines had underestimated Sandino's strength and guile. More ambushes had been readied for the approaching troops. Bloodied by the Sandinistas, the Marines didn't reach the downed plane until October 30. By then, it was far too late: Sandino had executed the two aviators. The pursuit of the rebel leader intensified. On November 23, a reconnaissance flight finally discovered Sandino's mountaintop fortress at El Chipote. Initially, the stronghold was bombed and strafed. Then Colonel Louis M. Gulick dispatched two well-armed patrols to drive the Sandinistas from their mountain stronghold. Unfortunately, Sandino was again

Above: A Marine on "Mounted Patrol" somewhere in the Caribbean. He carries his rifle across his lap, ready for use. As Europe was embroiled in World War I, troublespots in the Caribbean also drew a large Marine presence to that area.

"No troops, guerrilla or otherwise, will stand in the face of a well-directed fragmentation bombing attack."

Below: Marines take a break in their search for Sandino's forces in the rugged Nicaraguan countryside. Forced to use trails to cross this forbidding terrain, most of it unchartered, the Marines' progress would be extremely slow.

underestimated and the patrols were severely undermanned. Gulick's plan called for one column of Marines and *Guardias*, under the leadership of Captain Richard Livingston, to depart Jinotega, while another group was dispatched from the town of Telpaneca. The two patrols, with a total of only 200 men, were to converge in the town of Quilali and establish a forward base before advancing toward El Chipote.

On December 30, Livingston's patrol was ambushed south of Quilali, on the banks of the Jicaro River. In slightly more than an hour, 7 members of the patrol were dead, another 25 wounded. The Marines continued to advance and were hit again. The second patrol was no more fortunate, intercepted by Sandino's forces at Sapotillal. Machine-gun fire and dynamite bombs ripped through the patrol, causing several casualties. Gunnery Sergeant Edward G. Brown managed to rally the men and take the high ground at Las Cruces Hill. The Marines dug in and waited for what was left of Livingston's patrol to arrive. The combined patrols spent the night on hill, then battled their way back to Quilali. Sandino seized the opportunity and laid siege to the town. The situation was desperate: the Marines were surrounded and had no way out, supplies were low, and several men were critically wounded. They requested the wounded be evacuated by air. There was, however, no airstrip at Quilali. The Marines decided to construct one. Marine aircraft dropped tools to the men on the ground, and within a short period of time, the Leathernecks had filled holes and demolished buildings to clear the town's main street. This emergency landing strip was dangerously short, only 500 ft. (152 m) in length, and ended abruptly at the top of a cliff.

First Lieutenant Christian F. Schilt volunteered for the dangerous mission. In order to carry more supplies, and evacuate more wounded, Schilt ordered his plane stripped. The aircraft was disarmed, the parachute left behind. On January 6, 1928, flying his new Vought

O2U-1 Corsair through low clouds and rebel fire, Schilt approached the makeshift airfield. Marines on the ground ran forward to grab the wings as he came down, and hauled the aircraft to a stop. The Corsair had no brakes. It seemed like a recipe for total disaster, but over the course of three days, Schilt was able to make a total of ten landings. The most seriously wounded Marines were evacuated and some 1,400 lb. (635 kg) of food, ammunition, and medicine were delivered. For his "incredible display of flying skill and Marine courage," Christian Schilt was awarded the Medal of Honor.

On January 10, reinforcements arrived. The Marines, once again, moved north toward El Chipote and Sandino. A few days later, a four-plane strikeforce led by Major Roswell hit the rebel stronghold. The Sandinistas responded with primitive, but very heavy anti-aircraft fire. The Marine aviators strafed the rebel positions and dropped bombs and white phospherous grenades. Major Roswell later wrote, "No troops, guerrilla or otherwise, will stand in the face of a well-directed fragmentation bombing attack." Nonetheless, the tenacity of Sandino's forces led to the reinforcement of the Marines deployed in Nicaragua. The 11th Marines returned and moved into Nueva Segovia. The Sandinistas were driven out of the stronghold and into eastern Nicaragua.

A new strategy was proposed by the commander of the Marine detachment aboard the U.S.S. *Denver*. Captain Merritt A. Edson's plans centered on the Coco River. He recommended the river be reconnoiterred, and the lower section garrisoned. A series of combat patrols would then be sent upriver into Sandino's territory and the rebels trapped between them. Sandino would either have to flee into neighboring Honduras or surrender. Edson was ordered to begin patrols. His mission was to map the wild terrain, and gather information on the Sandinistas. On March 7, Edson and five Marines hired a boat and a guide and set out up the Coco River. It was not an easy trip, but the Marines penetrated

Above: Marines patrol the Coco River. Often these patrols lasted for months, the Marines living off the land and depending on Marine aviators for resupply of ammunition and food. In March 1928, one group, led by Captain Merritt A. Edson, traveled 260 miles (418 km) up the Coco River on a reconnaissance patrol and came back with a wealth of information.

"I have a territory of some 200 miles [322 km] long by 50 [80.5 km] miles wide to cover with a force of 60 men ... If you can supply me with food and clothing by air, I believe that my command can make it decidedly uncomfortable for the outlaws ..."

Below: This Marine has been ambushed by the forces of Augusto Sandino. After the Sandinistas were routed at Ocotal, the bandits became masters of concealment and ambush.

260 miles (418 km) into Nicaragua's forbidding interior and returned with a wealth of information. Sandino, Edson reported, had forces at large as far east as Bocay. He recommended that a strong Marine force be based at Waspuc.

In early April, the Sandinistas seized two goldmines and Edson moved up the river to lay an ambush. The Marine patrol hit rough water and its boat overturned. Weapons and rations were lost. Edson managed to reequip the patrol, but after two days march, no sign of the enemy was found. Edson returned to Waspuc convinced that more men were needed. His troops were too few in number and too far-flung to deal with Sandino's forces. In late April, the Marines in the eastern region of Nicaragua finally received reinforcements, when two companies of the 11th Marines arrived. Edson's commanding officer, Major Harold H. Utley, began planning an operation against the Sandinistas. He ordered Edson to move up the Waspuc River and block Sandino's escape to the west.

On May 4, Edson and 31 Marines left Waspuc. For three months, the patrol pursued the rebels through the mountainous wilds of Nicaragua. The shoes on the Marine's feet rotted in the wet jungle. Malaria struck. Rations were short and the men had to forage for food. Canned beans gave way to bananas and monkey meat, which Edson later described as "the sweetest and most tender of any meat I have ever eaten." The patrol stopped for a few days in the village of Musawas, along the Waspuc River. There, they had a chance to recover. On May 20, reinforcements and supplies arrived. Edson and his men moved out on the morning of the 25th, heading for Bocay and Sandino's new stronghold. It was the rainy season and the elements proved as tough an adversary as the Sandinistas. Intelligence indicated that the rebel forces would be in Bocay on June 3. The Marines reached there on the 2nd. Sandino's forces, though, had been and gone. Edson's patrol returned to the coast.

Thorn in America's Side

The Sandinistas were a thorn in the side of the United States. The American Government wanted an end to the conflict and new elections held in Nicaragua. Sandino's fierce nationalism, however, could undermine the stability of any new government; he had to be neutered. By late June, intelligence reports placed a large Sandinista force in the village of Poteca. Edson was once again ordered to take a patrol up the Coco River. The Marines were to seize the town and drive Sandino into a trap. On July 26, Edson and his patrol, only 46 Marines strong, started out from Bocay. The hellish rains made overland travel impossible, so the Marines planned to move by river. It rained steadily for the next five days. One of the boats overturned, and invaluable weapons and rations were lost. As the rains continued to fall, the

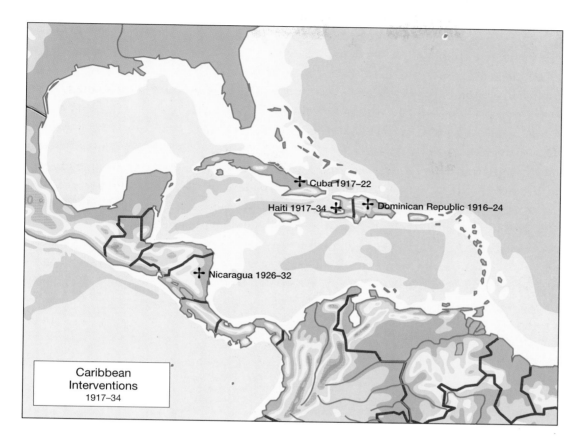

Caribbean
Interventions
1917–34

Cuba 1917–22

Haiti 1917–34

Dominican Republic 1916–24

Nicaragua 1926–32

Left: A map showing the interventions by the Marine Corps in the Caribbean during the interwar period. Much of the Marine Corps' strength was tied down in the area, thus weakening their presence in other areas of the world.

river rose, becoming a raging torrent, and travel became virtually impossible. A few days later, more provisions were lost to the weather: medical supplies, ammunition, weapons, and rations all plunged to the bottom of the swollen river.

By August 6, the Marines saw increased signs of enemy activity in the area. The patrol proceeded up the river toward Ililiquas, with a squad advancing on each bank. The terrain rose steeply on each side of the river, and the heavy brush and bamboo along the banks were impenetrable. As the Marines got into the boats to maneuver through the difficult territory, an enemy guerrilla was seen on the shore. The patrol began firing, at which point enemy machine guns opened up and rifle fire from the western bank cut through the Marines. Edson's patrol regrouped and advanced on the Sandinista positions from each side of the river. Initially, the Marines met little resistance but soon encountered rifle and machine-gun fire. As the patrol returned fire, however, the guerrillas retreated. Private Myer Stengel was killed in the exchange, and another four Marines were wounded. For his actions that day, Captain Merritt Edson was awarded his first Navy Cross.

The patrol spent the night recovering. Edson planned on continuing the advance up the river, but was concerned. Intelligence indicated a large Sandinista force in the area and the Marines were short on both men and ammunition. He prudently decided to withdraw and link up with another patrol. Frustrated, he wrote to Major Utley, expressing his concerns:

"I have a territory of some 200 miles [322 km] long by 50 miles [80.5 km] wide to cover with a force of 60 men. … If you can supply me with food and clothing by air, I believe that my command can make it decidedly uncomfortable for the outlaws. … If this is approved, I shall cut loose from boats, and using captured animals, move by trail."

As weather conditions improved, Edson's patrol received regular aerial resupply, and on August 17, the patrol reached the town of Poteca. The Marines lost no time strengthening their hold on the town and by September, barbed-wire fences were in place, trenches had been dug, and three Browning heavy machine guns were in place. From there, they were able to expand their patrols. To the west, Marine–*Guardia* patrols engaged Sandinista forces sporadically; however, a lull in the fighting occurred during the November elections. For the first time in Nicaragua, the Liberals were victorious. General Jose Maria Moncada was elected president of Nicaragua.

By early 1929, the fighting resumed. As the *Guardia* became more effective, Marines Corps strength in Nicaragua was decreased. By August 20, only some 2,000 Marines remained, though the campaign against the Sandinistas continued. Sandino, who had left Nicaragua to seek financial help, returned to the country. A Marine reconnaissance plane discovered his camp, and the area was bombed and heavily strafed. Sandino was wounded and retreated into the wilderness to recover, but ordered his forces to step up the guerrilla war. Both the *Guardia* and Marines responded with increased patrols, engaging the Sandinistas

Below: This Curtiss "Falcon" saw duty over Nicaragua. Marine aviation proved invaluable during the campaign, providing medical evacuation, resupply, reconnaissance, as well as close air support for the men on the ground.

frequently in bloody, no-quarter fighting. Particularly troublesome to Sandino was the Marine company led by Lieutenant Lewis B. "Chesty" Puller. On September 20, Puller, Gunnery Sergeant William "Iron Man" Lee and 40 men left the town of Jinotega to search for a trail used by the Sandinistas as a supply route. Six days later, the patrol was ambushed by some 150 rebels armed with automatic weapons and dynamite bombs. The rebel fire was intense. Lee was wounded, but firing a Lewis machine gun, managed to pin the enemy forces down. Puller's men climbed the ridges above the trail and fired on the rebels, killing at least ten of them. The patrol itself suffered two dead and three wounded. Puller headed back toward Jinotega, but the patrol was forced to fight its way through two more ambushes. Puller was awarded his second Navy Cross; Gunnery Sergeant Lee, his third.

On November 6, 1932, the Liberals, once again, won the election. Juan B. Sacasa became president of Nicaragua. The day after his inauguration, the remaining elements of the 5th Marines sailed for the United States, their intervention at an end. However, Sandino still roamed the countryside. In 1934, under the pretense of negotiating a truce, Sacasa lured Sandino to Managua. There, elements of the *Guardia* assassinated the rebel leader.

While the Marines assigned duty in the Caribbean often endured hardships, duty in China was initially much more pleasant. During the early 1920s, China was descending into chaos. The Nationalists, under the leadership of Chiang Kai-shek, fought both the warlords of the north and the Communists. The country dissolved into general panic. Trade was disrupted and anti-foreign sentiment grew. In 1927, Chiang Kai-shek's forces marched on Shanghai. The International Settlement, the very center of foreign trade in China, was threatened. On March 16, the 4th Marines landed. Their mission was to aid the British in keeping the Chinese out of the International Settlement. Nine days later,

Above: This mounted patrol prepares to depart. Searching the Nicaraguan jungles for the forces of Sandino was a time-consuming and arduous task for the Marines involved in the operation. Mounted Marines were used in July 1927, when a force of 225 scoured Nueva Segovia in search of the rebel leader.

As diplomatic relations with Japan worsened, the 4th Marines were withdrawn. In late November 1941, the Marines marched to the docks. Cheering crowds lined the streets as the last transport departed Shanghai.

Brigadier-General Smedley Butler arrived with aviation and artillery units. By early May, most of the 6th Marines were ashore. Butler assumed command of all Marines stationed in China, organized as the 3rd Marine Brigade. As war raged in the north, Butler left the 4th Marines in Shanghai. The remainder of the 3rd Marine Brigade traveled to Tientsin, ready to aid Peking in the event of trouble. When Chiang Kai-shek became president of China, the 3rd Marine Brigade was withdrawn. The Legation Guard remained in Peking, while some 1,150 men of the 4th Marines stayed in Shanghai.

The Invasion of Manchuria

Duty in China was very pleasant for the Marines. Paid $21 a month, a Marine could live very well. Spacious quarters were inexpensive, as were servants. The women were beautiful, accommodating, and affordable. Food and drink were cheap. A bottle of Chinese beer was priced at two cents a quart and even the enlisted men could afford a houseboy to maintain their equipment and uniforms. The idyll ended in September 1931 when the Japanese launched a campaign of conquest against China. In a grab for land and resources, Japan invaded Manchuria. Its iron ore and coal were seized, the puppet state of Manchukuo established. In January 1932 Japanese forces attacked the Chinese in Shanghai. Only the narrow Soochow Creek separated the fighting from the International Settlement. Fearing a Japanese attack, the Marines manned the barricades that surrounded the settlement. By March, however, the burst of fighting had ended.

On July 7, 1937, the Second Sino–Japanese War began when fighting broke out between the Chinese and the Japanese on the Marco Polo Bridge in Peking. By August 8, the ancient city had fallen. Chiang Kai-shek and Communist leader Chou En-Lai agreed to suspend the civil war that had raged for several years and instead to fight the Japanese.

Right: A Marine Corps transport plane in Nicaragua unloading casualties. The speed of casualty evacuation by air undoubtedly saved the lives of many of the wounded Marines.

Once again, the Marines were ordered to man the perimeter defenses of the International Settlement. There were 58 fortified positions to take care of, and the Marine forces were stretched very thin. The 6th Marines, in San Diego, were ordered to prepare for expeditionary duty, and they arrived in China six weeks later.

By late October, the Chinese were in retreat. The Japanese conquered the city of Nanking, taking it with a brutality that quickly became infamous, then moved on to Hankow and Canton. Shanghai slipped into a quiet, if nervous, existence. The 6th Marines returned to the United States, while the 4th Marines remained in Shanghai. During this time, however, the Marines had the opportunity to observe—and to learn from their observations. Major Merritt Edson, veteran of the Coco River patrols, had a particular interest in Japanese amphibious tactics and the Special Naval Landing Forces. First Lieutenant Victor Krulak, who served as assistant intelligence officer for the 4th Marines, was also impressed by their prowess—or rather, alarmed. The Japanese, he felt, far surpassed the U.S. in landing craft design. Captain Evans Carlson returned to Shanghai and learned to speak the language. With the permission of Mao Tse-tung, he visited the Communist armies to study the art of guerrilla warfare. He also began warning that war with Japan was imminent. His experiences in China, and further study of the British Commandos, would later play a profound role in the formation of the Marine Raider battalions. In 1939, World War II began and the Marines in China became increasingly isolated. As diplomatic relations with Japan worsened, the 4th Marines were withdrawn from the area. In late November 1941, the Marines marched to the docks in order to board ship. Cheering crowds lined the streets as the last transport departed Shanghai.

Above: The 2nd Battalion, 6th Marines on parade through the streets of Tientsin, China, in May 1928. The life of a Marine in China was comfortable; the men could afford spacious accommodation, good food, and house servants. But the good life was abruptly brought to an end when the Japanese invaded Manchuria in 1931.

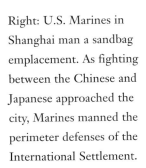

Above: One of the legendary "Horse Marines" as depicted by Charles Waterhouse, with the Great Wall of China in the background. The "Horse Marines" were unique in the Corps, as they rode on ponyback.

Right: U.S. Marines in Shanghai man a sandbag emplacement. As fighting between the Chinese and Japanese approached the city, Marines manned the perimeter defenses of the International Settlement.

During the "interwar" years, while Marines served in China and fought the bloody little wars of the Caribbean, doctrinal changes were developing within the Marine Corps. These began with Earl H. "Pete" Ellis. A brilliant lieutenant-colonel, Ellis had long been fascinated by the concept of advanced base defense. By 1921, convinced that a major war with Japan was looming, Ellis perceived a naval mission for the Marine Corps. In a report which he entitled *Advanced Base Operations in Micronesia*, Ellis anticipated the use of Marines as amphibious shock troops. The Marines would be required, he predicted, in order to seize the heavily defended islands which were at that time under the control of the Japanese:

"… it will be necessary for us to project our fleet and land forces across the Pacific and wage war in Japanese waters. To effect this requires that we have sufficient bases to support the fleet. … We cannot count upon the use of any bases west of Hawaii except those which we may seize from the enemy after the opening of hostilities. Moreover, the continued occupation of the Marshall, Caroline, and

Pelew Islands by the Japanese invests them with a series of emergency bases flanking any line of communications across the Pacific throughout a distance of 2,300 miles [3,700 km]. The reduction and occupation of these islands and the establishment of the necessary bases therein, as a preliminary phase of the hostilities, is practically imperative."

The Commandant of the Marine Corps, General John A. LeJeune, agreed with him. In a memorandum which was dated February 11, 1922, LeJeune declared that it was absolutely necessary to develop and maintain "a mobile Marine Corps force adequate to conduct offensive land operations against hostile Naval bases." In the winter of 1923, amphibious exercises were held in the Caribbean. Results were far from encouraging. Transports were badly loaded, landing boats capsized, and troops landed on the wrong beaches. In the words of Colonel Dion Williams, "Chaos ruled the beach." Events in the Caribbean prevented any further amphibious exercises. With Marines in Haiti, the Dominican Republic, and Nicaragua, there were simply not enough Marines to take part in field manuevers.

Admiral Ernest J. King was invited to ride in the new aluminum "Alligator." Traversing a reef, the vehicle broke a track and the Admiral was forced to wade ashore.

Earl "Pete" Ellis

Certainly one of the more intriguing figures in all of Marine Corps history is Lieutenant-Colonel Earl Hancock "Pete" Ellis. Simultaneously described as intellectual, eccentric, prophetic, and unstable, Ellis was an alcoholic who became one of the most portentous thinkers in Marine Corps history. Born in Kansas in 1880, Ellis enlisted in the Marine Corps at the age of 20 and received his commission a year later. In April 1902 he arrived at Cavite, the American naval base in Manila Bay. It was the first of two postings to the Philippines. By December 1907, he had returned. It was during these two tours that Ellis mastered Japanese and became convinced that a war with Imperial Japan was inevitable. While the U.S. military began to examine its defense of the Philippines, Captain Ellis was made executive officer of Company E which oversaw the fortification of Grande Island at the mouth of Subic Bay. Here, his work on advanced base capabilities earned him high praise. It was, apparently, the one thing in his career he found intellectually stimulating. In two years at the Naval War College, Ellis continued to focus on advanced base operations.

During World War I, Ellis served as adjutant of the Marine Brigade, performing his duties brilliantly. Reportedly, when faced with the mission of taking Mont Blanc, General LeJeune summoned Ellis. Told that Ellis was "indisposed," LeJeune said "Ellis drunk is better than anyone around here sober." Although the truth of this story remains suspect, there is no doubt as to the capabilities once again displayed by Ellis. He was subsequently awarded both the Navy Cross and the French Croix de Guerre. After the war, Ellis became increasingly intrigued with the idea of war with Japan. On July 23, 1921, he submitted a 31,000 word plan for amphibious operations in the Pacific. Entitled "Advanced Base Operations in Micronesia, 1921," the plan outlined an amphibious advance across Japanese-held islands toward the homeland. Events of the future proved Ellis uncannily accurate. In an effort to discover whether the Japanese were fortifying their Pacific islands, Ellis received permission to travel to the area. Disguised as an American businessman, he visited first Japan, then the Central Pacific islands. Lieutenant-Colonel Earl Ellis died on May 12, 1923, under mysterious circumstances, on Koror, in the Japanese-held Palau islands.

By 1931, however, work had begun on a viable amphibious doctrine. After the defeat of British and Australian troops at Gallipoli in the Dardanelles in 1915, it was widely concluded by military theorists that the effectiveness of assaults from the sea had come to an end. Too many advantages were held by the defenders. However, the Marine Corps sought to disprove that theory and to learn from the unmitigated disaster that was Gallipoli. Four years later, the *Tentative Landing Operations Manual* was released. Essentially the bible of amphibious warfare, the manual covered the essential elements of amphibious operations. Included were naval bombardment and close air support, as well as ship-to-shore movement, logistics, and the use of landing craft.

Exercises held between 1935 and 1941, however, still proved the inherent difficulties in launching an amphibious assault. Finally, training was turned over to Brigadier-General Holland M. Smith, the leading expert on amphibious warfare. While he sought to teach the principles of amphibious doctrine, he also fumed at the lack of suitable landing craft; the early "Beetle boats" and Christie amphibian tractors had proved useless. The solution was a landing craft built by Andrew Higgins. Flat-bottomed, with a shallow draft, the Higgins boat also had a retractable bow ramp, which overcame the difficulty of ship-to-shore movement. Over the next several years, the Higgins boat would prove invaluable. Tank lighters had also presented a problem: early models had capsized, with the result that valuable tanks had been simply dumped into the surf.

The answer was, once again, provided by the innovator Andrew Higgins. He developed a vessel which was 50 ft. (15.25 m) in length and which was fitted with a retractable bow. This vehicle was capable of landing a 30-ton medium tank. Initially it seemed as if political infighting would spell the end for Higgins' tank lighter, but with support from Senator Harry S. Truman, the craft eventually became the standard LCM.

The invaluable LVT, Landing Vehicle Tracked, was produced by Donald Roebling, Jr. He modified his "Swamp Gator," a tracked vehicle which had been designed for use in the Everglades. The modified craft could travel at a speed of 29 mph. (46 km/h) on land, and 9.7 mph. (15.6 km/h) in water. It was capable of handling rough terrain and could carry large payloads. This was exactly what the Marine Corps needed. However, the LVT was not without teething problems. In 1940 the commander of the Atlantic fleet, Admiral Ernest J. King, was invited to ride in the new aluminum "Alligator." While traversing a reef, the vehicle broke a track and the Admiral was forced to wade ashore. Roebling eventually solved this problem. Further work on the design produced a steel-welded "Alligator," the model which was to become the backbone of amphibious assault.

The "interwar" years had provided the Marine Corps with experience in guerrilla warfare, with a new amphibious capability, and with tactical development in Marine aviation. All of these experiences would prove priceless, for although its men didn't yet realize, the United States Marine Corps was about to enter World War II.

The Higgins Boat

Throughout the 1920s and 1930s the Marine Corps struggled to develop its amphibious assault doctrine. In a series of Fleet Landing Exercises, the problems inherent in conducting an amphibious assault became apparent. The seemingly simple task of putting Marines and weapons ashore brought about an obsessive search for suitable ship to shore landing craft. Early experiments with the "Beetle boat" were unsatisfactory, as were the first attempts at using commercial fishing boats. General Holland Smith was unhappy at the pace at which the Navy's Burea of Ships addressed the problem and began to look elsewhere. The answer, ultimately, was to be with civilian engineer Andrew Jackson Higgins.

As early as 1926, Higgins had attempted to interest the Navy in one of his designs. He was unsuccessful, but was certain he held the answer to the Marines' problem of finding suitable landing craft. Higgins had developed the "Eureka" boat, designed for use in the bayou waters of Louisiana. It was high-powered, with a shallow draft and a protected propeller. In comparison to previously tested craft, the "Eureka" was a marked improvement. The Marines, however, wanted a retractable bow ramp which would allow rapid debarkation of troops. In April 1941 Higgins was shown photographs taken by Lieutenant Victor H. Krulak of Japanese landing craft while in China in 1937. One of those photographs showed a craft with a ramp in its bow. Higgins quickly redesigned the "Eureka" to include the retractable ramp. Built and tested in 1941, the 36-ft. (11-m) boat became the Navy's Landing Craft Vehicle, Personnel. (LCVP). It was the Higgins boat that would put thousands of Marines onto Japanese-held islands during World War II.

CHAPTER FOUR

WORLD WAR II

The Pacific campaign between 1941 and 1945 was a defining moment for the Marine Corps. The legendary names which feature so prominently on the Corps' roll of honor were added in those four short years: Tarawa, Peleliu, Iwo Jima, Okinawa to name only a few. Thousands of Marines lost their lives clearing the Pacific of the Japanese invaders, but their sacrifice was not in vain.

Left: Men of the 4th Marines Division hit the beach on Iwo Jima, running into a storm of Japanese fire.

The Japanese force of 350 aircraft climbed to 9,000 ft. (2,740 m) and turned south toward the U.S. naval base at Pearl Harbor. At 07:53 hours, Mitsuo Fuchida radioed the code words "Tora, Tora, Tora."

It was early in the morning of Sunday December 7, 1941. North of Oahu, the Japanese First Air Fleet crashed through heavy swells. Behind a phalanx of destroyers, battleships, and heavy cruisers were the aircraft carriers. In the lead was the *Akagi*, behind her, the *Kaga*; to port were the *Soryu* and the *Hiryu*; behind them rushed the *Shokaku* and the *Zuikaku*. In the *Shokaku*'s ready room, a pilot smiled over breakfast, commenting "Honolulu sleeps." At 05:50 hours, the carriers and her escort vessels turned to port and launched 183 planes. An hour later, a second wave took to the skies. The Japanese force of 350 aircraft climbed to 9,000 ft. (2,740 m) and turned south toward the U.S. naval base at Pearl Harbor. At 07:53 hours, Mitsuo Fuchida radioed the code words "Tora, Tora, Tora."

At Ewa Mooring Mast Field, the Marine airfield west of Pearl Harbor, Captain Leonard W. Ashwell had just finished breakfast. Walking out of the mess hall, he heard the roar of engines. Two formations of aircraft flew overhead. The first, flying at about 1,000 ft. (305 m), were torpedo bombers headed for Pearl Harbor. The second formation of fighters flew in low and commenced firing. Forty-seven planes of Marine Aircraft Group 21 were parked wingtip to wingtip. Bursts of 0.3 in. (7.7 mm) and 0.78 in. (20 mm) machine-gun fire ripped through the aircraft, setting them ablaze. Explosions rocked the field. The Marines fought back valiantly. Pilots and ground crews alike attempted to get the planes off the ground, but all the aircraft had been destroyed or badly damaged. Men fired pistols and rifles at the attacking Japanese. Others manned battle stations with machine guns pulled from the burning wreckage. The Japanese returned at 08:35 hours. The dive bombers off the *Shokaku* strafed barracks and hangars, then sprayed the Marine defenders with machine-gun fire. The attacking Japanese flew off to the west, leaving the Marine airfield in flames. Thirteen men had been wounded, another four killed.

At Pearl Harbor, similar destruction: as the bombs fell and the Pacific Fleet burned, Marines of the 1st and 3rd Defense Battalion raced to battle stations. The commander of

Right: Marine antiaircraft positions at Pearl Harbor firing at the Japanese aircraft flying overhead. The 1st and 3rd Defense Battalions were based on shore, but a number of Marines also served on the ships which were moored in the harbor.

the Marine Barracks ordered his men to set up machine guns and 3 in. (76 mm) antiaircraft (AA) guns. However, ammunition for the anitaircraft guns was stored in a facility miles away. Marines serving in ship's detachments courageously manned antiaircraft batteries. Beneath the fury of the assault, surrounded by smoke and flames, the Marines occasionally inflicted damage on the attacking Japanese. In less than two hours, the Japanese crippled the Pacific Fleet. Four battleships had been sunk, another four more sustained heavy damage. Casualties numbered 2,403 dead, another 1,178 wounded. Among those killed were 108 Marines, defenders who had met the Japanese attack with courage and daring.

Elsewhere throughout the Pacific, Marines faced Japanese aggression. On December 8, some two hundred Leathernecks stationed in Tientsin and Peking heard of the attack on Pearl Harbor. Japanese troops surrounded the barracks and demanded their surrender. Chief Gunner William A. Lee, who had earned three Navy Crosses in Nicaragua, began organizing a defense. He issued weapons to his men and prepared to take on the Japanese. However, the commanding officer concluded that a defense served no useful purpose and surrendered. The Marines were taken prisoner and held in Shanghai. The same

Above: A Marine recruiting poster from the beginning of World War II. The painting shows men during an amphibious assault, and shows that the Marines still wore the old World War I-era helmet at the beginning of the conflict. Shortly after the outbreak of World War II, they would adopt the familiar M1 helmet.

fate awaited the Marines stationed on Guam. For two days, Japanese bombers pounded the small island. Then, on December 10, 5,500 Japanese troops came ashore. The Marine garrison, barely 200 men strong, mounted a spirited defense, but the situation was hopeless. The garrison commander, Captain George J. McMillan, U.S. Navy, was forced to surrender the island to the Japanese invaders.

When news of the attack on Pearl Harbor reached Wake Island, the Marines stationed there immediately began preparing for a Japanese assault. Major Paul A. Putnam, commanding officer of Marine fighter squadron VMF-112, ordered the Grumman F4F Wildcats dispersed and the squadron to be placed on a war footing. Marines of the 1st Defense Battalion, under the command of Major James P.S. Devereaux, also swung into action. Observation posts were manned, weapons were unpacked and issued to civilian volunteers, grenades were distributed throughout the island. Although they were lacking in manpower, both the 5 in. (127 mm) and 3 in. (76 mm) gun batteries were readied for use against the oncoming invaders from Japan.

Wake Island didn't have long to wait—Japanese bombers struck that afternoon. Seven of the squadron's Wildcats were destroyed on the ground, and no supplies survived the attack. Spare parts and tools were gone, the gasoline storage tanks blown. Five pilots and ten enlisted men were wounded. Most of the maintenance crew was killed in the attack. For two more days the Marines endured air attacks. Then on the night of December 10, the

Left: Exactly eight months
after the attack on Pearl
Harbor, U.S. Marines hit
the beaches of
Guadalcanal. The tracks
on their LVT vehicles
helped propel them
through the water toward
the beach, but the sea had
to be relatively calm or the
LVT would be swamped
by high waves.

submarine *Triton* spotted a Japanese destroyer on the horizon. She was in the forefront of an invasion fleet bearing down on Wake. Putnam ordered his remaining Wildcats into the air. As the Japanese began shelling, Devereaux ordered his Marines to hold their fire. The fleet moved in closer, coming to with 4,500 yards (4,920 m) of the beach. At 06:15 hours, the Marines commenced firing. The flagship *Yubari* took three hits. The destroyer *Hayate* exploded, killing all hands. As the Japanese force retired, Putnam's Wildcats struck, sinking the destroyer *Kisaragi*. Naval historian Samuel Eliot Morison later wrote, "The eleventh day of December 1941 should always be a proud day in the history of the Corps. Never again, in this Pacific War, did coast defense guns beat off an amphibious landing." Nevertheless, Wake Island was doomed. As the Japanese continued to bomb, the cost in men and equipment continued to escalate. At Pearl Harbor, a relief force put to sea, only to be turned around again, because the Navy High Command was unwilling to risk the carriers *Lexington*, *Saratoga*, and *Enterprise* in the battle.

4th Marines

Throughout 1941 the Japanese continued to tighten their grip on embattled China. In late November, with Shanghai's streets filled with well-wishers and bands playing, the 4th Marines, under the command of Colonel Samuel L. Howard, marched to the city's dock. There the Marines boarded transports that took them to the Philippines. They arrived only a week before war began. On December 8, 1941 the Japanese began bombing the Philippines, catching American airpower on the ground at Clark Field. Less than two weeks later, General MacArthur requested the transfer of the 4th Marines to his command. Manila was declared an "open city" and American forces moved to the narrow Bataan Peninsula. The Marines proceeded to destroy the U.S. bases at Olongapo and Cavite, before moving on to Mariveles on the southern tip of Bataan. Leaving one battalion behind at Mariveles in order to protect against a Japanese amphibious assault, Colonel Howard moved the rest of the 4th Marines to the island fortress of Corregidor.

On the night of January 22, 1942, 900 men of the Japanese 20th Infantry landed at Quinauan Point behind the American–Filipino lines. For the next five days, the Allied forces battled the Japanese, with Marines often serving as squad and platoon leaders. Finally, on the 29th, a battalion of Filipino scouts, supported by Marine machine guns and mortars, drove the Japanese from Mariveles. On March 12, MacArthur left the Philippines for Australia. By mid-April, the Japanese were pounding the Bataan Peninsula. The men who were valiantly defending Bataan were suffering from malnutrition, disease and the strain of neverending bombardment. But there could be no resupply of food, or ammunition or medicine. As many men as possible were evacuated to Corregidor, but on April 9, Bataan fell. Some 75,000 Americans and Filipinos stumbled through the Death March and into Japanese POW camps. Among them were 105 Marines.

On Corregidor, the 4th Marines dug in, strung barbed wire, laid minefields, and waited for the Japanese to come. After dark on May 5, the enemy landed. The battle raged all night, the Marines putting up a fierce defense, but by noon the following day, it was over. As General Jonathan Wainwright prepared to surrender Corregidor, Colonel Howard burned the regimental colors of the 4th Marines. Altogether 1,283 Marines would become prisoners of the Japanese that day; a total of 239 would not survive the three years of brutal confinement and torture at the enemy's hands.

By December 22, VMF-112 had lost all of its fighters. In the early morning hours of December 23, the Japanese landed on Wake Island. The Marines, along with sailors and civilians, defended the island valiantly, fighting off several hundred Japanese. Naval Commander Winfield Cunningham sent a final, terse message to Pearl Harbor, "Enemy on island; issue in doubt." Vastly outnumbered, with no relief en route, Cunningham and Devereaux ordered the surrender of Wake

Above: Marines engage the Japanese 36th Infantry Brigade during the Battle of Bloody Ridge.

Island. The survivors were accepted as prisoners of war and taken to Shanghai. Forty-nine Marines died in defense of the isolated outpost, including aviator Captain Hank Elrod. He died on the ground while fighting the invading Japanese troops. For his courage in defending Wake Island, he would become the first Marine aviator of World War II to receive the Medal of Honor.

In the Philippines, the 4th Marines, assigned to MacArthur's command on December 20, heroically held out against the advancing Japanese. With no hope of relief or reinforcement, the American defense of Bataan and Corregidor became an important symbol of courage and sacrifice. When Bataan finally fell to the invading Japanese on April 9, 1942, 75,000 Americans and Filipinos, including 105 Marines, were forced into captivity. Corregidor held out another 27 days. Then, on May 5, Lieutenant-General Jonathan M. Wainwright surrendered. The soldiers and Marines spent the next three years in Japanese prison camps, where brutal mistreatment and death were commonplace.

While the Marines struggled against the Japanese in the western Pacific, Admiral Yamamoto, the brilliant strategist behind the attack on Pearl Harbor, planned a massive assault on Midway Island and the Aleutians. This time, however, there would be no surprise: U.S. codebreakers had cracked the Japanese code and were aware that an attack on Midway was imminent. On May 2, Admiral Chester W. Nimitz, commander of the Pacific Fleet, flew to the island to inspect the defenses. Within a few weeks of his visit, supplies began to arrive. These included AA guns and search radars. Two rifle companies of the 2nd Raider Battalion then proceeded to go ashore. On May 26, a force of 7 F4F Wildcats and 19 SBD-2s arrived aboard U.S.S. *Kitty Hawk*.

The Marines had a total of 64 planes on Midway Island, and when the Japanese struck on June 4, Marine Air Group-22 met the attack. It was destroyed. Only 2 Marine fighters

Naval Commander Winfield Cunningham sent a final, terse message to Pearl Harbor, "Enemy on island; issue in doubt." Vastly outnumbered, with no relief en route, Cunningham and Devereaux ordered the surrender of Wake Island.

and 11 dive bombers survived the action. The antiquated planes were no match for the Japanese Zeroes, but the sacrifice was not in vain: the Japanese attack was disrupted. AA fire from the Marines ashore damaged or destroyed several enemy aircraft. The Japanese ordered a second attack wave. By then, the U.S. fleet was position. Four Japanese carriers were sunk, ending the last Japanese offensive action of the war.

Shortly after the Battle of Midway, the 1st Marine Division arrived in New Zealand. Commanded by Major-General Alexander Vandegrift, the division was understrength and in need of more training. Vandegrift hoped to have at least six months before his men were committed to a combat mission. He would not get it. On June 26, Vandegrift was summoned to the office of Vice Admiral Robert L. Ghormley. Intelligence reports and aerial reconnaissance showed the Japanese were constructing an airfield on the jungle-covered island of Guadalcanal. They had to be stopped: enemy bombers staging out of the Solomons would be able to disrupt the flow of materials between the U.S. and her allies in Australia and New Zealand. In an action codenamed "Operation Watchtower," Guadalcanal and the nearby island of Tulagi were to be seized with all possible speed.

Vandegrift's 1st Marine Division was given the task, augmented by the 1st Raider Battalion, the 1st Parachute Battalion, and the 3rd Defense Battalion. Since the division's 7th Marines were serving in Samoa, the 2nd Marines of the 2nd Division would sail from San Diego. The landing was scheduled for August 1, 1942. Vandegrift argued for more time, but the invasion could be delayed until no later than August 7: the Marines had less than five weeks to prepare. Those preparations quickly turned into a logistical nightmare. When the division sailed for New Zealand, the ships had not been loaded for combat operations—economy of space had been the priority. Once in Wellington, New Zealand, the ships had to be completely emptied, then reloaded with weapons, ammunition, and rations positioned to offload first. Difficulties with the dockworkers' union arose. Leaders demanded regular tea breaks and refused to work in the heavy rains that fell daily. The Marines had to do the job themselves. The docks descended into confusion as the tired, wet Marines struggled to reload supplies. Vandegrift's problems were exacerbated by the lack of intelligence information on the target areas. No accurate maps existed of Guadalcanal and the strength of the Japanese garrison on the island was largely unknown. On July 17, an Army B-17 with Lieutenant-Colonel Merrill B. Twining and Major William McKean aboard, flew over the proposed landing beaches. No significant defenses were seen. This was welcome news for the Marines.

Below: This Grumman Wildcat was set afire when Japanese bombs hit the hanger. Leathernecks pulled the plane into the open and extinguished the flames with shovels of dirt.

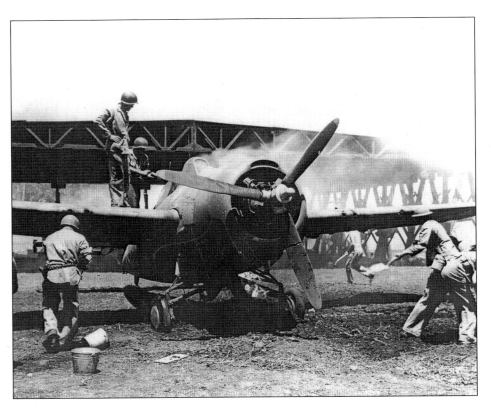

Left: This Marine machine-gun team ascend one of Guadalcanal's ridgelines. The invasion fleet is visible in the background. The man in front carries the machine gun's tripod; the man behind, the Browning M1917 gun itself.

On July 22, the ships bearing the 1st Marine Division departed New Zealand. After a limited rehearsal in the Fiji Islands, later described by Vandegrift as "a fiasco," the task force sailed for Guadalcanal. At 06:13 hours on August 7, the heavy cruiser *Quincy* trained her guns upon the landing beaches and opened fire. Carrier-based planes bombed and strafed the shoreline. Twenty-eight minutes later, the signal was given to "land the landing force." The first major offensive of the war was underway. The Marines expected a hard fight, but the 1st and 3rd Battalions, 5th Marines came ashore near the Tenaru River with no Japanese resistance. The 1st Marines followed closely behind. Through an eerie silence, which was broken only by the haunting sounds of the jungle, the Leathernecks entered the darkness of Guadalcanal's tangled rainforest and advanced toward the airfield.

The Marines who landed on Tulagi, across the Sealark Channel, weren't so fortunate. The 1st Raider Battalion, under the command of Lieutenant-Colonel Merritt "Red Mike" Edson encountered *rikusentai*, members of the 3rd Kure Special Landing Force. Despite meeting pockets of heavy resistance, the Marines advanced steadily. By evening, they held the high ground overlooking the ravine where the Japanese had dug into coral caves. The 2nd Battalion, 5th Marines moved into position along the crest of the hill to support the Raiders. Throughout the night, the Japanese hit the Marine positions in savage counterattacks. These were classic *banzai* charges: the Japanese troops emerged from hiding, screaming and firing their weapons while hitting the Marine lines at a dead run. By morning, most of the Japanese troops were dead, the survivors holed-up in the caves of the

Throughout the night, the Japanese hit the Marine positions in savage counterattacks. These were classic banzai *charges: the Japanese troops emerged from hiding, screaming and firing their weapons while hitting the Marine lines at a dead run.*

ravine. A barrage of 2.36 in. (60 mm) mortar fire pounded the Japanese positions. As the Leathernecks moved through this last stronghold, dynamite and grenades eliminated any remaining resistance. At 15:00 hours, Tulagi was declared secured.

The fight for Gavutu and Tanambogo, tiny specks of land raising out of the ocean, was equally intense. The 1st Parachute Battalion made an amphibious landing against a heavily defended beachhead. One out of ten Marines became a casualty. Reinforcements from the 2nd Marines came ashore, but were raked by concentrated machine-gun fire and forced to withdraw. Point-blank gunfire from the *Buchanan* as well as the commitment of 3rd Battalion, 2nd Marines helped to overwhelm the Japanese defenders.

On August 8, the Marines managed to secure the airfield on Guadalcanal. By evening, almost 11,000 Leathernecks were ashore on Guadalcanal, and another 6,805 were on Tulagi. However, that night, the Japanese delivered a staggering response to the American offensive. The Japanese Eighth Fleet moved down "The Slot," a wide channel between Bougainville and Guadalcanal, and then struck. In the ensuing Battle of Savo Island, the Japanese sent three cruisers to the bottom. The Australian Navy's HMAS *Canberra* was scuttled. Both the *Chicago* and the *Talbot* sustained heavy damage. It would be one of the worst defeats ever to be suffered by the U.S. Navy.

Raiders

In February 1942, the Commandant of the Marine Corps, Lieutenant-General Thomas Holcomb, ordered the formation of a highly trained guerrilla unit similar to the British Commandos. Designated the 1st Raider Battalion, the origin of the unit and its sister battalions could be traced to two separate sources. The first was the friendship between President Franklin D. Roosevelt and Evans F. Carlson. Between 1937 and 1938, Carlson was posted to duty to China. There he visited the Communist forces of Mao Tse-tung. After observing their tactics in guerrilla warfare, Carlson was convinced this was the future of war. Roosevelt's son, Captain James Roosevelt agreed. In January 1942, the younger Roosevelt wrote a letter to General Holcomb, recommending the creation of a unit similar to the British commandos and Chinese guerrillas.

Concurrently, General Holland M. Smith was attempting to put amphibious doctrine into practice. During Fleet Landing Exercises, Smith's ideas about amphibious operations took real shape. He foresaw the use of a highly trained battalion to precede the main assault. During the summer of 1941 at New River, North Carolina, Smith utilized the 1st Battalion, 5th Marines in a series of exercises. To this battalion, which was commanded by Lieutenant-Colonel Merritt A. Edson, Smith added a company of tanks, as well as a company of parachutists. During the exercises, this combined unit made a "spearhead thrust around the hostile flank."

In August, Edson wrote a lengthy report on the mission of his unit. He foresaw a focus of reconnaissance and special operations. At the beginning of 1942, the 1st Battalion, 5th Marines was redesignated to become the 1st Separate Battalion. On February 4, the 2nd Separate Battalion was established. Based in California, the unit was commanded by Major Evans Carlson. The units were quickly redesignated as Marine Raider Battalions which received priority in both men and equipment. Training emphasized rigorous physical conditioning, hand-to-hand combat, weapons practice, and demolitions.

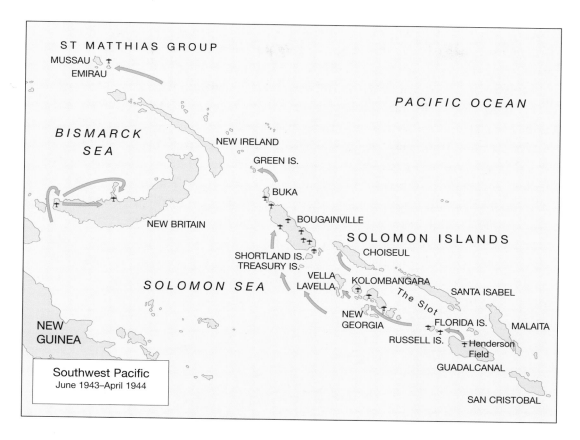

Left: A map showing the progress of the American forces during "Operation Cartwheel," the recapture of the Solomon Islands.

ST MATTHIAS GROUP
MUSSAU
EMIRAU

PACIFIC OCEAN

BISMARCK
SEA

NEW IRELAND

GREEN IS.

BUKA

NEW BRITAIN

BOUGAINVILLE

SOLOMON ISLANDS
CHOISEUL

SHORTLAND IS.
TREASURY IS.

VELLA
LAVELLA

KOLOMBANGARA

SANTA ISABEL

SOLOMON SEA

The Slot

NEW
GEORGIA

FLORIDA IS.

MALAITA

RUSSELL IS.

Henderson
Field

GUADALCANAL

NEW
GUINEA

Southwest Pacific
June 1943–April 1944

SAN CRISTOBAL

Vice Admiral Frank J. Fletcher, the Expeditionary Force commander, feared the loss of his aircraft carriers and obtained permission to withdraw from the area. Rear Admiral Kelly Turner, in command of the amphibious force, had no choice but to evacuate the amphibious ships as well. Vandegrift was stunned—and alarmed. The Marines were alone, with only a four-day supply of ammunition and rations for 17 days. He was forced to rethink his objectives, for the 1st Marine Division was no longer capable of an offensive drive across Guadalcanal. Instead, the Marines dug in and prepared to hold the airfield. Once completed, the island could be resupplied, the wounded evacuated.

By August 12, resourceful Marine engineers had managed to have the airfield up and running. An American flag was raised over the newly renamed Henderson Field, named in honor of Major Lofton Henderson, a Marine aviator who was killed leading the dive-bomber attack against Japanese carriers in the battle for Midway. A PBY-5 Catalina flying boat set down on the tiny airstrip and declared the field fit for use, then departed with a plane-load of wounded Marines. By August 20, the forward echelon of Marine Air Group-23 was on Guadalcanal. The F4F Wildcats and SBD-3 Dauntless dive bombers were soon joined by Army and Navy planes. The interservice aviators dubbed themselves the "Cactus Air Force." Inspired leadership was given by seasoned Marine aviator Brigadier-General Roy S. Geiger. Within a day of beginning flight operations, the Cactus Air Force scored its first kill when Major John L. Smith shot down a Zero.

The presence of the Marines on Guadalcanal had become intolerable for the Japanese command. The Imperial General Staff ordered Lieutenant-General Haruyoshi Hyakutake to retake the island. Believing that only some 2,000 Marines were on Guadalcanal, Hyakutake ordered the 28th Infantry, under the command of Colonel Kiyono Ichiki, to

Vice Admiral Frank J. Fletcher, the Expeditionary Force commander, feared the loss of his aircraft carriers and obtained permission to withdraw from the area. Vandegrift was stunned—and alarmed. The Marines were alone, with only a four-day supply of ammunition and rations for 17 days.

land near the Marine perimeter and drive the Americans into the sea. The Marines were alerted to the Japanese presence on the island when sentries came across retired Sergeant Major Jacob Vouza of the British Constabulary. This native scout had been savagely beaten and tortured, then impaled by the Japanese and left to die. Just managing to free himself, Vouza then crawled to the Marine perimeter and reported to them the presence of hundreds of Japanese soldiers in the nearby thick jungle.

At 01:30 hours on August 21, the Japanese infantry proceeded to strike.

"They came flowing across the sandpit, sprinting, hurling grenades, howling. They came blundering into that single strand of barbed wire, and there they milled about in a jabbering frenzy. They hacked wildly at the wire with bayonets, tried to hurdle it, and they slung long thin lengths of explosive-packed pipe under it in the hopes of blowing gaps in it. Then the Marines opened fire, the flare-light faded, and the re-enveloping night seemed to reel with a thousand scarlet flashes.

Above: Japanese bombs ignite Marine aircraft on Henderson Field in this painting entitled "Raid by Moonlight" by Hugh Laidman.

Machine guns chattered and shook. Rifles cracked. Grenades whizzed and boomed. Fat red tracers sped out in curving arcs and vanished. Orange puffs spat from the mouth of the antitank gun. Howitzers bayed in the rear distance and their whistling shells crashed and flashed among the coconuts where mortar missiles … were falling with that dull *crrrunch* that tears and kills."

At daybreak, the 1st Battalion, 1st Marines crossed the sluggish Ilu River and pushed the Japanese toward the shore. Mortars and artillery slammed into the enemy. Overhead, Wildcats repeatedly strafed the Japanese positions. Vandegrift ordered five light tanks into the battle. They advanced mercilessly through a coconut grove, chasing the fleeing enemy, grinding their bodies beneath the tracks—it was, Vandegrift later said, "war without quarter." In the Battle of the Tenaru River, the Marines virtually annihilated one of the best infantry units in the Japanese Army. Vandegrift, however, knew his Marines were still vulnerable. He ordered the 1st Raider Battalion and the 1st Parachute Battalion (both under Edson's command) and the 2nd Battalion, 5th Marines from Tulagi to strengthen the perimeter. These reinforcements soon proved critical. Hyakutake ordered the 35th Infantry Brigade to take Henderson Field, so on August 31, this Japanese force landed on Guadalcanal, before disappearing into the heavy cover of the jungle.

The Marine perimeter was strongest on the flanks, which were close to the shoreline. Between those two positions, stretching southward, the line thinned markedly. Vandegrift moved the Raiders and the Parachutists to the most obvious enemy approach route; a kunai grass-covered ridge that ran south from Henderson Field. Aware of a large enemy force lurking somewhere "out front," Edson ordered his men to dig in. The Marines at the perimeter settled down for a long night of waiting and listening. One Marine described their silent ordeal with particular vividness:

"It was darkness without time. It was an impenetrable darkness. To the right and left of men rose up those formless things of my imagination, which I could not see, but I dared not close my eyes lest the darkness crawl beneath my eyeballs and suffocate me. I could only hear. My ears became my being and I could hear the specks of life that crawled beneath my clothing … I could hear the darkness gathering against me and the silences that lay between the moving things. I could hear the enemy everywhere about me, whispering to each other and calling my name."

Left: Marines loaded with backpacks and equipment climb down the cargo nets and into the landing craft which will take them to the beach on Bougainville for their assault against enemy positions.

After nightfall on the 12th, Japanese destroyers began pounding the ridgeline. The attack began at 21:00 hours, when Kawaguchi's infantry surged out of the darkness to hit Edson's left flank. The Japanese seemingly had no fear, plunging into a rain of machine-gun and rifle fire. Closing to bayonet range, the battle then dissolved into individual struggles for survival. The Japanese were thrown back, but Kawaguchi's men again and yet again boiled out of the jungle to assault the Marines lines. At 02:30 hours, Edson told Vandegrift his Marines would hold the ridge, though he told his men, "they'll be back."

On the morning of September 13, Edson pulled his lines toward the airfield. The 2nd Battalion, 5th Marines reinforced his position. That evening, the Japanese attacked with incredible ferocity, fighting the Marines hand-to-hand. Foxholes and machine-gun pits were overrun. Edson seemed to appear out of nowhere to wherever the fighting was toughest, encouraging and rallying his men to go on. Artillerymen from the 5th Battalion, 11th Marines added their firepower to the ferocious, unrelenting battle:

"The shells came whistling in from the … 105 mm [4.13 in.] pack howitzers a half-mile back. They fell in a curtain of steel not 200 yards [220m] from that desperate last horseshoe of defense. They shook the Marine defenders, squeezed their breath away, but they made a flashing white slaughter among the Kawaguchi's … The night was made hideous by their screams …"

As dawn approached, the Japanese pulled back into the jungle, leaving some 600 dead and another 600 wounded behind. The Cactus Air Force took to the skies, bombing and strafing the retreating enemy. Kawaguchi lost over half of his fighting force, but "Edson's Ridge" still belonged to the Marines. Edson and Major Kenneth Bailey, commander, C Company, 1st Raider Battalion were awarded the Medal of Honor for heroic and inspiring leadership. The fight for the ridge had exacted a heavy toll on the Leathernecks: 69 were dead, 194 wounded. The 1st Parachute Battalion ceased to exist as a fighting force.

The Japanese were thrown back, but Kawaguchi's men again and yet again boiled out of the jungle to assault the Marines lines. At 02:30 hours, Edson told Vandegrift his Marines would hold the ridge, though he told his men, "they'll be back."

Above: An LCVP moves at speed through Empress Augusta Bay toward Bougainville's shore. Landing craft were at their most vulnerable when fully laden and heading toward the enemy shore.

On September 18, the 7th Marines arrived on Guadalcanal. They would soon be needed. General Hyakutake committed his elite fighting force, the *Sendai* Division, to the battle. Throughout late September, Vandegrift attempted to expand the Marine perimeter to the banks of the Matanikau River. It proved a difficult endeavor. Japanese resistance was very strong and growing: the *Sendai* Division had brought with them 5.9 in. (150 mm) guns, capable of pounding the Marine perimeter and Henderson Field.

On October 7, Vandegrift launched an offensive against Japanese positions along the Matanikau. Battle plans called for five infantry battalions and a Scout-Sniper group under the command of Colonel William J. Whaling to trap the enemy along the river. The 2nd and 3rd Battalions, 5th Marines ran into Japanese in strength: an advance element of the Japanese 4th Regiment had crossed the Matanikau to establish forward artillery positions. The fighting was intense, much of it hand-to-hand. The Japanese troops were destroyed. Two days later, the 1st Battalion, 7th Marines, under the command of the fiery Lieutenant-Colonel Lewis B. "Chesty" Puller, found a battalion of the Japanese 4th Infantry Regiment bivouacked in a ravine. Creating a "machine for extermination," Puller called for artillery concentration in front of his position, and added fire from his own mortars: a rain of shells fell among the Japanese troops. Those who survived, desperately tried to escape by climbing the opposite slope of the ravine. Puller's Marines riddled the fleeing troops with machine-gun and rifle fire. These survivors then returned to shelter in the ravine, only to flee the artillery and mortar fire once again. Only when his mortar ammunition was expended did Puller cease firing. Seven hundred Japanese were dead, the Matanikau was cleared. The enemy plans, which had been to position artillery in order to support an assault on the Marines' perimeter, had now been totally thwarted.

The 5th Marines dug in along the eastern bank of the river. Welcome reinforcements arrived on October 13. The Army's 164th Infantry arrived on Guadalcanal. That same day, the Japanese began their bombing in earnest. During the night, both the infantry and the Marines came under a terrific, and terrifying, bombardment. To cover a landing of troops near Tassafaronga, the Japanese battleships *Kongo* and *Haruna* moved up into the Sealark Channel, now called Ironbottom Sound, and commenced firing. To all who experienced the bombardment, it was 80 minutes of sheer hell.

"Star shells rose, horrible and bright, scarlet with the fat red beauty of Hell, exploding like giant ferris wheels to shower the night with streamers of light. And then, the 14-inchers [355 mm] of the battleships, the 8-inchers [203 mm] of the *Isuzu*, the 5-inchers [127 mm] of the destroyers. … In that cataclysm … every shell seemed to explode with the pent-up flame and fury of a full thunderstorm …"

Henderson Field was left in ruins. General Geiger ordered that every remaining plane went into the air to strike at the Japanese transports.

Vandegrift knew an attack was imminent. Major-General Masao Maruyama, commanding the *Sendai* Division, planned to hit the Marine lines near Edson's Ridge. Puller's 1st Battalion, 7th Marines defended that part of the perimeter. On the night of October 24, the Marines strained to see into the blackness. A driving rain fell. Then out of the inky darkness, Maruyama's *Sendai* troops hit the Marine lines. Puller's Leathernecks threw back the first attack, but the Japanese regrouped and again smashed into the Marine perimeter. Sergeant "Manila John" Basilone, machine-gun section chief, mowed down the enemy. With ammunition running low and supply lines severed, Basilone battled his way through the enemy to resupply his machine-gun section. Puller credited him with aiding in the virtual annihilation of the Japanese regiment. For his extraordinary heroism, Basilone was awarded the Medal of Honor.

Puller realized the Japanese force was a strong one, and requested reinforcement from the 164th Infantry. When the Japanese attacked the following night, the soldiers of the 3rd Battalion were completely integrated into the Marine lines. In a hail of machine-gun, rifle, mortar, and artillery fire, the enemy forces were decimated. The brunt of the attack, however, was west of Puller's position. The 2nd Battalion, 7th Marines, under the command of Lieutenant-Colonel Herman H. Hannekan, repeatedly repelled the Japanese forces. Platoon Sergeant Mitchell Paige, another machine gunner, distinguished himself that night. When the enemy broke through the lines in front of his position, Paige directed the fire of his gunners until all of them were either dead or wounded. When his own gun was destroyed, Paige moved to his right, found another gun, and then continued to fire on the advancing Japanese. Then, with a few riflemen by his side, Paige gathered the blisteringly hot gun into his arms and led a bayonet charge against the enemy. He, like Basilone, was awarded the Medal of Honor.

The Japanese retreated and would not return: Maruyama's offensive was over. More than 3,500 Japanese soldiers lay dead before the Marine lines. Weeks of hard fighting were still ahead, but on November 29, after almost four months of constant combat, hunger, and

Above: "The Landing, Bougainville" painted by the artist W. F. Draper. The Marines came ashore on Bougainville under heavy fire from the Japanese defenders.

Joe Foss

By October, 1942, the battle for Guadalcanal had raged for two long months. Marines who fought in the air, as well as those on the ground, faced a shortage of equipment and mind-numbing fatigue. Finally, Guadalcanal began to receive reinforcements. Pilots of Marine Fighter Squadron-121 (VMF-121) arrived at Henderson Field in early October. Among them was a 27-year old captain named Joe Foss. Joseph J. Foss, a native of South Dakota, had taken private flying lessons. Over a period of five years, he accumulated over 100 hours of flying time. In 1940, Foss enlisted in the Marine Corps Reserve and two months later was called to active duty. After attending flight school in Pensacola, Foss was commissioned as a 2nd Lieutenant in March 1941. At 27, he was considered too old to fly fighters and instead was posted to a photo reconnaissance squadron. After submitting several requests for transfer, Foss was finally assigned to VMF-121. The newly-promoted captain served as the fighter squadron's executive officer.

Flying the Grumman F4F Wildcat, on 13 October, Foss scored his first victory against the Japanese, shooting down an attacking Zero. Nine days later, Marine aviators took to the skies to intercept a force of Betty bombers with a sizeable fighter escort. Foss was among them. He made his first kill of the day using his .50 caliber machine guns, raking the Japanese Zero and sending it plummeting to earth. Before the battle was over, he had gunned down three more. The following day, 25 October, Foss repeated the feat, shooting down five more enemy aircraft. By January 15, 1943, Captain Joseph Foss had shot down a total of 26 Japanese aircraft. This tied the World War I record of Eddie Rickenbacker for confirmed enemy kills. For his outstanding service during the Guadalcanal campaign, Foss was awarded the Medal of Honor.

disease, the Joint Chiefs of Staff ordered the 1st Marine Division be relieved. They left 681 men behind and another 1,278 had been wounded. The task of securing Guadalcanal fell to the joint forces of the Army and the 2nd Marine Division. However, it would take another two months of battle and several hundred more casualties before the Japanese were vanquished. Said the *New York Times* of the battle, "… Guadalcanal. The name will not die out of the memories of this generation. It will endure in honor."

While the 1st Marine Division was battling the Japanese at Guadalcanal, two companies of the 2nd Raider Battalion, under the command of Lieutenant-Colonel Evans Carlson, departed Hawaii on two large submarines. The *Nautilus* and the *Argonaut* were headed for the Gilbert Islands. Carlson's Raiders were to land on Butaritari Island and destroy the Japanese garrison, then go ashore on Little Makin Island. Their mission on Little Makin Island was to gather intelligence, to take prisoners, and to destroy enemy installations, as well as to serve as a diversionary force from Guadalcanal.

On the night of August 17, the Raiders went ashore. However, the element of surprise was lost when a Marine accidentally discharged his weapon. The Japanese garrison on Butaritari manned its machine guns and began firing. Twice the Japanese launched *banzai* attacks. Armed with a shotgun, Sergeant Clyde Thomason moved to the forefront to direct the fire of his platoon, but was killed by a sniper's bullet. For his bravery under fire, and leadership in repelling the Japanese attack, Thomason became the first enlisted Marine of World War II to be awarded the Medal of Honor. The Raiders threw back the Japanese attacks, killing most of Butaritari's garrison. Enemy planes flew overhead, bombing and strafing the Marines. Two Japanese flying boats landed in the lagoon and were met with a hail of machine-gun fire. Carlson's Raiders destroyed the planes.

Convinced the Japanese still had a sizeable force on the island, Carlson decided to withdraw. Heavy surf, however, caused disaster. Outboard motors on the rubber boats failed to function and the Raiders were unable to paddle against the heavy breakers. Boats capsized, weapons and equipment were lost. Carlson and 120 of his men were stranded. The next morning, Major James Roosevelt got four boats to shore and returned a number of the Raiders to the waiting submarines. However, 70 of Carlson's men remained on the beach. Helped by some islanders, the remaining Marines put the rest of their boats and a native canoe in the water. When the Raiders returned to Pearl Harbor, it was discovered nine men had been left behind. They eluded capture for sometime, but surrendered on August 30. They were then taken to Kwajalein and beheaded. Carlson and the Raiders were lauded as heroes and the raid portrayed as a great success, boosting the morale of the American public, now hungry for a victory over the Japanese. Ironically, it caused the enemy to recognize their vulnerability in the Gilbert Islands, resulting in very heavy fortifications at Tarawa.

Now secured, Guadalcanal provided the springboard from which to launch an offensive against Japanese-held territories in the Central Pacific. The attention of the Joint Chiefs of Staff turned to Papua New Guinea, specifically the port of Rabaul. More than 100,000 Japanese troops were believed to occupy the massive base there on the eastern shore of New Britain Island. General MacArthur wanted to attack the stronghold directly, but Vice Admiral William F. Halsey, the newly appointed commander of the South Pacific Force, had serious reservations about such a plan. The Joint Chiefs of Staff decided to neutralize Rabaul by pounding the base with a massive bombing campaign and seizing each of the Solomon Islands in turn. The Japanese stronghold could then simply be bypassed.

Carlson and the Raiders were lauded as heroes and the raid portrayed as a great success, boosting the morale of the American public who were hungry for a victory over the Japanese.

Left: Marines wade on to the beach through waist-deep water to come ashore, holding their packs up high to keep them from becoming waterlogged. The vehicle in the foreground is an LCVP, its antiaircraft gun pointed skyward.

Right: Marines of the 1st War Dog Platoon advance inland on Rabaul, moving up the Piva Trail with the 2nd Raider Battalion before then proceeding to establish a blocking position. The dogs of this platoon were useful for sniffing out Japanese positions during the war in the Pacific.

The decision to attack was a risky one for Halsey. He lacked sufficient troops to seize [Bougainville,] but the potential rewards were too great: to gain an airfield would be a major advance in the war effort.

The first step in the advance up the chain of islands was the seizure of the Russell Islands. On February 21, the 3rd Raider Battalion, under the command of Lieutenant-Colonel Harry B. Liversedge, landed on Pavuvu Island. Construction of an airstrip began on neighboring Banika and by mid-March, Marine Air Group-21 had three squadrons of Wildcats in the air. The next objective was to attack New Georgia. During the battle for Guadalcanal, aerial reconnaissance patrols had discovered that the Japanese were constructing an airfield at Munda on the northern end of the island. Only 175 miles (282 km) from Guadalcanal, it would pose a serious threat to American forces there. With the capture of Munda as its primary objective, "Operation Toenails" was launched.

The assault commenced on June 21, 1943, when two companies of Raiders landed at Segi Point. There, they rescued a Coast Watcher who had come under suspicion and was being hunted by the Japanese. The Raiders then set out across the island for Viru Harbor, surprising the Japanese force encamped there and destroying the 3 in. (76 mm) coastal guns. As the Army's 43rd Division and the 9th Marine Defense Battalion hit the beaches of Rendova Island on June 30, a fierce air war raged overhead. The Japanese put 130 planes into the sky in order to oppose the landing. Of those planes, 101 were shot down, including 58 by Marines aviators. All in all, it was a good day's shooting.

A few days later, Marine Colonel Harry B. Liversedge led ashore two battalions of the Army's 37th Infantry Division as well as the 1st Raider Battalion. Fighting through thick jungle, the soldiers and Marines made their way toward Bairoko Harbor. They were to serve as a blocking force which would cut off Munda's defenders from any reinforcement and from escape. On August 10, the Raiders managed to secure the village of Enogai and seize the Japanese 5.5 in. (140 mm) coastal guns.

When the 4th Raider Battalion arrived on July 18, Liversedge set out to take Bairoko Harbor. The Marines met very heavy resistance. The Japanese opened fire with automatic weapons hidden in coral bunkers and log emplacements. Snipers and Nambu machine guns laid down a heavy weight of fire. Lieutenant-Colonel Samuel B. Griffith II, one of the battalion commanders, committed his reserve platoon, but the Japanese opened up with 3.54 in. (90 mm) shells. The Marines had no weapons with which to reply and were sent back, reeling. Help was desperately needed. Meanwhile, an Army battalion was supposed to hit the enemy flanks, but had met stiff resistance in the jungle. Suffering 30 percent casualties, the Marines were forced to withdraw. This was intensely frustrating: they were only 300 yards (328 m) from their objective. The following day, when the 25th Division entered Bairoko, they found it had been deserted. The Raider battalions returned to Guadalcanal. Finally, on August 5, the Munda airfield was seized.

Ten days later, the lightly defended Vella Lavella was secured, and the heavily defended Japanese airfield at Kolombangara was also bypassed. The entire New Georgia group was now in the hands of the Allies. Admiral Halsey's staff looked toward the next objective: the northern Solomons. An airstrip in the Solomons would be a vital asset, and to secure one would bring the Allies within land-based fighter range of Japanese positions. Rabaul could then be targeted by dive bombers and torpedo bombers, as well as by Corsairs.

The island of Bougainville was the obvious choice. It was a mountainous place, thickly covered in rain forest with deep, murky swamps, crocodile-infested rivers, and daily heavy rains. A formidable Japanese force held the island: Lieutenant-General Haruyoshi Hyakutake commanded a garrison of some 35,000 troops, which held three airfields, as well as the northern and southern ends of Bougainville. However, the decision to attack was a risky one for Halsey, because he lacked sufficient troops to seize the island, Nonetheless, the potential rewards were too great: to gain an airfield would be a major advance in the war effort. The decision was made. The Marines would be sent to gain a foothold and to defend the position, while Navy Seabees built a pair of airstrips.

The mission was given to I Marine Amphibious Corps, under the command of General Vandegrift. The 3rd Marine Division were to spearhead the assault, with the Army's 37th Division in reserve. A total of 728 Allied aircraft would support the attack, including 14 Marine squadrons. In September 1943, the landing site was chosen: Cape Torokina on the northern side of Empress Augusta Bay. Here, the surf was treacherous, and the narrow beaches were backed by swamps and thick jungle. However, with Japanese forces at the northern and southern ends of the island, it would be the point of least opposition.

Vandegrift knew that any landing on Bougainville would be met with swift counterattacks. A diversion was needed. On October 27, the 8th New Zealand Brigade Group landed on the Treasury Islands, some 75 miles

Below: The mud on Bougainville was an unwelcome surprise to the Marines, and proved an unwanted complication in their plans for capturing the island.

Left: Knee-deep mud
slows these Marines'
advance across the island
of Bougainville. Such wet
conditions gave the
landing forces an added
risk of trench foot as well
as encouraging the local
insect life.

(121 km) southeast of Empress Augusta Bay. Another feint was sent against Choiseul Island. Just after midnight on October 28, the 2nd Parachute Battalion, under the command of Lieutenant-Colonel Victor "Brute" Krulak, stormed ashore. Its mission was to make enough noise to convince the Japanese a division had landed, and for several days the parachutists created havoc on Choiseul. Radio Tokyo reported that 20,000 Americans had come ashore. General Hyakutake dispatched reinforcements from Bougainville.

On the morning of November 1, 1943, the Marines landed on 12 beaches north of Cape Torokina. The landing was made by two teams. The 3rd Marines plus the 2nd Raider Battalion were on the right. The 9th Marines were on the left of the Koromokina River. The mission of the 3rd Raider Battalion was to secure the island of Puruata. It was not an easy landing. Heavy surf pounded the landing craft of the 9th Marines, and some 86 craft were destroyed, their hulks littering the beaches. The 3rd Marines met the strongest resistance. They were caught in a crossfire of machine-gun and artillery fire from Japanese positions on Cape Torokina and Puruata. A single 2.95 in. (75 mm) gun opened fire when the Marines had reached to within only 500 yards (547 m) from the beach, and it created havoc, sinking several landing craft and causing heavy casualties.

> "After the first shell hit, the men in the forward part of the boat fell back toward the center as if a big wave had pushed them. A shell fragment from the second hit me in the thigh. The boat grounded … It was an awful mess. Bloody men pulled themselves off the deck and forced themselves over the side. One man had part of his back blown off. Everyone kept hold of his rifle. Some of them only had half a rifle."

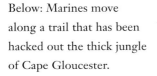

Below: Marines move along a trail that has been hacked out the thick jungle of Cape Gloucester.

As the Marines came ashore, machine guns, rifle fire, and 3.54 in. (90 mm) mortars pounded the beach. The heavy jungle provided concealment for the defenders, and the limited pre-invasion bombardment had done little to knock out Japanese positions. The

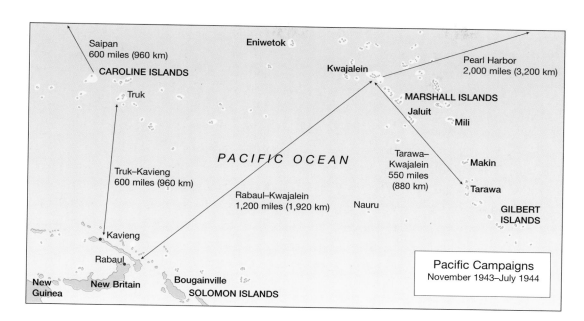

Left: A map showing the Caroline, Marshall, Gilbert and Solomon Island groups, and the large distances that were involved when moving the Marines fighting in the Pacific campaign.

assault of the 9th Marines began to falter. A 23-year-old sergeant, Robert A. Owen, took matters into his own hands, and single-handedly silenced the 2.95 in. (75 mm) gun and its crew before himself being killed. For these actions, he became the first member of the 3rd Marine Division to be awarded the Medal of Honor.

The Japanese command at Rabaul ordered a series of counterattacks against the Marines: 120 fighters and bombers strafed the beachhead and the exposed troops. Halsey ordered New Zealand and Marine fighters to meet them in the air, and 26 Japanese planes went down in flames. By nightfall, there were 14,000 Marines ashore, and the day's objectives had been met. Over the course of the next several days, the Marines advanced inland to extend and strengthen the perimeter. The 2nd Raider Battalion, with 29 dogs of the 1st Marine War Dog Platoon, moved up the Piva Trail and then proceeded to establish a blocking position. By November 5, they controlled 10,000 yards (10,936 m) along the beach, and an area 2,000 yards (2,187 m) deep.

Hyakutake planned his countermeasures. The 23rd Japanese Infantry Regiment was ordered to hit the Marine perimeter. On the morning of November 7, elements of the 17th Division landed west of American positions and dug in along the Koromokino River. Lieutenant-Colonel Walter Asmuth Jr, commanding officer of the 3rd Battalion, 9th Marines, ordered an attack. The Japanese were well equipped. It took the Marines two days of fighting to eradicate the Japanese threat. On November 7–8, Hyakutake's 23rd Regiment moved toward Marine positions along the Piva Trail. It was not unexpected, for the trails were the only way through the rainforest that covered Bougainville. The Japanese hit the roadblock the Raiders had established. The battle raged for five days. Finally, on November 9, all Japanese resistance crumbled. The Marines moved to the junction of the Piva and the Numa-Numa trails, and then dug in.

Navy Seabees selected an airfield site some 1,500 yards (1,640 m) beyond the Marine perimeter. The 2nd Battalion, 21st Marines were ordered to secure the area. At 11:00 hours on November 11, E Company was ambushed by a sizeable Japanese force. The situation was critical. The next day, tanks were brought into the fray, as well as torpedo bombers. Japanese positions were overrun and the area secured. The airfields could now be built.

"The boat grounded … It was an awful mess. Bloody men pulled themselves off the deck and forced themselves over the side. One man had part of his back blown off. Everyone kept hold of his rifle. Some of them only had half a rifle."

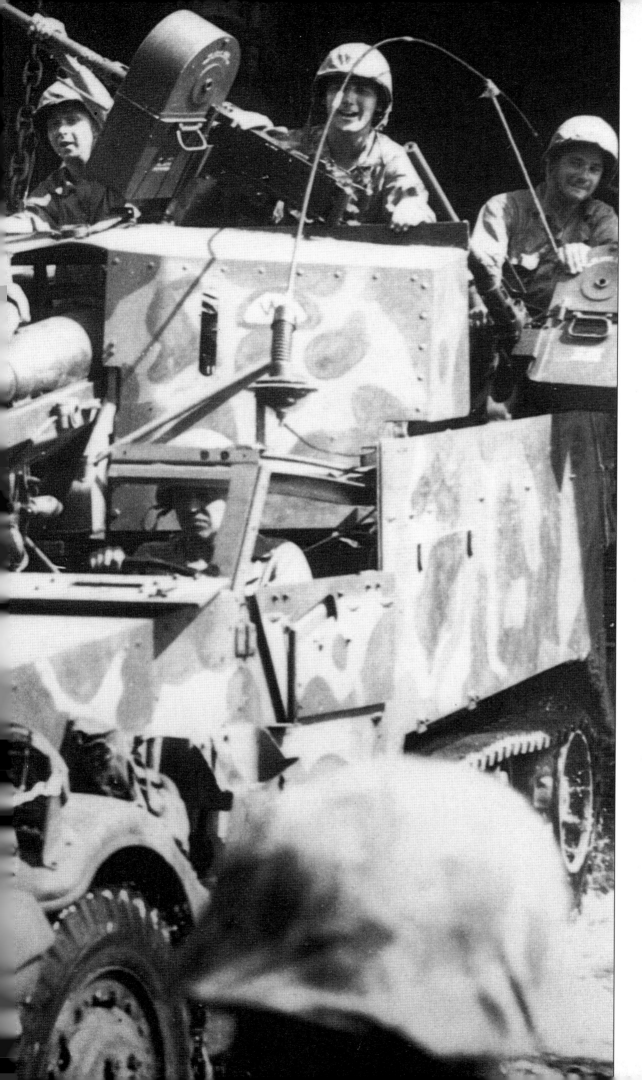

Left: A Marine half-track with a 2.95 in. (75 mm) gun moves out of an LST (Landing Ship Tank) on December 26, 1943, before moving inland to the airfield at Cape Gloucester. The invasion of Bougainville marked the first time the tank-landing craft was utilized.

Right: A Marine advances cautiously through the thick jungle of Cape Gloucester. The 1st Marine Division battled not only the jungle, but also rain and disease, as well as enemy forces, in this "Green Inferno."

Below: This drawing by Tech. Sergeant V.P. Donahue depicts the miserable conditions faced by the Marines on Cape Gloucester in 1943/44.

On November 18, patrols reported that the Japanese had established roadblocks along both the Numa-Numa and East-West Trails. The 2nd and 3rd Battalions, 3rd Marines hit the Japanese and routed the enemy, then established their own blocking positions. An expert scout from the 2nd Battalion found high ground—a 400-ft. (122 m) ridge with a commanding view of the area. First Lieutenant Steve J. Cibik and his platoon ascended the ridge, then dug in and waited for the Japanese to come. And they didn't have to wait long.

The next morning, the Japanese made three fanatical attempts to take the summit of the ridge, but they were repulsed each time; the Marines held their ground.

On November 23, preparation began for two battalions of the 3rd Marines to advance across the Piva River. Seven battalions of artillery were trained upon Japanese positions. On the morning of the 24th, a thunderous barrage began. As the two battalions advanced against the Japanese, the enemy responded with its own artillery fire. The Marines took the heaviest casualties of the Bougainville campaign, but continued to move forward.

"For 500 yards [547 m], the Marines moved in a macabre world of splintered trees and burned-out brush. The very earth was a churned mass of mud and human bodies. The filthy, stinking streams were cesspools of blasted corpses. Over all hung the stench of decaying flesh and powder and smoke which revolted the toughest."

Throughout the month of December, the Marines fought to control a series of hills, including the spur that Marines named "Hellzapoppin Ridge." It was a natural fortress: its steep slopes made ascent deadly, and the heavy jungle provided ample concealment. The Japanese troops were deeply dug in, fighting from bunkers and covering their forces with artillery fire. General Roy S. Geiger, who had taken over command of I Marine Amphibious Corps from Vandegrift, ordered airstrikes. Taking off from the newly constructed airfield at Torokina, Marine aircraft pounded the Japanese. On December 18, two battalions of the 21st Marines took the ridge. Marine casualties on Bougainville now numbered a total of 423 killed and 1,418 wounded. But Halsey's objectives, which had been laid out months before, had now been achieved: on December 10, the airfield at Torokina finally became operative. By January 9, 1944, U.S. fighters and bombers were flying out of Bougainville, and these aircraft, as had been planned, would soon be instrumental in the offensive against the island of Rabaul.

"The Black Sheep Squadron"

In 1943, over 100,000 Japanese soldiers occupied the massive base at Rabaul on New Britain. While General MacArthur wanted to storm the Japanese stronghold directly, the decision was made to neutralize the base. With that decision began the full-scale air assault on Rabaul. A total of 33 squadrons of Marine aircraft saw action in the skies over the Japanese base.

One of those squadrons was Marine Fighter Squadron-214, commanded by the colorful Major Gregory Boyington. Called "Pappy" because of his advanced age of 31 years, Boyington was a veteran of the Flying Tigers. He scored his first six kills as a volunteer P-40 pilot in China. After flying with VMF-122 at Guadalcanal, Boyington took command of "The Black Sheep Squadron," a hard-drinking, hell-raising group of misfits and replacements who, despite their lifestyles, quickly earned a reputation for their skills as aviators. Boyington led his men in fighter sweeps against the Japanese, and scored four more kills within the first week of combat.

Flying the bent-wing F4U Corsairs, larger, faster and more powerful than the Grumman Wildcats, the "Black Sheep" downed 57 enemy aircraft in their first month of battle. When results were less than satisfying, Boyington often tuned his radio to Japanese frequencies and dared the enemy pilots to come out and fight. Between September 16, 1943 and January 3, 1944 Boyington shot down 22 Japanese aircraft. Combined with his six kills in China, "Pappy" became the premier Marine ace of World War II. During his last mission, in which he destroyed two Zeros, Boyington was shot down off New Ireland. Badly wounded, he parachuted into the sea. Presumed dead, he was posthumously awarded the Medal of Honor for his outstanding service in the central Solomons. Boyington, however, had actually survived and was taken prisoner by a Japanese submarine. After 20 months of brutal captivity, "Pappy" Boyington returned a hero and was awarded his Medal of Honor by President Harry Truman.

The successful campaign, however, proved to be the final chapter in the history of the Marine Raiders: no unit ever saw combat again. The war in the Pacific was changing. No longer needed were those specialized units that could strike deep within enemy-held territory. Indeed, it was felt that the missions of the Raiders could have been accomplished by any well-trained unit. The necessity now was manpower. There were currently four Marine Divisions and two more were planned. On August 8, 1944, General Vandegrift, now Commandant of the Marine Corps, disbanded the Marine Raiders. Members of those units provided the core of the 4th Marines, re-established to honor those who had fought on Bataan and Corregidor. Others were to become part of the newly formed 5th Marine Division, which would fight at Iwo Jima.

In the early fall of 1943, General MacArthur believed that the isolation of Rabaul required three Japanese airfields on the western half of New Britain be neutralized. He looked to the veteran 1st Marine Division, "The Old Breed." It had spent a year in Australia recovering from the assault on Guadalcanal. Command had passed to Major-General William H. Rupertus. During that time the division was re-equipped. The Leathernecks traded their much-loved Springfield .03 rifle for the semiautomatic Garand M-1, and the seriously flawed Reising submachine guns for the more reliable Thompson.

In late December, the 1st Marine Division moved to staging areas in eastern New Guinea. New Britain was across the straits. Plans called for the division to land at Cape Gloucester, site of a Japanese airbase. Enemy strength in the area was estimated to stand at between 7,400 and 9,800 troops, and they were commanded by Major-General Iwo Matsuda, but a strong resistance at the beaches was not anticipated. On December 26, 1943, the Marines landed.

The 2nd Battalion, 1st Marines, commanded by Lieutenant-Colonel James M. Masters, Sr, and known as "Masters' Bastards," came ashore on the west side of the cape near the village of Tauali. Their mission was to establish a blocking position on the trail that ran along the coast, preventing Japanese reinforcements from reaching the Cape Gloucester airfields. The main assault hit the eastern side of the Cape. At 07:46 hours, the leading elements of the 3rd Battalion, 7th Marines landed on Yellow Beach 1, followed by the 1st Battalion, 7th Marines on Yellow Beach 2. Close behind was the 3rd Battalion, 1st Marines. There was no organized Japanese resistance and by evening, the 1st Marine Division had 11,000 men ashore.

Struggle for Cape Gloucester

Above: An exhausted-looking Marine from the 2nd Marine Division during the Tarawa island campaign in 1943. His helmet has a "beach"-camouflaged cover.

Victory at Cape Gloucester would require more than defeating the Japanese, however. The assault on New Britain was fought in the worst weather of the year: monsoon rains soaked the Marines; streams rose above their banks and trails became quagmires; insects and poisonous snakes thrived in the dripping, tropical jungle. What's more, pre-invasion bombardment had added its own dangers. The natural landscape, already difficult, was made worse by the hundreds of trees brought down by air and naval gunfire. Other trees were weakened and came crashing suddenly to the ground. The swamps covered shell holes and bomb craters; a mis-step could easily result in serious injury. As the Marines expanded the beachhead, they were forced to hack their way through the thick vegetation, rifle in one hand, machete in the other. This area behind the Yellow Beaches was an area marked on Marine maps as "damp flats." The men had been prepared to encounter mud, but found instead a dank, stinking jungle that was virtually impassable. Before the campaign for Cape Gloucester was finished, this difficult terrain claimed its own casualties.

On December 27, the 1st Marines moved toward Cape Gloucester's airfields. Initially, they met only sporadic resistance but aerial observation had spotted a series of trenches and bunkers in their path. The Marines would come to call this area "Hell's Point." Aided by airstrikes and an additional platoon of M4 Sherman medium tanks, the 3rd Battalion, 1st Marines moved against the Japanese positions. Protected by riflemen, the tanks succeeded in destroying the bunkers and routing the Japanese. On December 29, two battalions of the 5th Marines joined the 1st Marines and moved forward. By evening, they had secured the area and established a perimeter around the airfield. The Japanese officer responsible for defending the airfield fell back. He gathered his troops in the hills south of the airfield, along a ridge. The 1st and 2nd Battalions, 5th Marines attacked on December 30, supported in their efforts by tanks and artillery. By dusk, the Marines had reached the summit. Finally, on New Year's Eve, 1943, General Rupertus formally raised the flag over Cape Gloucester.

Above: A Marine patrol scouts Japanese positions along the Natamo River in New Britain. This patrol later came under enemy machine-gun fire which killed two of the Marines.

Brigadier-General Lemuel C. Shepherd, Jr, Assistant Division Commander, was given the task of enlarging the beachhead to the southwest and securing Borgen Bay. He was all too aware that Matsuda's forces remained essentially intact, and so on January 1 issued orders to probe the enemy's defenses in order to measure just how strong these defenses were. The Marines encountered a well-emplaced Japanese force on the far side of a wide stream: Matsuda had given three reinforced battalions to Colonel Kenshiro Katayama, commander of the 141st Japanese Infantry. Several attempts to cross that stream were unsuccessful and the area became a deathtrap for the Marines, known as "Suicide Creek."

Firepower was needed to punch through the Japanese defenses, but tanks were unable to advance. It was simply too wet, the mud too thick. Seabees from the 17th Marines succeeded in constructing a road of thick logs that would support the weight of the tanks. The steep banks of the creek remained an obstacle. Two Marines were killed by sniper fire while attempting to bulldoze a path. Finally, the ingenuity of Private First Class Randall Johnson prevailed. He positioned himself outside the bulldozer's cab and, using a shovel and an ax handle to manipulate the controls, opened the way for tanks and half-tracks. The

Japanese defenses were broken. The Marines crossed "Suicide Creek" and advanced on Aogiri Ridge, high ground heavily defended by some 1,300 Japanese troops.

On the morning of January 8, Lieutenant-Colonel Lewis W. Walt took command of the 3rd Battalion, 5th Marines. The previous day's fighting had left the battalion battered, but the Marines continued to advance, moving up a steep slope. The terrain was hellacious, the jungle undergrowth being very thick, dense, and tangled. Fire from Japanese machine guns was savage. The battalion needed the support of heavy firepower, but once again the ubiquitous rain and mud of Cape Gloucester stopped the tanks. The only weapon available to the Marines was a single 1.45 in. (37 mm) gun and half its crew lay dead. Walt asked for volunteers to manhandle the piece into position. None came. Putting his shoulder to the wheel, Walt began to push. The surviving members of the gun crew joined him. They pushed the gun up Aogiri Ridge, stopping every few feet to fire, then reload and push again. As Marines were hit by enemy fire and went down, others joined in the struggle. Walt would be awarded a Navy Cross for his actions that day. By nightfall, the men of the 3rd Battalion had reached the crest of the ridge. Only 10 yards (11 m) from enemy positions, the Marines dug in and waited for the Japanese to counterattack.

At 01:15 hours on January 10, the first of the Japanese attacks was launched in a pouring rain. Four more attacks followed. The 4.13 in. (105 mm) guns of the 11th Marines hammered the Japanese positions, which responded with artillery shells that fell within 50 yards (55 m) of the Marines. By first light, the last attack had been beaten back. Aogiri Ridge belonged to the Marines, and would thereafter be named "Walt's Ridge." The final Marine objective on Cape Gloucester was Hill 660. Its capture was the mission of the 3rd Battalion, 7th Marines. Captain Joseph W. Buckley, commander of the Weapons Company, 7th Marines led a detachment to block the trail behind the hill. Two platoons of infantry, a platoon of 1.46 in. (37 mm) guns, two light tanks, and two half-tracks mounting 2.95 in. (75 mm) guns established a roadblock and waited for the Japanese.

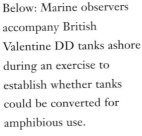

Below: Marine observers accompany British Valentine DD tanks ashore during an exercise to establish whether tanks could be converted for amphibious use.

Bombers, artillery, and mortars pounded the hill in preparation for the attack. The initial assault by the 3rd Battalion was repulsed, but the Marines regrouped and began the ascent of Hill 660 once again. They advanced slowly against a determined Japanese defense. The ground near the summit rose very steeply and the mud made footing precarious. The Marines were forced to sling their rifles and climb hand over hand, grasping tree roots and pulling themselves toward the crest of the hill. The Japanese were driven off the summit and down the trail—and into Buckley's roadblock. The Marines pursued the surviving Japanese as they moved eastward along the north coast. On March 6, a shore-to-shore landing by the 5th Marines, under the command of Colonel Oliver P. Smith, seized the airfield at Talasea. Total Marine casualties numbered 310 killed and 1,083 wounded, but the battle for Cape Gloucester was won. The isolation of Rabaul was complete. On April 24, 1944, the 1st Marine Division was relieved.

In August 1943, Vice Admiral Raymond A. Spruance flew to New Zealand to meet with Major-General Julian C. Smith, commander of the 2nd Marine Division. The subject was the Central Pacific offensive. The march toward Tokyo would take Allied forces through the Gilbert Islands, the Marshalls, the Marianas, and the Carolines. The first objective was the Gilberts. This would mean taking Tarawa Atoll, the Japanese airfield on Betio Island, to provide an advanced base for future campaigns. It was clear from the onset that "Operation Galvanic" would not be an easy task. The islands had the natural defenses of coral reefs and unpredictable tides that made an amphibious landing dangerous, at best. The reefs could easily be made impassable with barbed wire and mines, while the islands themselves were flat, offering fine fields of fire for Japanese defenders. The enemy had learned much from earlier attacks: after Evans Carlson's Raiders hit Makin in August 1942, they realized their vulnerabilities and turned Betio into a fortress. Tangles of barbed wire stretched over the coral reefs; the beaches were fortified with coconut logs and reinforced concrete; more than 500 pillboxes and blockhouses were built; some 200 guns sat at the

Betio [was] a fortress. Tangles of barbed wire stretched over the coral reefs; the beaches were fortified with coconut logs and reinforced concrete; more than 500 pillboxes and blockhouses were built; some 200 guns sat at the ready.

ready. In all, an estimated 4,800 Japanese troops of the 3rd Special Base Force and the 7th Sasebo Special Naval Landing Force stood in defense of the island.

The U.S. Navy felt that a short, heavy pre-invasion bombardment would smash the fortress-like defenses, while limiting the threat of Japanese air and naval counterattack. The Marines, though, realized that Tarawa could easily become a slaughterhouse. General Smith and his staff, including Colonel Merritt Edson and Lieutenant-Colonel David Shoup, requested that a small neighboring island be seized to provide artillery support. In addition, they wanted three full days of air and naval bombardment prior to the Marine landing. Both requests were denied. Pre-invasion bombardment was limited to just three hours.

The actual landing presented another problem. A coral reef lay some 600–1,000 yards (656–1,094 m) off the beach. Invasion planners gambled that high tide would cover the reef with enough water (4 ft./1.2 m) to float the landing craft; this was by no means a certainty.

Below: Marines take shelter on Tarawa as a naval bombardment targets Japanese positions on the island. The effects of earlier bombardments can be clearly seen, as the trees' foliage has been stripped away.

An erratic tide could also prove disastrous. The only solution was the use of LVTs, amphibian tractors. However, the 2nd Marine Division had only enough tractors to land the first three waves of Marines. Subsequent waves of troops would have to depend on high tide, or wade ashore. The situation became even more grim when General Holland "Howlin' Mad" Smith withheld the 6th Marines and made it the Corps' reserve. General Julian Smith tried desperately to retain the 6th Marines, for his plan to hit Tarawa needed two full regiments abreast and one held in reserve. "Howlin' Mad" Smith refused. The 2nd Marine Division would have to make a frontal assault on Betio with limited preparatory bombardment and too few Marines.

Dawn on November 20, 1943 brought surprise to the Japanese on Tarawa. They were surrounded by U.S. warships. Battle commenced at 05:07 hours, when the Japanese fired their 8 in. (203 mm) guns. Three U.S. battleships, survivors of Pearl Harbor, responded with their 14 in. (355 mm) batteries. Supported by carrier planes, they pounded Tarawa with one of the heaviest bombardments in naval history. In their landing craft, the Marines believed no one could have survived. Surely, the defenses on Tarawa had been obliterated. But no: the Japanese defenses remained strong. Furthermore, a lull in the bombardment served to let the enemy regroup.

At 08:55 hours, a scout-sniper platoon led by First Lieutenant William Deane Hawkins landed on the long pier jutting out from Tarawa. It divided Red Beach Two and Three. From here, the Japanese were assured flanking fire. Marines and Japanese Special Naval Forces met in hand-to-hand combat. Using explosives and flamethrowers, Hawkins and his men destroyed several gun emplacements that waited to fire upon the approaching Marines. The pier was now clear. Behind the scouts, three waves of the 2nd and 3rd Battalions, 2nd Marines and the 2nd Battalion, 8th Marines headed for the beach. The last 200 yards (219 m) were the most difficult for these men: LVTs were hammered by heavy machine-gun fire and the Marines fell by the dozen.

"We were 100 yards [109 m] in now and the enemy fire was awful damn intense and getting worse. They were knocking (LVTs) out left and right. A tractor'd get hit, stop, and burst into flames with men jumping out like torches. … I didn't want to put [my] head up. The bullets were pouring at us like a sheet of rain."

At 09:10 hours, the Marines hit the beaches of Tarawa. The 2nd Battalion, 8th Marines landed on Red Beach Three, east of the pier. Japanese resistance was tough in the center at Red Beach Two: the 2nd Battalion, 2nd Marines was badly shot up, its commanding officer killed by machine-gun fire while wading to the shore. On Red Beach One, to the west, the Japanese had four 2.95 in. (75 mm) guns trained on the approaching Marines. Major John Schoettel watched the slaughter, convinced he was witness to the annihilation of his men. He radioed Colonel Shoup, commander of the 2nd Marines: "Receiving heavy fire all along beach. … Issue in doubt." Told to land his reserve, Schoettel replied, "We have nothing left to land." Yet despite very heavy casualties, the 3rd Battalion, 2nd Marines came ashore. On the narrow beaches, they were pinned down in a hellish position between the water and a reinforced coconut-log seawall. Machine guns and artillery fire sliced through the Marines.

Above: In one of his most horrific works, Kerr Eby shows what was left of a Marine tank after being hit by Japanese mortar fire. Eby later said it was his responsibility as a combat artist to show the terrible, magnificent way Marines died.

Shoup sent the 1st Battalion, 2nd Marines ashore on Red Beach Two with orders to attack westward toward Schoettel's men, advancing inland as much as possible. Japanese fire was incredibly heavy. Vaulting over the seawall, 1st Sergeant Wilbur Burgess ignored the bullets whistling around him and spurred on the Marines. Echoing the words of Dan Daly at Belleau Wood, he asked, "Whatsa matter? Do you wanna live forever?" Singly, and in small groups, the Marines followed Burgess toward the Japanese positions. Colonel Shoup crawled ashore by 10:30 hours. It had taken him nearly four hours to reach the beach; three attempts to cross the reef had been thwarted by intense enemy fire. His LVT was disabled, two-thirds of his staff were dead, and he had taken a shell fragment in the leg.

Shoup led the remainder of his men ashore, into the shelter of the pier. Standing in waist-deep water amid the floating corpses of Marines, he began to take charge of the battle. He realized that the assault on Tarawa had stalled: the number of casualties was

Above: Two Marines drag a badly wounded man back to the cover of Tarawa's seawall. Tarawa was the Marines' bloodiest landing yet: a total of 997 Marines were to die during the landing, which took place over a period of only three days. A further 2,000 men were wounded.

horrific; Marines could not advance against the heavily defended Japanese positions; reinforcements could not reach the beach. Shoup hoped the new Sherman tanks would break the stalemate—in vain. The tanks crossed the reef easily, but several drowned in shell holes. Combat engineers had blasted a gap in the seawall to let the tanks move inland, but dead and dying Marines blocked the way. The commander refused to maneuver across the bodies and reversed instead, proceeding toward another opening in the seawall. Only two tanks made it ashore. On Red Beach Three, seven of the Shermans landed and were then ordered inland, with vague instructions to knock out any enemy positions they came across. All but one of the tanks succumbed to Japanese fire. Shoup radioed the flagship that the tanks had offered little assistance to the Marines' efforts.

General Julian C. Smith realized that the attack must be kept moving. The 3rd Battalion, 8th Marines was ordered to the line of departure, where it came under the tactical control of Shoup. At 11:03 hours, the battalion was ordered to land on Red Beach Three. Offshore, the Leathernecks faced other problems. Planners had gambled that by mid-morning, the tides would be high enough for Higgins boats to cross the reef. The gamble failed: the tides fluctuated no more than 1 ft. (30 cm). The Marines crashed into the exposed coral and some drowned under the weight of their equipment. The rest were forced to wade some 500–700 yards (547–765 m) ashore through withering machine-gun fire. Casualties were as high as 70 percent. Major-General Julian C. Smith radioed General Holland Smith: "Request release of Combat Team 6. Issue in doubt." On November 20, some 5,000 Marines assaulted the beaches of Tarawa. By evening, 1,500 of them were dead or wounded. The survivors were dug in along a very narrow beachhead. "There we were, toes in the water, casualties everywhere, dead and wounded all around us." The Marines expected a Japanese counterattack. It never came. Later, General Julian C. Smith stated that the Japanese had lost the battle for Tarawa that night by failing to attack; the beaches would never again be so vulnerable as they were during those hours of darkness.

As morning dawned on Tarawa, the stench of death lay over the island. Bodies floated near the beach and the dead covered the sands. The smell drifted across the water to the 1st Battalion, 8th Marines, which had spent the night in landing craft. On the morning of the 21st, it was to come ashore and move west toward Red Beach One. Such a task would prove no easier than it had on the day before. Wading ashore, the Marines were hit by flanking machine-gun fire. Their numbers were decimated.

> "It was terrible seeing Marines shot down. … I saw one Marine coming in carrying a heavy load and saw him get hit. He continued coming in and I saw him get hit again, and still he kept coming, and then he was hit a third time. When he reached the shore, I grabbed him, saying, 'You stupid S.O.B., why in hell didn't you drop that load and crouch in the water so you wouldn't make such a target? … I heard him mutter, 'They said we had to get this ammo to the Marines on the beach—that they were running short—I had to bring it in.' "

Seeing the carnage in the water spurred First Lieutenant Hawkins into action. Although wounded the day before, Hawkins hit one Japanese bunker after another, obliterating four pillboxes before being mortally wounded. He was later awarded the Medal of Honor. By 08:00 hours, half the men of the 1st Battalion hit the beach. It was the men under the command of Major Michael P. Ryan, including members of the 1st Battalion, who made

Below: A Marine throws a grenade at a Japanese pillbox while his buddy watches from the safety of stacked sandbags. Grenades, rifle grenades, flamethrowers and satchel charges were all used to knock out the deadly Japanese pillboxes.

The fighting on Tarawa was still intense, but the Marines were on the move. They inched forward, assaulting Japanese positions with grenades and flamethrowers. At 16:00 hours, Shoup radioed Julian Smith: "Casualties: many. Percentage dead: unknown. Combat efficiency: we are winning."

the greatest contribution on the second day of the battle. Ryan, a company commander of 3rd Battalion, 2nd Marines, had taken command of stragglers from the previous day's landing. The men of four different landing teams, known as "Ryan's Orphans," established a small beachhead at the western tip of the island. Utilizing two surviving Sherman tanks and a working radio, Ryan then launched an assault north to south across the island. The Marines obliterated two 3.15 in. (80 mm) guns, cleared out a maze of pillboxes, and routed a company of Japanese Special Naval Landing Forces. Major-General Julian Smith was overjoyed. He now had a secure beach upon which to land the 6th Marines.

The advantage began to shift. The fighting on Tarawa was still intense, but the Marines were on the move. They inched forward, assaulting Japanese positions with grenades and flamethrowers. At 16:00 hours, Shoup radioed Julian Smith: "Casualties: many. Percentage dead: unknown. Combat efficiency: we are winning." The third day of the battle for Tarawa began as the 1st Battalion, 6th Marines pushed along the southern shore. By 11:00 hours, they had established contact with the 1st Battalion, 2nd Marines. With the exception of a pocket of resistance between Red Beach One and Two, the Japanese on the western half of the island was now crushed. Sandwiched between the 3rd Battalion, 2nd Marines on the west and the 1st Battalion, 8th Marines on the east, the resistance would not be long-lived.

On Betio's northern side, the 8th Marines attacked fortified Japanese positions to the east. Several strongpoints had proven effective against the Marines the previous day: coconut-log machine-gun emplacements, a bombproof shelter, and a steel pillbox. Luck was with the Leathernecks: at 09:30 hours, a 2.36 in. (60 mm) mortar hit the coconut-log emplacement, igniting the ammunition stores. The bunker exploded. A few minutes later, one of the medium tanks directed several 2.95 in. (75 mm) shells into the steel pillbox. An infantry-engineer team went after the bombproof shelter in the toughest battle of the day.

Right: Combat artist Richard Gibney's painting shows a Marine flamethrower in action. Flamethrowers were ideal for clearing Japanese pillboxes, but as they were easily spotted, the men using them attracted heavy fire from the enemy. Gibney landed on Tarawa with the Marines.

Left: As one Marine prepares to throw a grenade from within the shelter of a sandbagged emplacement, his buddy, who is armed with an M1 carbine and carries a belt of ammunition, stands ready to advance.

The surviving Japanese launched a series of counterattacks that night, but few survived. By early afternoon of the 23rd, General Julian C. Smith declared the island secured. The Allies gained four new airfields, which could be used to launch strikes in its march across the Pacific. Viewing the carnage on Tarawa brought tears to the eyes of General Holland Smith. Marine dead remained unburied and the stench of death was overpowering. Seizing the bloody beaches of Tarawa had been a difficult and costly task: in three days, a total of 997 Marines had been killed and more than 2,000 had been wounded.

A *TIME* correspondent wrote:

"Last week some 2,000 or 3,000 United States Marines, most of them now dead or wounded, gave the nation a name to stand beside those of Concorde Bridge, the *Bon Homme Richard*, the Alamo, Little Big Horn, and Belleau Wood. The name was 'Tarawa.' "

As the assault on Tarawa progressed, plans were being made for the next step. This was to be the offensive thrust on the Marshalls. These strategic islands had been under Japanese control since World War I, and consequently little was known about them. Naval intelligence had estimated that some 30,000 Japanese troops defended the Marshalls, but it

"Last week some 2,000 or 3,000 United States Marines, most of them now dead or wounded, gave the nation a name to stand beside those of Concorde Bridge, the Bon Homme Richard, the Alamo, Little Big Horn, and Belleau Wood. The name was 'Tarawa.' "

was believed that the majority of those forces were garrisoned on the eastern rim. Nearby lay the island of Truk, home port of the Japanese Combined Fleet.

Admiral Nimitz made the bold decision to strike Kwajalein Atoll, in the heart of the Marshalls. The objective was the seizure of Kwajalein Island to the south, and the connected islands of Roi-Namur to the north. The offensive was to begin with a Marine Force Reconnaissance Company securing Manjuro Atoll in the eastern Marshalls to serve as an advanced base. The assault on Kwajalein itself was to be made by the Army 7th Infantry Division. Roi-Namur was to be taken by the 4th Marine Division under the command of Major-General Harry Schmidt. After several delays, D-Day was scheduled for January 31, 1944. The lessons of Tawara having been learned, a massive pre-invasion bombardment began on January 29. Navy ships pounded Japanese artillery positions and blockhouses, mapped by submarine and aerial reconnaissance. Air strikes continued mercilessly. A total of 6,000 tons of shells and bombs struck the Japanese defenses.

Above: Men of the 24th Marines hit the beaches of Namur Island under enemy fire. The 23rd Marines had better luck, facing little opposition on neighboring Roi.

On January 31, the 25th Marines landed on five small islands adjacent to Roi-Namur. Communications problems plagued the Marines and landings were uncoordinated. Resistance was light. By evening the beaches were secured. The 14th Marines 2.95 in. (75 mm) and 4.13 in. (105 mm) howitzers were dug in, ready to support the main landings. That morning, Marines came ashore on Manjuro against minimal enemy forces. Captain James L. Jones, of 5th Amphibious Reconnaissance Company, raised the first American flag over the Marshall Islands.

On the morning of February 1, a furious bombardment of Roi-Namur began. The battleship *Tennessee* opened fire. Carrier planes strafed the islands. The artillery of the 14th Marines added to the fray. Plans called for the 23rd Marines to come ashore on Roi; the 24th Marines were to land on Namur. Complications hampered the movement of the Marines from ship-to-shore. The hour of the attack was postponed several times. Finally, after running out of patience, Colonel Louis Jones, commander of the 23rd Marines, ordered the assault on Roi. The Japanese offered scant resistance. In a radio message to General Schmidt, Jones said: "This is a pip … no opposition near the beach." By evening, the 23rd Marines had secured Roi's airfield and reached the northern shore of the island.

The 24th Marines were in a much more difficult situation. The Japanese had dug a line of trenches along the beach, It was reinforced with machine-gun emplacements and foxholes. As the Marines approached the shore, they were raked by enemy fire. A young Second Lieutenant, John C. Chapin, was in the first wave.

"The beach lay right before us. However, it was surrounded in such a pall of dust and smoke from our bombardment that we could see very little of it. As a result we were unable to tell which section we were approaching … I turned to my platoon sergeant, who was manning the machine gun right beside me. He was slumped over—the whole right side of his head disintegrated into a mass of gore. Up to now, the entire operation had seemed almost like a movie, or like one of the numerable practice landings we'd made."

As the Marines moved inland toward the day's objective, resistance stiffened. Demolition teams began attacking the enemy's strongholds. At 13:05 hours, Marines of the 2nd Battalion were assaulting a large concrete structure, hurling satchel charges inside the building. It was a deadly mistake. The structure was actually a munitions bunker full of torpedo warheads and heavy ammunition. A tremendous explosion rocked Namur. One aerial observer thought the entire island had been obliterated, as it disappeared in a cloud of brown dust. Ashore, the damage was staggering. Trees and slabs of concrete were strewn

Below: Marines man a Browning 0.50 caliber (12.7 mm) machine gun during the invasion of Namur. The 0.50 caliber is still in regular service today with the Corps as well as with the forces of many other nations.

Right: The 2nd Marine Division is shown in this painting poised to strike the southwestern shore of Saipan, an small island with rugged mountains, ridgelines, cliffs, jungle, and dense sugarcane fields. A total of 32,000 Japanese Imperial Army soldiers and *rikusentai* awaited the Leathernecks' arrival.

The Allied offensive in the Pacific was gathering momentum. Victory in the Marshalls had been surprisingly swift. Nimitz made the decision to seize the opportunity that presented itself, and strike again quickly.

around like matchsticks. Twenty Marines of the 2nd Battalion, 24th Marines were dead, and 100 others wounded, accounting for half the casualties on Namur.

By 16:30 hours, the 2nd and 3rd Battalions, 24th Marines renewed the attack. General Schmidt ordered the 3rd Battalion, 23rd Marines and supporting medium tanks into the fray. They crossed the sandbar from Roi to Namur and formed the spearhead of a push along the west coast to the northernmost part of the island. By nightfall, the Marines held half of Namur. On the morning of February 2, the tanks shattered a Japanese counterattack. Fighting continued throughout the day, but by afternoon two battalions of the 24th Marines met on the northern shore of Namur. The island was secured. To the south, the fighting on Kwajalein Island continued until February 4, when the Army 7th Infantry Division declared the island secured. Two days later, Marine aircraft began arriving at Roi. By February 7, Kwajalein Atoll was in American hands. It was a job well done. Japanese casualties were estimated at 3,563. There were far fewer Marine casualties than anticipated. The 4th Marine Division had lost 313 men and another 502 wounded.

Momentum in the Pacific

The Allied offensive in the Pacific was gathering momentum. Victory in the Marshalls had been surprisingly swift. Nimitz made the decision to seize the opportunity that presented itself, and strike again quickly. The next step in the advance against the Japanese, the assault on Eniwetok Atoll, would now take place on February 17 rather than the planned date of May 1. Initially, the 2nd Marine Division was to be given the task of taking Eniwetok. In the event, it was decided to utilize the V Amphibious Corps reserve. The 22nd Marines and two regiments of the Army 106th Infantry Regiment, under the command of Marine Corps General Thomas Watson, were to take Engebi, Eniwetok, and Parry Island.

Aerial reconnaissance indicated that both Eniwetok and Parry were lightly defended and that the strength of the Japanese forces appeared to be gathered on Engebi. Pre-invasion strikes began in conjunction with the assault on the Marshall Islands. The airfield on Engebi was neutralized in order to prevent enemy aircraft from refueling and striking American forces which were at that point hitting Kwajalein. Additional strikes throughout early February attempted to batter the small islands into submission. Already the Japanese defenders found themselves to be in seriously dire straits.

On February 17, Marines of the V Amphibious Reconnaissance Company came ashore on small islands adjacent to Engebi. As at Kwajalein, the mission was to capture support bases which could be used for Army and Marine artillery units. The Marines lost little time in selecting firing positions, and by evening, registration was complete. These artillery units would add their firepower to a massive bombardment of the island.

On the morning of February 18, the 22nd Marines hit the beaches of Engebi. Enemy defenses were clustered in a thick palm grove and many of the Japanese were dug into "spiderholes." Fallen trees provided additional cover. Eradicating those positions proved perilous work for the Marines, but by the afternoon Engebi belonged to the Americans. That night, surviving Japanese soldiers harassed the Leathernecks with grenades and automatic rifle fire. The following morning, after a formal flag-raising, demolition teams and flamethrower operators set out to eradicate the remaining Japanese threat.

Securing Eniwetok was more difficult. Pre-invasion bombardment had been much lighter than on Engebi, and contrary to intelligence reports, a large Japanese force defended the island. A maze of "spiderholes" greeted the soldiers of the 106th Infantry Regiment. The tough Japanese resistance convinced Colonel Russell G. Ayers, commander of the 106th, that more force was needed. The 3rd Battalion, 22nd Marines was ordered to land and take

Above: Marines head for Saipan's shore. Many Marines were killed when the highly skilled Japanese artillery launched a concentrated salvo against the landing craft as they approached the beach.

Japanese strategy changed ... any Japanese forces coming under attack were to hold fast. Every inch of Japanese territory taken by American forces was to cost as many American lives as possible.

the left half of Eniwetok. At 15:15 hours, the two battalions began the advance on Japanese positions. It was not an easy task. As darkness approached, the Marines encountered a series of coconut-log emplacements, well concealed in the heavy underbrush. They had been unharmed by the heavy shelling. Repeated use of satchel charges and flamethrowers let the advance proceed slowly and by the night of the 19th, the Marines were several hundred yards from the westernmost tip of the island. The morning, however, brought an unwelcome surprise: the Army battalion supporting the right flank of the Marines had pulled back during the night and enemy troops had then entered the gap to launch a desperate counterattack against the Marine command post. Clerks and radiomen joined riflemen to resist and the Japanese were thrown back. By afternoon, the southwestern half of the island was secured. With additional Marine tanks and engineers, the Army finally overran the northern portion of Eniwetok on the afternoon of February 21.

General Watson was concerned about the ability of the Army to take the heavily defended Parry Island quickly. Changing plans, he decided to bring in the 1st and 2nd Battalions, 22nd Marines from Engebi, as well as the 3rd Battalion from Eniwetok. For three days prior to the invasion, Parry Island was pummeled by aerial and naval gunfire. The battleships *Tennessee* and *Pennsylvania* moved to within 850 yards (930 m) of the shore and and turned their big guns on the island. A total of 944 tons of shells, supplemented by artillery fire from the neighboring islands, fell on Parry. On February 22, the 22nd Marines hit the beaches. Despite the heavy bombardment, the Japanese were determined to defend the island. The 2nd Battalion met only light resistance, but the 1st Battalion faced heavy enemy fire. Machine guns and mortars opened up on the Marines as they came ashore. Fighting was hand-to-hand as the Leathernecks cleared out the Japanese defenses. With the support of tanks and artillery, the 22nd Marines pushed across the island. Bulldozers buried the Japanese hiding in "spiderholes." By 19:30 hours, Parry Island was American. The Japanese still had four major bases in the Marshalls, but these were without reinforcements; Marine air operations prevented this. The conquest of the Marshall Islands was complete.

Victory had been swift and casualties were considered light. U.S. forces would not, however, be so fortunate throughout the rest of the Pacific campaign. Japanese strategy changed, the Imperial General Headquarters establishing the Absolute Defense Zone around the home islands. This included the Marianas and the Carolines, strategically important targets in the march across the Pacific. Defenses there were to be strengthened and any Japanese forces coming under attack were to hold fast. Every inch of Japanese territory taken by American forces was to cost as many American lives as possible.

Above: A group of Marines comes under enemy sniper fire. The Leatherneck in the center has just been hit. The Japanese used snipers to try to sap the Marines' morale.

Out of a series of Allied conferences, a plan emerged for the invasion of the Marianas. Codenamed "Operation Forager," it was a bold strike westward toward Japan. The seizure of Saipan, Tinian, and Guam would bring American airpower within some 1,200 miles (1,932 km) of the homeland. The power of the new long-range bomber, the B-29 Superfortress, could then be brought to bear against Japanese targets. The first objective was Saipan, 72 square miles (187 sq km) of rugged mountains, ridgelines, cliffs, jungle, and dense sugarcane fields. Here, the Japanese had an airfield as well as an administrative center. Once seized, this could serve as an advance base as well as provide artillery support for an invasion of Tinian, only 3 miles (4.8 km) to the southwest.

No one expected Saipan to fall easily. A total of 32,000 Imperial Army and Navy troops defended the island and the terrain favored the Japanese. Field artillery regiments of the Japanese Army were fully armed and Navy coastal defense batteries ringed the island. General Holland Smith expected the seizure of Saipan to result in "a lot of dead Marines." For four days prior to the Marine landing, the island was pounded by aerial and naval gunfire. Some 71,000 Marines, commanded by General Holland Smith, waited offshore to storm the beaches of Saipan. The landing force consisted of the 2nd and 4th Marine Divisions. Smith's plan called for the Marines to come ashore in the southwest corner of the island, on either side of the town of Charan-Kanoa. Major-General Thomas Watson's 2nd Division was to land on the left. Marines of Major-General Harry Schmidt's 4th Marine Division were to storm the beaches to the south, and on the right.

On the morning of June 15, as H-hour approached, the bombardment of Saipan reached a truly thunderous climax. U.S. warships hammered the beaches; carrier planes dropped bombs and strafed the shoreline with machine-gun fire. At exactly 08:12 hours,

Above: A drenched Marine crawls to shore on Saipan after his landing craft was disabled or destroyed. The confusion and apprehension among these crouching men is easy to see in this picture. Enemy fire, the prospect that confronted every Marine who came ashore on the beaches of Saipan, was appalling to witness.

the first LVTs headed toward Saipan. As the tractors approached the reef, the Marines were caught in a hail of fire: Japanese artillery units were committed to expending a full 15 percent of their ammunition total on the approaching landing craft. Mortars and machine guns opened up against the Leathernecks. A concentrated salvo of artillery fire hit as the Marines closed with the shore. Some LVTs took direct hits; equipment, crew, and Marines disappeared in a cloud of smoke and a froth of surf. Despite some losses, the assault pushed toward the beach. By 08:43 hours, the first Marines were landed on the thick sands of Saipan's

Above: With bayonets fixed, these Marines take cover behind a captured Japanese field artillery piece. The fighting on Saipan was particularly brutal, in a bloody campaign for the island which would last for three long weeks.

shores. Within a short 20 minutes after that, there was a huge total of 8,000 Leathernecks on the shore, waiting for their next order to be issued.

The beachheads were a scene of confusion. First Lieutenant John C. Chapin vividly recounted his experience of those confusing moments:

"All around us was the chaotic debris of bitter combat: Jap and Marine bodies lying in mangled and grotesque positions; blasted and burnt-out pillboxes; the burning wrecks of the LVTs that had been knocked out by Jap high velocity fire; the acrid smell of high explosives; the shattered trees; and the churned-up sand littered with discarded equipment."

A strong northerly current had caused the 6th and 8th Marines, the regiments that formed the 2nd Marine Division, to land too far to the north. Artillery, mortars, and automatic weapons fire ripped through the 6th Marines. Enemy fire was hellacious. By afternoon, the advance of the 6th Marines had been stopped. Thirty-five percent of the regiment lay dead or wounded. To confuse matters further, both assault battalions of the 8th Marines landed on the same beach, some 600 yards (656 m) from the planned boundary with the 4th Marine Division. A dangerous gap was created. This delayed the seizure of Afetna Point, a Japanese stronghold located in the center of the beachhead. Enemy fire from this position raked the Marines of both divisions. Artillery and mortars added to the destruction. Casualties were staggeringly high: one-third of the 8th Marines were lost.

To the south, the 4th Marine Division was meeting equally heavy resistance. Most of the 23rd Marines had been stopped at the beach. On the far right, the 25th Marines received very heavy fire from Agingan Point and held only a sliver of shoreline. At 09:30 hours, the

Japanese attacked from the south, but were repulsed by naval gunfire and aerial strikes. An advance toward the ridgeline proved hazardous:

"Suddenly, WHAM! A shell hit right on top of us! I was too surprised to think, but instinctively all of us hit the deck and began to spread out. Then the shells really began to pour down on us: ahead, behind, on both sides, and right in our midst. They would come rocketing down with a freight-train roar, and then explode with a deafening cataclysm that is beyond description. ... It finally dawned on me that the first shell-bursts we'd heard had been ranging shots and now that the Japs were 'zeroed in' on us, we were caught in a full-fledged barrage."

By sunset, some 20,000 Marines held a slim beachhead. This was only half the width that planners had hoped for, and it had cost nearly 2,000 Marines dead or wounded.

That night, the 6th Marines bore the brunt of a desperate Japanese counterattack. Hoping to overwhelm the narrow beachhead and annihilate the American invaders, some 2,000 Japanese troops and 40 medium tanks roared out of the night. The 2nd Division had only two howitzer battalions ashore and could not cover the Japanese approach. Offshore, the *California* illuminated the night with star shells. A hail of fire from machine guns, antitank guns, and M-1 rifles greeted the Japanese charge. As the Japanese broke, the *California* opened fire with her secondary batteries. In the morning, the Marines found the smoking remnants of the enemy tank battalion. Some 700 Japanese soldiers lay dead.

On the morning of June 16, the 2nd Battalion, 8th Marines succeeded in clearing the Japanese defenders from Afetna Point. To the south, the 4th Marine Division pushed the attack: the 25th Marines advanced to within a half-mile (800 m) of Aslito Airfield. while the 23rd and 24th Marines fought a tough battle against the tanks of the Japanese 47th Independent Mixed Brigade. In two days, the 4th Division took some 2,200 casualties. General Holland Smith ordered the Army 27th Infantry Division ashore to reinforce the Marine lines.

Offshore, Admiral Spruance received word that the Japanese Combined Fleet had sailed. Admiral Jisaburo Ozawa's carriers were closing on the Marianas. Task Force 58, under the command of Admiral Marc Mitscher, headed out to meet the threat. The resulting engagement was the Battle of the Philippine Sea, the greatest carrier action in history. In the ensuing aerial battle, U.S. pilots downed some 476 Japanese planes in what became known as the "Great Marianas Turkey Shoot." This decimation of their air forces was an event from which the Japanese would never recover.

Above: Marine Corps combat artist Richard Gibney captures a patrol moving cautiously through Saipan's jungle. The dense foliage gave the Japanese plenty of cover from which to ambush Marine patrols.

Above: A Marine peers carefully through a hole in the wall. In securing the town of Garapan, the Marines faced their first street fighting since the battles in Veracruz in Mexico during 1914.

On Saipan, the Marines looked nervously at the open ocean and continued to push inland. In the early morning hours of June 17, the Japanese commander launched a major attack on 2nd Marine Division positions on the northern edge of the beachhead. Realizing that the Marines could not be crushed in a single stroke, the Japanese planned a coordinated attack utilizing the 9th Tank Regiment, the 136th Infantry Regiment, and the 1st Yokosuka Special Landing Force. The executive officer of the 1st Battalion, 6th Marines called that night a "madhouse of noise, tracers, and flashing lights." The Marines hit the oncoming Japanese with everything they had. Rocket and grenade launchers, antitank guns, tanks, and 2.95 in. (75 mm) guns essentially obliterated the enemy tanks. Machine guns, mortars, and rifle fire cut through the Japanese troops. Marine casualties were once again numerous, but the Japanese had been beaten back. At 07:30 hours, battle plans called for the 2nd Marine Division to push inland. Encountering only light resistance, the 2nd Marines advanced halfway to Garapan, the largest town on Saipan. The 6th Marines fought their way to the foothills of Mount Tipo Pale, which stood at a height of 1,133 ft. (345 m). By evening, the Marines had managed to double the area they previously held.

To the south, the 4th Marine Division and the Army's 27th Division surged forward from the beachhead. The Army 165th Infantry moved toward Aslito Airfield. The 24th and 25th Marines pushed across the island toward Magicienne Bay, encountering increasingly heavy resistance. Advancing across open ground, the Leathernecks were vulnerable. Japanese defenders, dug into the face of a cliff, raked the Marines with gunfire, causing heavy casualties. Twice, the Marines fell back to gain a better defensive position. The attack progressed no further that day, but support from the 2nd 4.13 in. (105 mm) Howitzer Battalion ensured additional support when the assault was renewed.

On June 18, the 4th Marine Division successfully bisected the island, reaching Magicienne Bay on the east coast of Saipan. By 10:00 hours, the Army had secured Aslito

Airfield. Most of southern Saipan was now in American hands. The Japanese established a new line of defense running south of Garapan, along the cliffs of Mount Tapotchau to Magicienne Bay, but any glimmer of Japanese hopes for a victory were fading.

The second phase of the invasion of Saipan began when the three divisions swung northward toward the newly formed enemy defense line. The terrain faced by the Americans was a nightmare: Saipan was riddled with cliffs, caves, and steep ravines. The Japanese were dug in and prepared to fight to the death. On the morning of June 23, the offensive began. The 27th Infantry Division was in the center, flanked by the Marines. The 6th Marines, positioned on the far left, took Mount Tipo Pale. Towering Mount Tapotchau was secured by the 8th Marines. In the center, the advanced of the 27th Infantry Division had become bogged down, thus exposing the flanks of the Marines. Holland Smith was not pleased, and by evening, Major-General Ralph C. Smith had been relieved of command of the 27th. "The Battle of the Smiths" would soon become a newspaper sensation and would result in a long and bitter dispute between the Marines and the Army.

Meanwhile, the Americans moved inexorably northward, eliminating the fortified Japanese positions. By June 30, Japanese defenders no longer held central Saipan. On July 2, the final offensive began. The 2nd Marines faced a particularly brutal fight in the town of Garapan, where Japanese troops were holed up in the rubble, but despite this setback, methodically the enemy strongpoints across the island were wiped out. On the evening of July 5, the commander of the Japanese forces committed suicide. His final orders were carried out during the following morning, when some 4,000 screaming, frenzied Japanese soldiers rushed at the Marines in the largest *banzai* attack of the war.

Below: Two Marines take shelter on a landing beach in this painting by Marine Corps combat artist Richard Gibney. Marines took many of their casualties on the beaches of the Pacific campaign.

"Jap soldiers were … firing their weapons at us and screaming 'Banzai' as they charged toward us … Our weapons opened up and machine guns fired continually. No longer do they fire in bursts of three or five. Belt after belt of ammunition goes through that gun, the gunner swinging the barrel right and left. Even though the Jap bodies build up in front of us, they still charged at us, running over their fallen comrades' bodies. The mortar tubes became so hot from the rapid fire, as did the machine gun barrels, that they could no longer be used … Although each [attack] had taken its toll, still they came in droves … Bullets whizzed around us, screams are deafening,

the area reeks with death, and the smell of Japs and gunpowder permeate the air. Full of fear and hate, with the desire to kill … [Our enemy seems to us now to be] a savage animal, a beast, a devil, not a human at all, and the only thought is to kill, kill, kill."

The 1st and 2nd Battalions of the 105th Infantry were crushed under the onslaught. The 3rd Battalion, 10th Marines were hit next. Firing its 4.13 in. (105 mm) howitzers at point-blank range, the battalion slowed the Japanese attack. The 106th Infantry counterattacked and regained the ground that had been lost. Casualties among the American forces were high: 451 killed, another 592 wounded. On the afternoon of July 9, Saipan was declared secured. The bloody three-and-a-half week campaign had resulted in 3,426 American dead and another 13,099 wounded. Holland Smith stated that the battle for Saipan was one that had never been fought before, a brutal campaign where men clubbed, burned, shot, and bayoneted each other to death. The cost had been high, but by late November, the first B-29s left the airfields of Saipan to bombard Tokyo.

Attention was turned toward Tinian. Only a few miles to the southwest, this island was smaller and flatter than Saipan, and already had three airfields. Navy Seabees planned to expand these and build three more to accommodate the heavy B-29s. Tinian was also less heavily defended than Saipan. Just 9,000 Japanese troops were garrisoned on the island. However, invasion planners faced other challenges. Tinian was protected by steep coral escarpments. The only obvious beach for the Marines to land upon was heavily fortified and invasion routes had been mined. Two very narrow points on Tinian's northwest coast intrigued General Holland Smith. Both beaches were within artillery range from Saipan, and their close proximity would promote ease of resupply. However, Admiral Turner, the Navy's amphibious expert, expressed serious doubts about utilizing these beaches. In a heated exchange, he refused to land the Marines. Smith's response was terse: "Oh yes you

Right: Marines drop over the side of an amphibian tractor (amtrac) and into the waters off the coast of Tinian. The island's coral outcroppings prohibited amtracs from moving onto the beach. Amtracs had machine guns mounted for use against enemy ground and air targets.

will. You'll land me any goddamned place I tell you to." After a series of scouting missions by Captain Jones' Recon Marines, the decision was made to put the Marines ashore.

The 4th Marine Division, now under the command of General Clifton B. Cates, was to lead the assault from the northwest. Tanks and artillery units were stripped from the 2nd Marine Division and diverted to Cates' forces. Although still understrength, these would thus have greater firepower when they hit the beaches of Tinian. Meanwhile, the 2nd Marine Division would create a ruse on the wide beach near Tinian Town. It was hoped the feint would occupy the Japanese defenses and ensure surprise as the real landing force came ashore. Since June 20, Tinian had been pounded by artillery fire. As D-Day drew nearer that pounding steadily increased. On July 23, the day before the Marines hit Tinian, 13 artillery battalions opened fire. Some 25,000 high-explosive shells rained down on the Japanese defenders. The *Tennessee* and the *California* fired another 1,200 5 in. (127 mm) and 14 in. (355 mm) shells. Army Air Force P-47s joined carrier-based aircraft in pummeling targets on the island. A squadron of B-25s landed on Saipan and soon joined the fray. For the first time, a new weapon from the American arsenal was utilized: napalm. Essentially a "fire bomb," napalm was a concoction of diesel oil, gasoline, and a salt from the naptha used in the manufacture of soap. On Tinian, 147 "fire bombs" were dropped and were very effective in clearing the thick sugarcane fields, leaving only charred Japanese bodies behind.

At 06:00 hours, on July 24, the 2nd Marine Division began the deception. Landing craft were lowered. Marines climbed up and down the cargo nets, simulating the debarkation of the landing teams. As the empty boats moved ashore under the cover of naval gunfire, the Japanese fired artillery and mortars at them. Admiral Hill withdrew the boats to reform, then began a second run toward the beach. Once again, the boats took fire from Japanese shore batteries. At 10:00 hours, the transports began recovering landing craft. The ruse was convincing: the Japanese radioed Tokyo they had repulsed an American invasion force.

Above: Marines wade ashore at Tinian. Landing on two narrow points on the island's northwest coast, 16,000 Marines were safely ashore by the evening of July 24.

On the beaches to the northwest, the real landing went very well. By mid-morning, both the 1st and 2nd Battalions, 24th Marines were ashore on the smaller beach, White Beach 1. The 25th Marines landed on the larger beach. It was more heavily defended, but by evening 16,000 Marines established a beachhead on Tinian. General Cates, commanding the 4th Marine Division, was sure of an imminent Japanese attack. He ordered the 23rd Marines ashore and they strung barbed wire around the perimeter and dug in.

The Japanese hit the Marine lines at 02:00 hours. With a barrage of mortar fire, some 600 Japanese naval troops attacked the 24th Marines on the left flank of the beachhead. The Marine perimeter exploded with machine-gun and rifle fire. In three hours of brutal combat, the Leathernecks beat back the Japanese assault. Another Japanese force, including a few tanks, hit the boundary between the 24th and 25th Marines. The initial assault was repelled, but 200 Japanese soldiers broke through the line in a second attack. As they approached the artillery positions of the 14th Marines, enfilading fire from .50 caliber (12.7 mm) machine guns tore through the Japanese. They were slaughtered. Naval star shells burst over the action and turned night to day. On the right side of the beachhead, a column of Japanese tanks was spotted. The enemy ran straight into a maelstrom of Marine Corps firepower: bazookas, 2.95 in. (75 mm) half-tracks, and 1.46 in. (37 mm) guns ripped into the Japanese tanks. Five were quickly destroyed, but enemy soldiers continued their advance, charging the lines of the 23rd and 25th Marines. By dawn, 267 Japanese bodies lay scattered among the Marine foxholes. Enemy dead resulting from that night's counterattack numbered close to 2,000. General Cates later stated that the night's action "broke the Jap's back in the battle for Tinian."

The 2nd Marine Division landed the following morning and the push across the island resumed. By evening, the 8th and 24th Marines occupied Ushi Airfield. Within a few days, it was in use; P-47s were flying missions from the field. The toughest resistance was met by the 25th Marines on the slopes of Mount Mapa. The commanding officer, Colonel Batchelder, felt that a frontal assault of the Japanese defenses would cost too many Marine lives. So, in a double envelopment, he positioned the 1st Battalion to the right, while the 2nd Battalion was to position itself in front to deliver suppressive fire. The 1st Battalion was ordered to attack the right front, then encircle Mount Mapa and join forces with the 3rd Battalion. By 17:15 hours, the position had been secured.

By July 26, the two divisions were positioned across the width of Tinian and prepared to sweep southward. Supported by field artillery, aircraft, and the thunder of naval guns, the Marines moved through the cane fields, obliterating Japanese positions. The surviving Japanese made a final stand on the cliffs along Tinian's southern coast. On August 1, American patrols reached the southern beaches. General Harry Schmidt, now commanding the V Amphibious Corps, declared the island secure. Holland Smith called the invasion of Tinian the "perfect amphibious operation of the Pacific War."

The Recapture of Guam

The battle to recapture Guam was concurrent with the invasion of Tinian. While the Marines swept swiftly across Tinian, General Roy Geiger's III Amphibious Corps faced bitter fighting on Guam. Captured by the Japanese early in the war, Guam is the largest island in the northern Marianas, roughly 225 square miles (580 sq km). Its terrain is much

Opposite: Only eight minutes after the Marines hit the beaches of Guam on July 21, 1944, captains Paul S. O'Neal and Milton F. Thompson carry the Stars and Stripes ashore.

The Japanese hit the Marine lines at 02:00 hours. With a barrage of mortar fire, some 600 Japanese naval troops attacked the 24th Marines on the left flank of the beachhead. The Marine perimeter exploded with machine-gun and rifle fire. In three hours of brutal combat, the Leathernecks beat back the Japanese assault.

Right: The first assault
waves of Marine amtracs
move towards Peleliu, each
wave timed to hit the
beach at regular intervals.
This photograph was
taken from a U.S. carrier
fighter providing air cover
for the invasion fleet.

Right: The first assault
waves of Marine amtracs
move towards Peleliu, each
wave timed to hit the
beach at regular intervals.
This photograph was
taken from a U.S. carrier
fighter providing air cover
for the invasion fleet.

more rugged than both Tinian and Saipan; more mountainous, with more thick jungle but no cane fields. It was also more heavily defended. Lieutenant-General Takeshi Takashina commanded the Japanese garrison of some 13,000 Army troops, and another 5,500 men of the Imperial Navy were also based on the island of Guam. The most obvious landing beach at Tumon Bay had been heavily fortified by the Japanese.

Geiger's landing force consisted of the 3rd Marine Division, veterans of Bougainville, and the 1st Provisional Marine Brigade under the command of Major-General Lemuel Shepherd. The Brigade was a new outfit, but was comprised of the battle-tested 4th and 22nd Marines. Despite enemy expectations that the Marines would come ashore at Tumon Bay, Geiger decided to split his landing force and hit Guam on separate beaches, north and south of Apra Harbor. To the north, the three regiments of the 3rd Marine Division were to storm ashore. The two regiments of the 1st Provisional Marine Brigade were to land to the south. Both forces would independently fight their way inland, then join together.

By late June, Admiral Marc Mitscher's carrier planes began periodic strikes against Guam. On July 6, the pre-invasion bombardment began, intensifying as D-Day approached. For a full 13 days, Guam was pummeled by massive aerial and naval strikes. Underwater demolition teams cleared the approaches to the landing beaches and then paused long enough to leave a sign facing seaward, "Welcome Marines!"

Between 07:15 and 08:15 hours on the morning of July 21, 14 miles (22.5 km) of coastline was swept by carrier planes; 85 fighters, 62 bombers, and 53 torpedo planes pounded the beach. Naval gunfire accompanied the attack. Marine LVTs moved toward the shore. As they approached the beach, the Japanese defenses sprang to life. The Marines took heavy casualties but, by 08:33 hours, they were ashore on all beaches.

*Underwater
demolition teams
cleared the
approaches to the
landing beaches
and then paused
long enough to
leave a sign facing
seaward, "Welcome
Marines!"*

On the far left, the 3rd Marines literally hit a wall. Chonito Cliffs, pockmarked with caves, rose 300 ft. (90 m) above the beach. The Marines could go neither up it nor around it until flamethrowers and tanks cleared out the Japanese defenders. That accomplished, they faced a ridgeline, 400 ft. (122 m) high, covered in thick jungle and bristling with mortars and machine-gun emplacements. Company A assaulted the ridge and reached the crest but could not hold it. In the center of the northern beachhead, the 21st Marines were to push the assault inland and secure a line of cliffs. Aerial reconnaissance had identified two defiles leading to the top of the high ground. The 2nd Battalion moved up the passage on the left, while the 3rd Battalion advanced on the right. The Marines suffered casualties from machine guns and mortars before the defenders were eliminated. By midmorning, however, the Marines had reached the high ground and began the battle for a series of fortified Japanese ridges. Some would remember it as the battle for Banzai Ridge.

To the south, the 1st Provisional Marine Brigade encountered less troublesome terrain, but equally tenacious Japanese defenders. Two 2.95 in. (75 mm) guns fired into the Marines, causing heavy casualties before being silenced. The 22nd Marines advanced through concentrated fire into the village of Agat and toward the high ground 1,000 yards (1,094 m) inland. By evening, the Brigade had established a beachhead some 4,500 yards (4,921 m) long and 2,000 yards (2,187 m) deep. Major-General Shepherd's greatest concern at this point was a critical shortage of fuel and ammunition.

That night, just before midnight, a hail of mortar shells hit the Marine positions. Japanese soldiers emerged from the darkness as star shells illuminated the front lines in the first major action of the night. There would be more attacks as the Japanese launched a three-pronged assault against the 1st Brigade. But the Japanese were beaten back: over 600 were killed.

For the next several days, the Marines continue to advance across Guam, meeting stiff Japanese resistance but systematically annihilating the enemy positions. One particularly brutal struggle took place in an area called Fonte Plateau. Here, the advance stalled. The number of dead and wounded rose to more than 2,000, but the Japanese defenses showed no signs of weakening. On the night of July 24, the 2nd Battalion, 9th Marines, under the command of Lieutenant-Colonel Robert Cushman, was ordered to the area to reinforce the 3rd Marines. The following morning. the battalion passed through 3nd Marine lines and pushed toward the summit, driving a wedge into the Japanese defenses.

Below: A Marine comes to the aid of his buddy under withering enemy fire on Peleliu. However, he himself would come under attack and would become one of a total of 1,124 Leathernecks to die in the month-long campaign for the island.

Takashina ordered a desperate counterattack. That night, 5,000 Japanese troops hit the Marine lines in wave after wave. Lieutenant-Colonel Cushman's embattled battalion bore the brunt of the assault, repelling seven separate attacks during the night. The Marine lines held, but only by the slimmest of margins. Casualties mounted and ammunition ran alarmingly short. Before dawn, the enemy delivered one final, frantic blow: surging out of the night in seemingly endless numbers, the Japanese again hit the 2nd Battalion, 9th Marines. The air filled with the sounds of weapons fire and the screams of men caught up in hand-to-hand combat. At first light, a platoon of Sherman tanks moved to the front and helped crush the last Japanese onslaught. Half of Cushman's men had been killed or wounded; some 600 Japanese soldiers lay dead in and around the 9th Marine positions.

Below: These Marines advance on enemy positions along Bloody Nose Ridge, a series of coral crags and sheer cliffs pockmarked by caves which had been fortified by the Japanese before their arrival.

Takashina's counterattack resulted in the loss of 3,200 men, but he gained little. In the morning, the Marines renewed their advance across Guam. At 07:00 hours, the 4th and 22nd Marines attacked Orote Peninsula. On July 28, the 22nd Marines recaptured the charred ruins of the Marine Barracks. The next day, the American flag was raised over Guam, the first time since it fell to the Japanese in 1941. Within a few days, aircraft from Marine Aircraft Group 21 were flying out of Orote Field. On August 10, Major-General Geiger declared the island secured. Jungle was cleared for two airfields to support the B-29s. American airpower was within striking distance of the Japanese homeland.

In a short seven months, American forces had crossed 2,500 miles (4,025 km) of the Pacific, capturing Japanese territories in the Gilberts, the Marshalls, and the Marianas. The

enemy had exacted a heavy toll. Some 6,902 Marines had lost their lives; over 19,000 had been wounded. And despite this, the bloodiest days of the Pacific campaign still loomed ahead: the islands of Peleliu, Iwo Jima, and Okinawa lay to the east.

The decision to invade Peleliu was largely based on support for MacArthur's plan to liberate the Philippines. MacArthur was obsessed with retaking the islands from which he had fled, convincing President Roosevelt that unless he returned to the Philippines, "all Asia would lose faith in American honor." Admiral Nimitz had initially considered an invasion of Peleliu months before, since the island would provide a forward base from which to hit the Japanese strongholds of Yap, Truk, and Ulithi. By March 1944, securing Peleliu had another purpose: to neutralize the enemy bases at Yap and Babelthuap, thus securing the approaches to Mindanao. The right flank of MacArthur's Army would then be protected and a U.S. return to the Philippines could become a reality. "Operation Stalemate," the amphibious assault against Peleliu, was put into motion. The Marines were to hit the beach on September 15, 1944.

Only 6 miles (9.6 km) long, and 2 miles (3.2 km) wide, Peleliu lies at the westernmost edge of the Caroline Islands, about 500 miles (805 km) from both the Philippines and New Guinea. A volcanic island of limestone and coral, Peleliu's terrain is a hellish nightmare of cliffs, natural caves, and steep hills. The Umurbrogol Ridge, a series of sharp coral highlands and rugged mountain peaks, towering 550 ft. (167.5 m) in height, dominates the northern arm of the island. Stinking mangrove swamps and thick jungle cover the lowlands. Heat and overwhelming humidity make the climate unbearable. Colonel Kunio Nakagawa commanded the Japanese garrison of some 10,000 troops on Peleliu. With almost a year's warning that the island might come under attack, Nakagawa had turned Peleliu into a fortress. He had also formed a new strategy: no longer would the Japanese squander men on

MacArthur was obsessed with retaking the islands from which he had fled, convincing President Roosevelt that unless he returned to the Philippines, "all Asia would lose faith in American honor."

Right: This drawing by
Walter Anthony Jones
depicts a body recovery
team on Peleliu. The body
recovery teams were kept
busy during the struggle
for the island, which was
transformed from an
invasion, to a long, bloody
war of attrition.

*Admiral Halsey
recommended a
last-minute
cancellation of the
operation. He
judged the assault
on Peleliu
unnecessary and
expected that it
would exact a high
price: "I feared
another Tarawa—
and I was right,"
he later said.*

desperate *banzai* attacks, or in attempting to obliterate American forces as they came ashore. Instead, using lessons they had learned on Saipan, the Japanese dug in. The battle for Peleliu was to become a long, bloody war of attrition.

Nakagawa brought engineers from Japan to turn the natural caves into military fortresses. Some of them were fitted with rolling steel doors. Other were blasted out and turned into deadly honeycombs hiding field artillery and heavy machine guns. Beaches were strung with barbed wire and heavily mined, sometimes as much as 100 yards (109 m) inland. Antitank obstacles were built, and trenches dug, those trenches being covered by fields of fire from reinforced pillboxes and gun casements. Artillery was zeroed-in on those positions, waiting to cut into the Marines as they came ashore. The Americans would have to annihilate these positions one by one, in a long, bloody struggle.

The 1st Marine Division, its battle-hardened veterans of Guadalcanal, was to hit Peleliu's western beaches. The division's commanding officer, Major-General William H. Rupertus, was absent during much of the planning, but had great faith in the fighting ability of his men. He predicted a tough battle, but expected his Marines to take Peleliu within a few days. Major-General Roy Geiger and Brigadier-General O.P. Smith, assistant division commander, were much less optimistic. Admiral Halsey recommended a last-minute cancellation of the operation. He judged the assault on Peleliu unnecessary and expected that it would exact a high price: "I feared another Tarawa—and I was right," he later said. Originally, only two days of pre-invasion bombardment of Peleliu was planned. Geiger was bluntly told not to expect the support that his troops had gotten at Guam; the Navy had neither the time nor the ammunition. Geiger argued that insufficient naval bombardment would result in far greater Marine casualties. Admiral Wilkenson acquiesced and added another day to the scheduled barrage. However, this extra time did not mean a larger number of shells were to be fired. Instead, the same amount of ammunition would be expended, but it was to be used over a longer period of time.

On September 12, 1944, the bombardment of Peleliu began. It would later be called the "least adequate" bombardment of the Pacific War. Rear Admiral Jesse B. Oldendorf, commander of the Naval Gunfire Support Group "blasted away at suspected positions and hoped for the best." There was no Japanese response. Believing that all targets had been destroyed, Oldendorf ordered the cessation of the bombardment a day early. To the naked eye, Peleliu had been turned into a wasteland, but the Japanese defenses remained unscathed. All three regiments of the 1st Marine Division were to land abreast on Peleliu's southwestern coast. Only one battalion was held in division reserve. The 1st Marines, under the capable command of Colonel Lewis B. "Chesty" Puller, were ordered to the left, to seize the high ground of the Umurbrogol Ridge. Colonel Harold D. "Bucky" Harris was to land his 5th Marines in the center and drive straight across the airfield. The 7th Marines, under the command of Colonel Herman Hannekan, were to come ashore on the right flank in order to then sweep the southern end of the island.

At 08:00 hours, the first of the LVTs crossed the line of departure. Chesty Puller was in the first wave heading toward White Beach Two. "We'll catch hell is my guess," said Puller. As the LVTs approached the beach, the Japanese defenses opened up with a searing curtain of mortars, machine guns, and artillery fire. The coral promontories on each flank hid 1.85 in. (47 mm) guns, which cut into the Marines. LVTs were transformed into burning hulks that littered the landing beaches: 26 had taken direct hits, another 60 were damaged or destroyed. Private First Class Eugene B. Sledge described the landing:

"Huge geysers of water rose around the amtracs ahead of us as they approached the reef. The beach was now marked along its length by a continuous sheet of flame backed by a thick wall of smoke. It seemed as though a huge volcano had erupted from the sea … we were being drawn into the vortex of the flaming abyss."

Left: The island of Iwo Jima, on whose black sands the blood of many a Marine ran red. Iwo was to be used as an fighter base to provide escorts for the bombers which would be engaged in attacking the Japanese mainland.

"I saw a ghastly mixture of bandages, bloody, and mutilated skin; Marines gritting their teeth resigned to their wounds; men groaning and writhing in their agonies."

"Huge geysers of water rose around the amtracs ahead of us as they approached the reef. The beach was now marked along its length by a continuous sheet of flame backed by a thick wall of smoke. It seemed as though a huge volcano had erupted from the sea, and rather than heading for an island, we were being drawn into the vortex of the flaming abyss. … Shells crashed all around. Fragments tore and whirred, slapping on the sand and splashing into the water a few yards behind us.… Machine gun and rifle fire got thicker, snapping viciously overhead in increasing volume. … Up and down the beach and out on the reef, a number of amtracs and DUKWs were burning. Japanese machine-gun bursts made long splashes on the water as though flaying it with some giant whip. The geysers belched up relentlessly where the mortars and artillery shells hit. I caught a fleeting glimpse of a group of Marines leaving a smoking amtrac on the reef. Some fell as fragments splashed among them."

The 3rd Battalion, 1st Marines faced the toughest resistance. The Japanese were dug into a coral outcropping on the left flank, an area called The Point. Heavy enfilading fire from a 1.85 in. (47 mm) gun and six 0.78 in. (20 mm) guns ripped through the Marines. Company K, under the command of Captain George P. Hunt, was hardest hit. Within an hour, both his 2nd and 3rd Platoons had been decimated.

"I saw a ghastly mixture of bandages, bloody, and mutilated skin; Marines gritting their teeth resigned to their wounds; men groaning and writhing in their agonies; men outstretched or twisted or grotesquely transfixed in the attitudes of death; men with their entrails exposed or whole chunks of body ripped out of them. …"

The Japanese positions had to be obliterated. In a classic example of a small unit attacking a fortified position, Hunt committed his reserve platoon and assaulted The Point from the east. In the face of concentrated enemy fire, the remnants of the 3rd Platoon and

Right: The black, volcanic sands of Iwo Jima which were found to make particularly durable concrete by the Japanese defenders. Mount Suribachi can be seen in the background. Japanese spotters on the mount could observe any movement by the Marines and call down artillery fire on them.

the reserve 1st Platoon moved toward the crest of the outcropping. The 1.85 in. (47 mm) was heard firing below. The 1st Platoon leader eased himself down the cliff and lobbed a smoke grenade into the Japanese position. Another Marine fired a rifle grenade into the gun port and ignited the ammunition. Japanese soldiers burst from the casement in flames, the ammunition on their cartridge belts exploding, and were cut down by the Marines. By 10:15 hours, Company K had silenced the enfilading fire from The Point, but Marine casualties were such that Hunt found only 32 survivors for a perimeter defense on the crest.

To the south, the rest of Puller's 1st Marines faced vicious circumstances. The general confusion of landing was exacerbated by a rain of heavy fire. Mortars and artillery shells slammed into the shallow beachhead. Rifle and machine-gun fire from Japanese positions on a coral ridge swept the area. For several hours, the Marines determinedly assaulted the ridgeline where the Japanese were dug in. By afternoon, Company A had gained a foothold on the southern slopes, but the Marine advance was halted. On the far right flank, Hannekan's 7th Marines encountered underwater obstacles and mines, forcing the LVTs to approach the beach in a single column. Fierce fire from a coral promontory added to the destruction. Many Marines were forced to wade ashore. Once on the beach, the regiment faced tangles of barbed wire, dense minefields, trenches and reinforced pillboxes. Hannekan reported: "We've got our hands full with problems. ... we're pretty much pinned down ... and we need some help from reinforcements."

Colonel Bucky Harris's 5th Marines also came ashore with difficulty. Three rows of mines stretched across the landing beach, their metal tips protruding from the sand. They also came under heavy fire, though fortunately they were not subjected to the heavy enfilading fire that plagued the flanks of the invasion force. Advancing inland through a coconut grove, they encountered only scattered Japanese resistance. By 09:00 hours, they had reached the edge of Peleliu's airfield and set up a defensive perimeter. Later that afternoon, Nakagawa launched a counterattack, sending a column of tanks across the airfield to hit the 5th Marine lines. Harris responded with heavy machine guns, 1.46 in. (37 mm) antitank guns, and fire from three Sherman tanks initially and then four more. The thin-skinned Japanese tanks were destroyed, the accompanying infantry obliterated.

Once on the beach, the regiment faced tangles of barbed wire, dense minefields, trenches and reinforced pillboxes. Hannekan reported: "We've got our hands full with problems ... we're pretty much pinned down ... and we need some help from reinforcements."

By the evening of September 15, the Marines had established an irregular beach head, 2 miles (3.2 km) long, on Peleliu. It ranged in depth from several hundred yards to the south, to a few feet along The Point. D-Day objectives had not been met and casualties were much higher than anticipated; Marine dead numbered 210, another 901 had been wounded. General Rupertus, however, remained optimistic. On September 16, the Marines on Peleliu had to fight thirst and the oppressive heat almost as much as they fought the Japanese defenders. Temperatures soared to 105 °F (45 °C) and water was in terribly short supply. Tongues swelled, making it difficult to talk or to swallow. Nonetheless, the Marine advance continued. The 7th Marines swept southward, battling Japanese troops holed up in pillboxes and spiderholes. The front lines of Harris's 5th Marines were heavily shelled, but at 08:00 hours the 1st Battalion moved onto the open runways of Peleliu's airfield. Despite heavy casualties, the Marines reached the main hanger on the northeast side of the field in an hour. Later, the battalion commander said that the Marines' advance across that fireswept airfield was "a sight to be forever remembered." Private First Class Sledge remembered it as the worst combat experienced of the war.

Below: Progress off the beach at Iwo Jima was slow, and Japanese snipers were active, picking off Marines at leisure. The beach gave the Marines no cover, but it took time to clear the Japanese defenses to allow the Marines to move inland.

"We moved rapidly in the open, amid craters and coral rubble, through ever-increasing enemy fire. I saw men to my right and to my left bent as low as possible. The shells screeched and whistled, exploding all around us. ... The sun bore down unmercifully, and the heat was exhausting. Smoke and dust from the barrage limited my vision. The ground seemed to sway back and forth under the concussions. I felt as though I were floating along in the vortex of some unreal thunderstorm. Japanese bullets snapped and cracked and tracers went by me on both sides at waist height. This deadly small-arms fire seemed almost insignificant amid the erupting shells. Explosions and the hum and the growl of shell fragments

filled the air. Chunks of blasted coral stung my face and hands while steel fragments spattered down on the hard rock like hail on a city street."

To the north, Puller's 1st Marines battered headlong into the Umurbrogol Ridge. Calling it "Bloody Nose," they clawed forward, taking horrific casualties. On September 19, Captain Everett Pope led 90 men forward to take Hill 100. Upon reaching the crest, the Marines discovered that it was not a hill at all, but just another ridge, and that the Japanese held the high ground all around their position. Pope had only a few dozen survivors left. They set up a flimsy defensive perimeter and waited for the Japanese to attack. By dawn, the Marines had run out of ammunition and resorted to using bayonets, chunks of coral, and fists to fight off the enemy. Pope led nine Marines to safety. The 1st and 2nd Battalions flung themselves at the hill, with severe losses. Within a few days, the regiment would lose 1,749 men, the highest regimental losses in the history of the Corps. Rupertus was still convinced the 1st Marines were a viable fighting force and could take the Umurbrogol Ridge. However, on September 21, Major-General Geiger ordered the 1st Marines be replaced by the Army's 321st Infantry of the 81st Infantry Division. The second phase in the battle for Peleliu had begun.

While the 7th Marines continued the attack on the Umurbrogol's central ridges, the 321st Infantry moved up the western coast to the north of the broken highlands. There, they found a trail to the east and attacked along a broad front, while the 5th Marines, using flamethrowers and fighting cave-to-cave, cleared the northern end of Peleliu. On September 28, the 3rd Battalion, 5th Marines hit nearby Ngesebus Island in a shore-to-shore landing. Colonel "Bucky" Harris had developed a savage fire support plan: coordinating fire from naval guns, the Army's 4.13 in. (105 mm) guns, howitzer fire, and close air support from the newly arrived Corsairs of VMF-114, he made sure the Japanese positions on Ngesebus were annihilated. The arrival of the Marine Corsairs brought a huge morale boost to the troops on Peleliu. Under the command of Major Robert "Cowboy" Stout, the Marine aviators brought rockets and napalm into the battle. Napalm proved more useful on Peleliu than on Tinian, burning off vegetation hiding cave entrances and spiderholes and roasting the Japanese lurking inside.

The Japanese still ruled the Umurbrogol Ridge and by the beginning of October, the 7th Marines were no longer a viable fighting force. What was left of the regiment was replaced by the 5th Marines. By October 15, the remnants of the 1st Marine Division, "The Old Breed," were replaced by the 81st Infantry Division. It would take the Army another six weeks of hard fighting to obliterate the Japanese defenders holed up in the craggy highlands. Rupertus's promised battle of a few short days had turned into a month-long nightmare that had cost the Marines 6,265 casualties, of whom 1,124 were dead.

Peleliu Overshadowed

Sadly, the fight for Peleliu was largely ignored by the media, overshadowed by MacArthur's return to the Philippines and by the Allied push against Germany's Seigfried Line. Nor did the airfields on Peleliu provide support for MacArthur's return to the Philippines, and the island was never used as an advanced base. Instead, a regiment of the 81st Infantry division took Ulithi Atoll with no casualties, and it was within its huge anchorage that the Fifth Fleet would assemble for the invasions of Iwo Jima and Okinawa.

Pope had only a few dozen survivors left. They set up a flimsy defensive perimeter and waited for the Japanese to attack. By dawn, the Marines had run out of ammunition and resorted to using bayonets, chunks of coral, and fists to fight off the enemy.

Although the invasion of Peleliu had been fought in support of MacArthur's return to the Philippines, few Marines were actually with the Army forces that landed on Leyte. Marine Major-General Ralph Mitchell offered use of the 1st Marine Aircraft Wing to the Army, but initially his offer was refused: it had been decided that the recapture of the Philippines was to be an all-Army operation. Yet, when four Army divisions came ashore, 1,500 men of V Amphibious Corps Artillery landed north of Dulag and supported the Army's advance. The heavy artillery for XXIV Corps had been assigned to the Marine assault of the Marianas and was, as a result, not available for the Leyte campaign. Instead, Marine artillery was ordered to be shipped out of Pearl Harbor in order to support the Army's landing in the Philippines. By December 13, Marine artillery had

Above: A Marine throws a grenade at a Japanese position from his rock-infested ridge. This Marine is armed with the M1 carbine, while the Marine closest to the camera has a Browning Automatic Rifle. The stark outline of bare trees blasted during the fighting can be seen in the photograph's background.

earned an Army commendation for "splendid performance" in fire support missions.

It was, however, Marine aviation that would play a major role in the campaign. In late November, MacArthur arranged for the transfer of Marine Fighter Squadron VMF(N)-541 to Leyte. The first planes to arrive at the airfield in Talcoban were 12 Grumman F6F Hellcats, followed a few hours later by 66 F4U Corsairs of Marine Air Group -12. Air operations began immediately. On December 7, the Japanese attempted to reinforce their garrison near Ormoc while the 77th Infantry Division was executing an amphibious landing just a few miles to the south. By 06:10 hours, the Hellcats had bagged four enemy escort planes. Later in the afternoon, Marine Corsairs set out to find Japanese destroyers and cargo ships. It was to be a productive day for the Marine aviators. Marine Corps records for that day show one enemy transport and four cargo ships sunk, and two destroyers seriously damaged. A few days later, the Japanese made yet another attempt to reinforce Leyte. Again, aircraft from MAG-12 managed to send several enemy planes into the sea, and they also succeeded in sinking both transports and destroyers.

In February, General MacArthur ordered the 1st Cavalry Division into Manila in order to free American prisoners there and also to seize the Malacanan Palace. For the first time in history, the Marine aviators flew close air support for the Army troops. SBD Dauntless bombers provided a dawn-to-dusk screen, attacking enemy positions when necessary as well as protecting the flanks of the division. The Army was generous in its praise, stating that "Much of the success of the entire movement is credited to the superb air cover, flank protection, and reconnaissance provided by Marine Air Groups -24 and -32."

Such praise convinced the 6th Infantry Division to utilize Marine air strength in its push against the heavily defended Shimbu Line, northeast of Manila. Additionally, the SBDs pounded Japanese strongholds in and around Manila Bay and flew close air support for Filipino guerrillas. In March, Marine Air Groups -12, -14, and -32 were ordered to fly air support for the 41st Infantry Division's landing on the Zamboanga Peninsula on the island of Mindanao. Army infantry had come to rely upon the Marine aviators: to the soldiers on the ground, their support was invaluable. Casualties among Marine aviators during the Philippine campaign numbered 277, including 100 killed in action, and their accomplishments brought praise from every quarter. Army Major-General Jens A. Doe claimed there were no words to describe the value of the air support offered by the Marine flyers, but that "From all quarters, commanders down to the men with the bayonets, I have heard nothing but high tribute." The Marine aviators had proven their use—and that they could inflict devastating damage upon the enemy. As the American war machine pushed closer to the Japanese homeland, Marine aviators would play an ever-increasing role.

Attention was turned to a small, sulfuric island some 670 miles (1,080 km) south of Tokyo. Roughly 8 square miles (21 sq km) in size, Iwo Jima was essentially unknown to the world. Unlike Peleliu, where Marines wondered bitterly why the island had been assaulted, the reasons for taking Iwo Jima were clear. Throughout the war in the Pacific, the Marines' role had been in support of the strategic bombing campaign of the Japanese homeland, seizing islands to use as advanced airbases and putting the B-29 Superfortresses within bombing range of Japan. The results of that bombing campaign, however, had been disappointing. As the B-29s made the long trip between Saipan and Tokyo, they came within range of Japanese radar installations on Iwo Jima. The enemy therefore had advanced warning of every B-29 strike. Additionally, Japanese fighters based on Iwo Jima harassed the big bombers continuously. The Joint Chiefs of Staff decided the island had to be taken. The Japanese radar installation would then be destroyed and construction of an airbase would let U.S. fighters escort the B-29s. The base would also provide any bombers damaged by Japanese fighters or antiaircraft fire with an emergency landing field. In a plan codenamed "Operation Detachment," Admiral Nimitz was directed to seize Iwo Jima. No one expected it to be easy. After studying aerial reconnaissance photos, General Holland Smith declared Iwo "the toughest place we have had to take." He also predicted upward of 20,000 casualties.

Below: After the struggle for Iwo Jima is finally over, a helmetless Marine looks wearily towards the outline of Mount Suribachi in the distance, rifle in hand.

"I could not forget the sight of Marines floating in the lagoon or lying on the beaches of Tarawa, men who died assaulting defenses which should have been taken out by naval gunfire. At Iwo Jima, the problem was far more difficult."

In late May 1944, Japanese Prime Minister Tojo informed Lieutenant-General Tadamichi Kuribayashi that he had been chosen to defend Iwo Jima to the last. Kuribayashi was to utilize Iwo's forbidding terrain and dig in, then fight a long, bloody war of attrition. Upon his arrival on the island in early June, he began to turn Iwo into a fortress. Since surface installations could not withstand intensive naval bombardment, an extensive system of caves and tunnels was constructed; each cave had multiple outlets and ventilation tubes, and cisterns for the capture of rainwater were constructed. Engineers discovered that when they were mixed with cement, the black sands of Iwo Jima turned into a concrete of superior quality. Pillboxes and blockhouses were built from it and gun positions were hardened with it. Artillery and mortars were dug into the slopes of Mount Suribachi, as well as near the airfield. The result was an almost impenetrable field of interlocking fire, in which the defenders based not on the island, but rather within it.

What's more, reinforcements were sent to the island. The 2nd Independent Mixed Brigade and the 145th Infantry Regiment were both transferred to Iwo to aid in its defense, while the 26th Tank Battalion was ordered to the island from Pusan. Artillery units and five antitank battalions arrived. Kuribayashi had at his disposal a total of 23,000 Japanese defenders and an impressive array of weaponry. This included 361 artillery pieces of 2.95

Flag Raising over Suribachi

On the morning of February 23, 1943, First Lieutenant Harold C. Schrier and 40 men of E Company were ordered to secure the heights of towering Mount Suribachi. Lieutenant-Colonel Chandler W. Johnson, commanding officer, 2nd Battalion, 28th Marines, handed the Lieutenant a small American flag to raise atop the mountain's summit. The Marines moved cautiously up the steep slopes, heavily laden with weapons and ammunition. Surprisingly, they encountered only light opposition and reached the summit of Suribachi by mid-morning. After a brief firefight, a length of pipe was found and the small flag suddenly flew proudly over Iwo Jima. This moment was captured on film by Leatherneck photographer Staff Sergeant Louis Lowery.

The sight brought cheers from the Marines on the beaches below. At sea, the warships surrounding Iwo Jima sounded their sirens in celebration. Lieutenant-Colonel Chandler, however, realized the flag was too small to be seen from all over the island. Obtaining a larger flag from LST 799, Chandler handed the colors to PFC Rene A. Gagnon. Together with Sergeant Michael Strank, Corporal Harlon H. Block, PFC Franklin S. Sousley and PFC Ira A. Hayes, Gagnon climbed Suribachi. The smaller flag was lowered. The five Marines and Navy Corpsman Pharmacist's Mate, 2nd Class John H. Bradley raised the larger flag over Suribachi's windswept summit. In place to record the historic moment were Marine Staff Sergeant William Genaust, who filmed the motion picture footage, and Associated Press photographer Joseph Rosenthal.

Taking Suribachi was not the end of the battle for Iwo Jima. Fighting would rage for another month before the island was secured. Three of the men captured in Rosenthal's famous photograph did not survive. Strank and Block were killed in the assault on Nishi Ridge on March 1. PFC Sousley was killed in action on March 21. Staff Sergeant William Genaust, photographer, died in the final days of the battle for Iwo Jima.

in. (75 mm) caliber or larger, 12 12.6 in. (320 mm) spigot mortars, a total of 65 medium and light mortars, 33 naval guns, and some 94 antiaircraft guns of 2.95 in. (75 mm) or larger. In addition, Iwo's defenses also boasted more than 200 0.78 in. (20 mm) and 0.98 in. (25 mm) AA guns and 69 1.46 in. (37 mm) and 1.85 in. (47 mm) antitank guns. This was further supplemented by a variety of rockets.

The Americans mustered an impressive force to hurl against this Japanese fortress. Lieutenant-General Holland Smith, in his last combat assignment, served as Commanding General, Expeditionary Troops. In mid-October, Smith designated Major-General Harry Schmidt (Commanding General, V Amphibious Corps) as commander of the landing force that would hit the small island. Schmidt was to lead the largest Marine fighting force ever to go into battle: a combination of the 3rd, 4th, and 5th Marine Divisions were to storm the shores of Iwo Jima.

For 74 days prior to the Marine landing, Iwo Jima was pounded by regularly scheduled airstrikes. General Smith and his staff felt that a prolonged and heavy pre-invasion bombardment was needed to save Marine lives. Smith later

Above: This Marine, fighting with the 5th Marine Division on Iwo Jima, is helped to an aid station, the pain of injury clearly etched on his face. The Marine's wounds were caused by an enemy mortar shell.

said, "I could not forget the sight of Marines floating in the lagoon or lying on the beaches of Tarawa, men who died assaulting defenses which should have been taken out by naval gunfire. At Iwo Jima, the problem was far more difficult." With this in mind, the Marines asked for at least ten days of bombardment. The Navy agreed to three. At 06:40 hours on the morning of February 19, 1945, the *North Carolina, Washington, New York, Texas, Arkansas,* and *Nevada* began to pummel the shores of Iwo Jima with their big guns. Marine Corsairs flew in low and unleashed a barrage of rockets, napalm, and machine-gun fire. Smoke and flame rose above the island. It seemed to the Marines that the bombardment would blow Iwo Jima out of the sea.

At precisely 08:30 hours, the first assault waves crossed the line of departure and headed toward the landing beaches on the southeastern coast. Schmidt's plan was simple. The 4th and 5th Marine Divisions were to come ashore abreast, and the 4th Division was to land the 23rd Marines to the left. The 25th Marines, on the right flank, were to assault the area known as the Rock Quarry, and the 5th Division was to land the 28th Marines on the left flank. From there, they were first to cut across the island, then take the heights of Mount

Above: The beaches of Okinawa. A total of 14,000 new LVT-As were used to land the massive American force on the island.

Suribachi. The 27th Marines, along with the 23rd Marines, were ordered to capture Airfield No. 1 before turning themselves northward.

Within 90 minutes, eight assault battalions were ashore. As the Marines headed inland, the Japanese defenses came to life. Shortly after 10:00 hours, Kuribayashi signaled and hundreds of Japanese weapons opened fire on the exposed Marines. A moderate amount of mortarfire became a deluge of artillery shells and mortars. Enormous 12.6 in. (320 mm) spigot mortars fell from the sky, blowing Leathernecks into oblivion. Intense machine-gun and rifle fired ripped into the men. Kuribayashi's guns cut a wide swathe, turning Iwo Jima's black sands red with the blood of Marines. Later, many would comment that the barrage was the heaviest ever experienced by Marines. Others would wonder how any survived. Casualties mounted horrifically as the Marine advance continued. Sherman tanks came ashore. But both the volcanic sand and the 1.85 in. (47 mm) antitank fire coming from the slopes of Suribachi took a heavy toll. Both division commanders therefore committed their reserve forces and ordered artillery regiments ashore.

Marines up and down the beachhead were struggling to gain ground. As enemy fire rained downed from Suribachi's heights, the 28th Marines tried desperately to achieve a foothold. To the right of the 28th, the 27th Marines fought through savage artillery and mortar fire to the southern edge of Airfield No.1. "Manila John" Basilone, hero of Guadalcanal and winner of the Medal of Honor, was mortally wounded while leading his machine-gun platoon. On the right flank, men of the 25th Marines landed below a strongly fortified cliff and were shredded by enemy fire. General Cates was correct: "That right flank was a bitch if ever there was one." Throughout the day, the battle for the Rock Quarry cliffs raged on. The 3rd Battalion took staggeringly high casualties; a total of 22 officers and some 500 men fell to Japanese fire. Finally, after a protracted struggle that lasted eight hours, the 2nd and 3rd Battalions were able to reach the high ground on top of the quarry.

The day's advances were far short of D-Day objectives, but by evening Schmidt had 30,000 Marines were on Iwo Jima and the Leathernecks had established a foothold on the heavily fortified island. That night, the Marines shivered in the cold and waited for the Japanese to attack. In the darkness, small teams of Japanese infiltrators, "Prowling Wolves," probed the Marine lines. Enemy fire continued to take lives, but no desperate *banzai* attack occurred. With the arrival of first light, the Marines were at last on the move.

Mount Suribachi loomed over the southern beachhead. Two thousand Japanese troops were garrisoned on the slopes, well dug in to a honeycomb of machine-gun nests, hardened gun positions, and tunnels. Hundreds of caves and reinforced concrete blockhouses protected the approaches to Suribachi's heights. On the morning of February 20th, in a cold rain, the 28th Marines once again assaulted the mountain. Their 4.13 in. (105 mm) batteries opened up on the Japanese positions, but had little effect. Each enemy pocket had to be assaulted with flamethrowers, followed by Marines with grenades and satchel charges. By nightfall, the regiment had gained 200 yards (219 m), every inch paid for in blood.

> "As we started our advance the morning of February 20th, I recall seeing a Marine from a mortar platoon hit—he had received a direct hit from a Japanese shell, his jaw was blown away, exposing his teeth, and his skull was blown open. There was a ball of gray matter, part of his brains, about the size of a golf ball lying on top of his right ear. He was still alive, and was making a motion with his right hand for somebody to shoot him."

For the next two days, the 28th Marines battled to the base of Mount Suribachi. On Friday February 23, First Lieutenant Harold G. Schrier and 40 men of E Company, heavily ladened with weapons and ammunition, slowly climbed Suribachi's steep slopes to the summit. Reaching the crater's rim, the Marines found a length of pipe and attached a small American flag. Suddenly the Stars and Stripes flew proudly over Suribachi's heights. The warships surrounding Iwo Jima sounded their sirens. Whistles blew and the Marines below cheered. Secretary of the Navy James Forrestal remarked to General Smith, "Holland, the raising of that flag means a Marine Corps for the next 500 years." Three hours later, a second flag-raising took place. Six Marines hoisted a larger flag over Suribachi.

Five hundred Marines had been killed or wounded seizing the mountain. This was in addition to the horrific casualties the regiment had taken on D-Day, but the battle for Iwo Jima was far from over. As the 28th Marines battled to take Suribachi, the rest of the landing force continued to assault the fortified Japanese positions. Enemy machine guns, mortars, and artillery emplaced on the high ground near the airfield cut a bloody swath through the Leathernecks. By Tuesday, however, Airfield No. 1 was secured.

To the north, the 25 Marines, reinforced by the 1st Battalion, 24th Marines fought to take the cliffs west of the Rock Quarry against the fury of Japanese artillery.

Suddenly the Stars and Stripes flew proudly over Suribachi's heights. The warships surrounding Iwo Jima sounded their sirens. Whistles blew and the Marines below cheered. Secretary of the Navy James Forrestal remarked to General Smith, "Holland, the raising of that flag means a Marine Corps for the next 500 years."

Left: Amtracs head toward the enemy beach before an amphibious landing. Like LVTs, amtracs were fitted with paddles, which were attached to their tracks and which helped them move easily through water.

"There was no cover from enemy fire. Japs deep in reinforced concrete pillboxes laid down interlocking bands of fire that cut whole companies to ribbons. Camouflage hid all the enemy installations. The high ground on every side was honeycombed with layer after layer of Jap emplacements, blockhouses, dugouts, and observation posts. Their observation was perfect; whenever the Marines made a move, the Japs watched every step, and when the moment came, their mortars, rockets, machine guns, and artillery would smother the area in a murderous blanket of fire."

Below: A map of the landings on Okinawa, showing the progress of the U.S. forces during the lengthy struggle for control of the island.

The 1st Battalion, 24th Marines finally achieved a breakthrough. The sight of friendly aircraft cheered the Marines, who thought the airpower would add impetus to their advance. But their joy would soon turn to terror. "Friendly fire" ripped through the men of B Company. Only moments later, a barrage of naval gunfire slammed into the front lines of the battalion, resulting in some 90 casualties.

Schmidt decided to commit his corps reserve. The 21st Marines of the 3rd Marine Division were ordered to Iwo. On Wednesday February 21, weather and beach conditions finally let the Marines come ashore. They were attached to the 4th Marine Division and ordered to take Airfield No. 2 as the drive for Iwo Jima swung north. It was to be a frontal assault on Kuribayashi's toughest line of defense. The 145th Infantry Regiment defended the objective. Approaches to the airfield were mined, and 1.85 in. (47 mm) antitank guns sited to fire down the runways. Pillboxes, blockhouses, and heavy gun emplacements, as well as bunkers, formed a dense, interlocking field of fire.

On February 24, as Navy Seabees began repairs on Airfield No.1, the 21st Marines advanced into this killing zone. To support his troops, Schmidt ordered the Sherman tanks of all three divisions into the battle. The tanks ran into difficulties almost immediately. Fierce antitank fire, mines, and buried aerial torpedoes exacted a heavy toll. Many tanks were destroyed. "Hold at all costs," ordered the Japanese regimental commanding officer. But the Marine advance continued, the Leathernecks clearing out Japanese strongholds in brutal, hand-to-hand combat. By evening, the 21st Marines had a foothold along the southern perimeter of the field, with Marines holding the high ground near the intersection of the runways. Schmidt ordered the 9th Marines ashore and they, together with the 21st Marines, secured the airfield and moved toward the heavily fortified high ground. Hill Peter and Hill Oboe were the toughest obstacles for the Leathernecks to overcome. With support from flamethrowing tanks and Marine howitzers, the hills were taken after three days of bitter fighting. Ahead lay the Motoyama Plateau and Airfield No.3, and beyond that Hill-362C. It would be another nine days before those Japanese strongholds were obliterated and the 3rd Marine Division drive reached the sea.

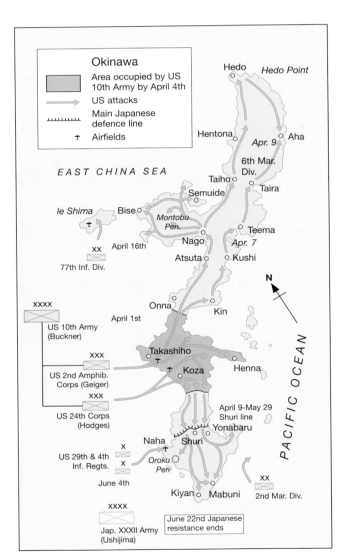

As the 21st Marines pushed into the center of the Japanese fortifications, the 4th Marine Division ran into what quickly became known as the "Meatgrinder."

"... dangling ledges, and caves carved by nature as well as the Japanese. Fissures of steam spewed from cracks in the ground, and evil-smelling sulfur fumes vied with the repulsive odor of decomposing bodies. Everywhere were Japanese defenses ..."

Here, in a maze of pillboxes, blockhouses, and hardened gun positions, the Japanese had five infantry battalions plus an artillery battalion. To the east of the airfield lay Hill 382. Just to the south was "The Amphitheater," to the east a hill called "Turkey Knob" surmounted by a large blockhouse. At 09:30 hours on February 25, 3,800 men of the 4th Marine Division assaulted the "Meatgrinder." The battle continued day after day, staggering casualties and exhaustion draining the division. Finally, after ten days of vicious combat, the Leathernecks secured the area, but the 4th Marine Division was spent and it stood at less than 50 percent of combat strength.

To the west, the 5th Marine Division faced some of the heaviest fighting on Iwo Jima. As the division pushed northward, relatively flat, sandy terrain gave way to heavily fortified cliffs throughout a series of ridges. Beyond that rose the heights of Hill-362A. From there, the Japanese had unobstructed views of the Marines below. Mortars and machine-gun emplacements formed deadly fields of fire. On February 28, the 27th Marines prepared to attack the hill looming above them. A 45-minute barrage from naval gunfire, artillery, and rockets commenced. Carrier-based aircraft flew overhead as the Marines began what would become one of the bloodiest encounters in the battle for Iwo Jima.

Above: Naval artist John Hamilton depicts K Company, 3rd Battalion, 5th Marines on the island of Okinawa. While corpsmen attend to the wounded in the foreground of this painting, a Marine mortar in the background can be seen launching another salvo against the enemy.

Taking the Heights of Iwo Jima

In two days of intense fighting, the Leathernecks assaulted Hill-362A. Sniper fire caused heavy casualties. The 28th Marines entered the fray and battled to the crest, where they came under concentrated fire from another ridgeline to the north, Nishi Ridge. Small-arms fire, machine guns, and mortars shredded the advancing Marines. The number of dead and wounded soared as men attempted to take Hill-362A and clear the ridgeline of Japanese. By March 2, the hill had been secured, but the fight was far from over. The Marines were dug in along the base of Nishi Ridge and facing the heights of Hill-362B. Despite heavily mined terrain and intense enemy fire, Nishi Ridge was seized the following day and the 26th Marines moved toward the hill. It was another bloody fight. Utilizing flamethrowers and demolitions, and exhibiting raw courage, two companies battled to the top of the Hill-

362B. The 26th Marines paid a high price for their victory: a total of 281 men lay either dead or wounded on the hill's slopes.

On March 7, H Company, 3rd Battalion, 26th Marines reached the crest of the small knoll. Flamethrowers and satchel charges sealed the Japanese caves. Machine-gun fire cut into the enemy troops who suddenly appeared. Then an eerie silence fell over the hill top. The entire hill seemed to shudder and then suddenly exploded—the Japanese had blown their own command post, taking with them 43 Marines who were gathered near the summit. Horror struck the 2nd Battalion, 27th Marines the same day. Personal sacrifice, courage, and heroism are not rarities in the annals of Marine Corps history, but the events surrounding First Lieutenant Jack Lummus are particularly poignant to read. In an area just east of the sea, the fighting was particularly bitter. Lummus, who was platoon leader of E Company, stormed the Japanese positions, and was knocked down by an exploding grenade. Nonetheless, he got to his feet and plunged ahead. Yet another grenade shattered his shoulder. However, once again, Lummus rose.

Below: Two Marines, one armed with a rifle, another a flamethrower, make their way along an outcropping on Okinawa. This Marine Corps photograph originally carried the simple caption, "Into the valley of death ..."

"Suddenly he was in the center of a powerful explosion obscured by flying rock and dirt. As it cleared his men saw him, rising as if in a hole. A land mine had blown off both his legs, the legs that had carried him to All-American football honors at Baylor University. They watched in horror as he stood on the bloody stumps, calling them on. Several men, crying now, ran to him and for a moment talked of shooting him to stop his agony. But he was still shouting for them to move out and the platoon scrambled forward. Their tears turned to rage, they swept an impossible 300 yards [328 m] over impossible ground, and at nightfall they were on a ridge overlooking the sea."

Finally, on March 16, Iwo Jima was declared secured. Heavy fighting would continue for several days in places named "Bloody Gorge" and "Cushman's Pocket." The Marine Corps' final casualties on the black sands of Iwo Jima totaled 25,851. Twenty-seven men were awarded Medals of Honor for conspicuous gallantry. Admiral Nimitz stated that "Among the Americans who served on Iwo Jima, uncommon valor was a common virtue." The seizure of the island produced immediate results in the bombing campaign against the Japanese homeland. While the battle still raged, Marines saw crippled B-29s landing. By early April, P-51 Mustangs were flying escort for the big bombers.

Before the war's end, a total of 2,251 damaged B-29s landed on Iwo Jima. "Whenever I land on this airfield, I thank God for the men who fought for it," said one grateful pilot.

Okinawa

As the Army mopped up on Iwo Jima, an invasion force gathered for the largest amphibious assault of the Pacific War. The target was Okinawa, the largest island in the Ryukyus chain, only 360 miles (580 km) from the Japanese island of Kyushu. Wresting Okinawa from the enemy would provide American forces with the military facilities from which to launch an invasion of Japan. The island had the requisite ports and anchorages; its airfields could also be used to step up the bombing campaign against the enemy. Perhaps most importantly, Okinawa was large enough to train and stage the massive number of troops that would be used in the final leap across the Pacific.

The Americans massed a truly awesome force for the task. Under the command of Lieutenant-General Simon Bolivar Buckner, Jr, the landing force was organized as the U.S. Tenth Army. This 183,000-man juggernaut consisted of Army XXIV Corps and Marine III Amphibious Corps, still under the command of Major-General Roy Geiger. Four Army divisions were to hit Okinawa's western shores, as well as the 1st and 6th Marine Divisions. The 2nd Marine Division was to be used as a diversionary force.

Above: A Marine war dog and his handler wait for orders to proceed. The Marine war dogs were trained to sniff out hidden snipers, as well as searching for stragglers, and scouring out caves and pillboxes.

The Japanese strategy to meet this massive force was simple. The Thirty-Second Army, a force 100,000 men strong, was to dig into the southern end of the island and wage a long, bloody defensive war that would give the *kamikazes* time to ravage the American fleet. Lieutenant-General Mitsuru Ushijima commanded the Japanese garrison. In an order issued in March 1945, Ushijima stated, "We must make it our basic principle to allow the enemy to land in full." The beaches would not be defended. Instead, three major lines of defense were established inland. The first ran along Kazuka Ridge. The second, the strongest position, reached from the capital city of Naha on the western coast, across the front of Shuri Castle in the center, and through the hills to Yonaburo in the east. A third line of defenses ran further to the south. Okinawa's numerous caves were reinforced and improved, tunnels dug to provide access to hardened gun positions. Pillboxes, machine-gun emplacements, and rifle pits were constructed. Both forward and reverse slopes of Okinawa's many hills were fortified, with machine guns, artillery, and mortars hidden within caves. A arsenal of antitank guns, spigot mortars, 5.9 in. (150 mm) howitzers, and 4.7 in. (120 mm) mortars awaited the American forces.

Above: This Leatherneck runs for cover in an area known as "Death Valley." Marines fought their way through interlocking fields of Japanese machine-gun, mortar and artillery fire to breach the defenses along the Shuri Line.

In late March, the campaign began. *Kamikazes* hit the invasion fleet, including Admiral Turner's flagship, the *Indianapolis*. Fortunately, the Army's 77th Infantry Division and a Marine reconnaissance battalion succeeded in capturing the Kerama Retto, a small group of islands west of Okinawa, whose anchorages would make possible the repair of ships damaged by *kamikaze* attacks. The additional seizure of Keise Shima let the 420th Field Artillery Group register their 6.1 in. (155 mm) guns on targets in southern Okinawa. Seven days before the landing, a pre-invasion bombardment began, but the Navy's 27,000 rounds proved largely ineffective.

On the morning of Sunday April 1, the invasion of Okinawa began. The 2nd Marine Division was given the task of executing a diversionary feint on Okinawa's southeastern beaches. Higgins boats and LVTs were loaded with Marines and launched toward Okinawa's shores. At precisely 08:30 hours, the time scheduled for the actual landing, the Marines veered off and returned to their transports. The deception was successful: the Japanese commanders believed they had repelled an American landing on the eastern shore. However, the deception exacted a high price. Upon return of the Marines to the transports, the Japanese struck. A massed *kamikaze* attack slammed into the small force. All air support had been assigned to the main assault force on the other side of the island. There was no air cover. Antiaircraft crews fought valiantly, but were no substitutes for fighters. *Kamikazes* crashed into both the *Hinsdale* and *LST 844*. A total of 50 Marines were either killed or wounded.

On the western coast, an attack by 500 carrier-based aircraft, including four Marine squadrons, preceded the landing. Planes dropped napalm and strafed the assault beaches. Naval gunfire pounded the coast. The U.S. Tenth Army stormed ashore. XXIV Corps landed to the south, the 1st and 6th Marine Divisions to the north. By 09:00 hours, eight assault battalions were ashore. The landing was unopposed. By early afternoon, advancing against light opposition, the 6th Marine Division secured Yontan Airfield. Nearby Kadena Airfield had fallen to the 77th Infantry Division. As the invasion force moved inland across Okinawa, the transfer of troops and supplies from ship-to-shore continued. By evening, Buckner had Sherman tanks, Marine 6.1 in. (155 mm) guns, and the Army's 8 in. (203 mm) howitzers ashore. A total of 60,000 American troops held a beachhead which was 8 miles (13 km) in length and 2 miles (3.2 km) deep.

Over the next two days, the 1st Marine Division seized the Katchin Peninsula, bisecting the island. General Shepherd's 6th Marine Division swung north toward the Ishikawa Isthmus. The terrain became more rugged and the Marines encountered pockets of stiff Japanese resistance. However, by April 3, the division was poised at the base of the isthmus, ready to advance. They were 12 days ahead of schedule. The division's next objective, the seizure of the town of Nago, was achieved on April 7. Within a week, the 22nd Marines moved up the length of the island and secured the northern point of Hedo Misaki.

Navaho Code Talkers

In May, 1942, with the approval of the Navajo Tribal Council, the Marine Corps began recruiting young native Americans in Window Rock, Arizona. Each recruit was required to meet the physical requirements of the Marine Corps and to speak both English and Navajo fluently. Many of these recruits would serve as radio operators for the Marine infantry units, as part of the legendary group of Navajo Code Talkers.

The Navajo language is one of the most unique dialects in the world. The idea of utilizing this language for communication in combat originated with Technical Sergeant Philip Johnston. Many were skeptical; others held the idea in complete disdain. Johnston apparently succeeded in convincing his superiors with a two-minute Navajo dispatch. The Code Talkers proved a boon to Marine communication. Urgent messages could be sent and received without the time-consuming process of encoding and decoding. The Navajos simply read the original message in English, mentally translated it into their native tongue, and transmitted. There was no fear of interception by the Japanese, who were never able to translate the Navajo language. Navajo Code Talkers served with infantry units throughout the war in the Pacific. On New Georgia, Code Talkers of the 1st Raider Battalion served with the Army's 3rd Battalion, 148th Infantry. Marine Corporal Eugene Roanhorse Crawford was assigned to the command of Lieutenant-Colonel "Dutch" Schultz to send secure situation reports while the fighting on New Georgia raged.

The skills of the Navajo were utilized heavily, and with great success, on Iwo Jima. Two dozen Code Talkers served with each Marine division. Communications, which had proved problematic in the past, were nearly perfect during the long struggle for Iwo. After their service on Okinawa, however, the Navajo Code Talkers were no longer needed. They slipped quietly into the annals of Marine Corps history.

The ease with which the 6th Marine Division had advanced, however, was about to end abruptly. Beyond Nabo was the Motobu Peninsula. The Japanese, under the command of Colonel Takesiko Udo, manned heavily fortified positions near Mount Yae Take. In an area roughly 6 by 8 miles (10 by 13 km), the enemy had hardened gun emplacements, 2.95 in. (75 mm) and 5.9 in. (150 mm) artillery pieces, and two 6 in. (152 mm) naval guns. All approaches to the area were heavily mined. The terrain made the use of tanks impossible. Shepherd decided it was too much for the 29th Marines to handle alone, and ordered the 4th Marines into the area. They came under intense enemy fire. Shepherd called in naval gunfire to support the Leathernecks. Marine Corsairs flew overhead, dropping bombs and napalm on enemy positions. The battle waged fiercely for five days. The 6th Marine Division took high casualties; 213 men killed, another 757 wounded. In securing the Motobu Peninsula, the Marines gained valuable experience in utilizing close air support to assault fortified Japanese positions. That experience would prove invaluable when the division was ordered south to the Shuri Line.

The Shuri Line

While the Marines had great success to the north, XXIV Corps encountered serious problems in its move southward. It hit Kazuka Ridge, the first line of Japanese defense. Stiff enemy resistance and heavy artillery fire stopped its advance. In an effort to break through, a massive bombardment of the fortified positions was ordered. The amount of firepower directed against the Japanese was truly awesome: gunfire from battleships, cruisers, and destroyers pounded the area; some 650 Navy and Marine aircraft targeted rockets, bombs, and napalm on the enemy; 27 battalions of artillery fired everything from 2.95 in. (75 mm) guns to 8 in. (152 mm) howitzers. To those who witnessed the bombardment, it seemed that nothing could have survived. But the Japanese did. When three divisions of XXIV Corps attacked, they failed to achieve a breakthrough. For five days, the Army threw itself against Ushijima's defenses. Little progress was made and casualties mounted. Commandant Vandegrift, who was visiting Okinawa, and General Geiger suggested that the 2nd Marine Division be landed near Nakagusuku Bay behind the Shuri Line. The division, now waiting in Saipan, could be ready to sail in six short hours. General Shepherd agreed, advising Buckner that establishing a beachhead would make the Japanese pull forces from their main line of defense. Buckner and the Tenth Army staff maintained that ammunition was too short, that a second front would break down his supply system. He also feared high casualties in "another Anzio, but worse."

The bloody battle still continued. The Tenth Army ordered pieces of the 1st Marine Division to join the others in the bitter struggle against the enemy. The artillery regiment was committed, and then the 1st Tank Battalion was also thrown in to battle. On May 1, the division replaced the 27th Infantry Division on the right flank.

> "Shortly a column of men approached us on the other side of the road. They were the army infantry from 106th Regiment, 27th Infantry Division that we were relieving. Their tragic expressions revealed where they had been. They were dead beat, dirty and grisly, hollow-eyed and tight-faced. I hadn't seen such faces since Peleliu. As they filed past us, one tall, lanky fellow caught my eye and said in a weary voice, 'It's hell up there, Marine.' "

"They were dead beat, dirty and grisly, hollow-eyed and tight-faced. I hadn't seen such faces since Peleliu. As they filed past us, one tall, lanky fellow caught my eye and said in a weary voice, 'It's hell up there, Marine.' "

Opposite: Marine PFC Galen A. Brehn, who was fighting with the 6th Marine Division, directs his flamethrower toward a Japanese cave to burn out its inhabitants on the island of Okinawa.

On May 8, Nazi Germany surrendered. The war in Europe was over, but for the men fighting on Okinawa, it was another day of battling the Japanese in a cold, heavy rain.

The following morning, the 1st Marine Division battled toward the Asa River. Driving rain limited its air support and artillery from the Japanese pounded the Leathernecks. Small-arms fire and automatic weapons cut a bloody swath right through the Marine lines.

"There was the brassy, metallic twang of the small 50 mm [1.97 in.] knee mortar shells as little puffs of dirty smoke appeared thickly around us. The 81 mm [3.18 in.] and 90mm [3.54 in.] mortar shells crashed and banged all along the ridge. The *whizz-bang* of the high velocity 47 mm [1.85 in.] gun's shells, which was on us with its explosion almost as soon as we heard it whizz into the area, gave me the feeling the Japanese were firing them at us like rifles. The slower screaming, whining sound of the 75 mm shells [2.95 in.] seemed almost abundant. Then there was the roar and the rumble of the huge enemy 150 mm [5.9 in.] howitzer shell, and the kaboom of its explosion."

Repeatedly, the Marines were forced to withdraw from their positions.

Ushijima's subordinates convinced the Japanese commander that the time had come to launch a massive counterattack. To support the attack, the guns, mortars, and howitzers of the 5th Artillery Command were removed from their hidden positions and brought into the open. On the night of May 3/4, Japanese troops were transported by barge behind American lines. On the right flank, the Marines intercepted the enemy before they ever got ashore, killing 700 Japanese soldiers. The 1st Reconnaissance Company and war dog platoons mopped up any enemy forces that had landed elsewhere on the western coast. At 04:30 hours, the Japanese artillery began firing. Army positions were hardest hit, but supporting artillery and naval gunfire pummeled the Japanese positions. At daybreak, American airstrikes began. By 19:00 hours, "77 tons of bombs, 450 rockets, and 22,000 rounds of machine gun and cannon ammunition" rained down on the enemy. Ushijima lost 59 artillery pieces and over 6,000 men. Although it was later described as the decisive action of the campaign, the battle for Okinawa would rage on for another seven weeks.

On May 8, Nazi Germany surrendered. The war in Europe was over, but for the men fighting on Okinawa, it was another day of battling the Japanese in a cold, heavy rain.

Buckner ordered the redeployment of the 6th Marine Division south from the Motobu Peninsula. It was now a four-division front, with XXIV Corps on the left, the two Marine divisions on the right. Ahead of the 1st Marine Division lay Dakeshi Ridge, beyond that Wana Ridge and Wana Draw. The 6th Marine Division faced Sugar Loaf hill. On May 11, Buckner ordered a general offensive on Okinawa.

Elements of the 6th Marine Division crossed the Asa River and began the approach to Sugar Loaf. It was an unimposing looking cluster of hills, with Sugar Loaf at the top, flanked by Half Moon and Horseshoe. But there, the Japanese defenders had created a killing ground. Mortars and 1.85 in. (47 mm) guns were trained on the approaches to the complex.

Above: These well-armed Marines advance against Japanese positions on the island of Okinawa. Securing the island would eventually cost the Marine Corps a staggering total of 20,020 casualties.

Above: Marine Lieutenant-Colonel R.P. Ross, 1st Battalion, 1st Marines carries "Old Glory" to the heights of Shuri Castle on the island of Okinawa.

Any attempt they made to assault one hill would subject the Marines to searing bands of Japanese crossfire. It took several days of bitter fighting to secure the area. In one single day of fighting, the 6th Marine Division suffered a total of 600 casualties, but by May 23, the division had made it to the outskirts of Naha.

The advance of the 1st Marine Division was no less costly. The 7th Marines fought their way through machine-gun fire, mortars, and grenades to gain a foothold on Dakeshi Ridge. It was a significant breakthrough. The Shuri line was breached, but ahead were the defenses of Wana Ridge and Wana Draw. All approaches were mined. The surrounding cliffs bristled with machine guns and artillery, forming deadly fields of interlocking fire. For some 18 days, the 1st Marine Division battled the Japanese defenders. Casualties were staggeringly high. Any gains made against the enemy positions were "measured by yards won, lost, then won again." Torrential rains halted any advance. The ground became a sea of mud. One Marine described the experience as being a "misery beyond description."

"I had my first opportunity to look around our position. It was the most ghastly corner of hell I had ever witnessed … an area that previously had been a low grassy valley with a picturesque stream meandering through it was a muddy, repulsive open sore on the land. The place was choked with the putrification of death, decay, and destruction. In a shallow defilade to our right … lay about 20 dead Marines, each on a stretcher and covered to his ankles with a poncho—a commonplace, albeit tragic, scene to every veteran. … At least those dead were covered from the torrents of rain that had made them miserable in life and from the swarms of flies that sought to hasten their decay. But as I looked out, I saw that other Marine dead couldn't be tended properly. The whole area was pocked with shell craters and churned up by explosions. Every crater was half-full of water, and many of them held a Marine corpse. The bodies lay pathetically, just as they had been killed, half submerged in muck and water."

By May 28, the rains stopped, and the Marines continued to advance against Shuri. Ushijima retreated southward to the final line of Japanese defenses. On the morning of May 29, the 5th Marines entered Shuri Castle. There would be another two weeks of fighting before Okinawa was eventually secured.

General Shepherd's 6th Marine Division was ordered to take Oroku Peninsula. On June 4, the 4th Marines executed a shore-to-shore landing and hit the Japanese on their exposed flank. The 29th Marines were close behind. The 22nd Marines sealed off the peninsula, and the three regiments converged. By June 14, the Japanese defenders were eliminated. Only Kunishi Ridge remained. The Japanese were dug in and determined to fight to the bitter end. Taking this coral outcropping decimated all three regiments of the 1st Marine Division. Reinforcements arrived only when the 8th Marines landed on Okinawa.

On June 18, Buckner moved to the forward observation post to watch the 8th Marines in action. A Japanese shell exploded nearby, driving a coral splinter into the General's chest. He died minutes later. Major-General Roy Geiger was given command of the Tenth Army, thus becoming the first Marine to command a field army. At 13:05 hours on June 21, Geiger announced that Okinawa was secured. The Marine Corps had suffered 20,020 casualties in the conquest of Okinawa, including 3,561 killed in action. Those were the highest casualties for any Pacific campaign, but still the invasion of Japan loomed on the horizon. "Operation Downfall" was scheduled to begin on November 1, 1945. The 2nd, 3rd, and 5th Marines Divisions were to hit the beaches of Kyushu.

On August 6, an atomic bomb was exploded over the city of Hiroshima. Three days later, another was dropped on the city of Nagasaki. In the wake of these attacks, Japan sued for peace under the terms of the Potsdam Declaration. On August 15, 1945, World War II finally ended. Eugene B. Sledge recalled that day amongst the Marines:

> "Sitting in stunned silence, we remembered our dead. So many dead. So many maimed. So many bright futures consigned to the ashes of the past. So many dreams lost in the madness that had engulfed us. Except for a few widely scattered shouts of joy, the survivors of the abyss sat hollow-eyed and silent, trying to comprehend a world without war. ... War is brutish, inglorious, and a terrible waste. Combat leaves an indelible mark on those who are forced to endure it. The only redeeming factors were my comrades' incredible bravery and their devotion to each other. Marine Corps training taught us to kill efficiently and to try to survive. But it also taught us loyalty to each other—and love. That *espirit de corps* sustained us."

Below: U.S. Marines inspect a Japanese garrison in China before taking over duties from them after the Japanese surrender in August 1945.

"Sitting in stunned silence, we remembered our dead ... Except for a few widely scattered shouts of joy, the survivors of the abyss sat hollow-eyed and silent, trying to comprehend a world without war."

CHAPTER FIVE

KOREA

After their magnificent efforts
in the Pacific in World War II,
the Marines faced an uncertain future
in the new, nuclear age. The attack
on South Korea by its Communist
northern neighbour gave the Marines
an opportunity to prove their worth
to the Joint Chiefs of Staff in the new
world order, an opportunity they would
grasp firmly with both hands.

Left: Marines, carrying their kit and their weapons, are picked up by a
Sikorsky HS-1 helicopter from HMR-161.

Right: Amtracs loaded with men from the 1st Marines who were led by "Chesty" Puller head for Blue Beach during the landings at Inchon. These took place on September 15, 1950.

Below: The invasion of South Korea by the North caught the world by surprise. The defending forces were quickly reduced to a small perimeter around Pusan.

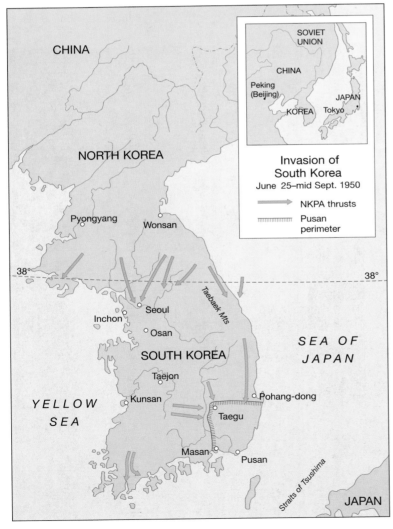

Invasion of
South Korea
June 25–mid Sept. 1950

→ NKPA thrusts

⟩⟩⟩⟩⟩ Pusan perimeter

In the years after World War II, the Marine Corps struggled for survival, not on the field of battle, but rather in the halls of Congress. A Senate bill was introduced in January 1946 which called for the restructuring of the Armed Services. Under the tenants of the legislation, the Marine Corps would be reduced to a force of 60,000 men, with no air component. Admiral Chester W. Nimitz argued vehemently against the bill. It would have virtually eliminated the Marine Corps as a combat force. General Vandegrift, Commandant of the Marine Corps, addressed the Senate Naval Committee: "We have pride in ourselves and in our past, but we do not rest our case on any presumed ground of gratitude owing us from the nation. The bended knee is not a tradition of our Corps. If the Marine as a fighting man had not made a case for himself after 170 years of service, he must go. But he has earned the right to depart with dignity and honor, not by subjugation to the status of uselessness and servility planned for him by the War Department."

The bill was never enacted. Another piece of legislation, however, was introduced that defined the roles and responsibilities of each branch of the Armed Services. The Marine Corps was defined as a separate service within the Navy Department with the responsibility for developing amphibious doctrine, for the seizure or defense of advanced naval bases, and for the conduct of land operations deemed essential to a naval campaign. In 1947, this legislation was passed as the National Security Act. The Marine Corps had survived the battle, but the war had not been won. This was the beginning of the Atomic Age, and many, including General Omar Bradley (Chairman of the Joint Chiefs of Staff) and Secretary of Defense Louis A. Johnson, felt an amphibious force was obsolete. The fight continued over the course of the next year, with cuts in the Defense Budget drastically reducing the strength of the Marine Corps. By June 1950, there were only 74,279 Marines—and they would soon be needed.

The Invasion of South Korea

In the pre-dawn hours of Sunday June 25, 1950, as many as nine infantry divisions and three tank regiments of the North Korean People's Army (NKPA) poured across the 38th Parallel and into South Korea. Combat veterans of the Chinese Civil War (1945–49), the soldiers of the NKPA were well equipped and well trained. The Army of the Republic of Korea (ROK) proved no match for the invading forces. Attacking at night, the North Koreans spearheaded their assault with Russian-built T-34 tanks, supported heavily by artillery and mortars. Within three days, the South Korean capital of Seoul had fallen, and the invaders had swept across the Han River. ROK forces were in full retreat.

Below: A Marine uses a flamethrower to clear defensive positions on Wolmi-do. The small island in the harbor had to be secured before the landing at Inchon.

Right: With the aid of
scaling ladders, the 5th
Marines go over the
seawall at Inchon. The
Marine leading the way
was identified as 1st
Lieutenant Baldomero
Lopez, who would later be
posthumously awarded the
Medal of Honor.

Below: A Marine as he
would have appeared
during the Inchon
landings—much the same
as at Iwo Jima or Okinawa.

The United States Government was shocked—and unprepared. An emergency meeting of the United Nations Security Council was convened in New York. On June 27, member nations were authorized to help repel the invasion. General Douglas MacArthur visited the Korean front and discovered that fully two-thirds of ROK troops could not be accounted for. Alarmed, MacArthur urged President Truman to commit combat troops. The President agreed. Within a week of the invasion, the United States was fully committed to the defense of South Korea.

The first troops sent to Korea were elements of the U.S. Army's 24th Division. Pulled from occupation duty in Japan, they were not ready for combat. When the division met NKPA forces at Taejon, they were shattered. Almost 30 percent of its 12,200 men were killed or wounded. The North Korean Army bore down on the port city of Pusan.

In those first few, frantic days, little thought was given to the Marine Corps. Some members of the Joint Chiefs of Staff even suggested that use of Marine Corps forces should not even be considered. General Clifford Cates, now commandant of the Corps, had other plans. Feeding units in piecemeal to reinforce the ROK lines had only delayed the enemy advance, and Cates knew exactly what the grave situation required: a combat-ready force supported by an air wing. He quietly told Major General Graves B. Erskine to place the 1st Marine Brigade on alert for expeditionary duty to Korea. On July 1, the chief of naval operations informed MacArthur that the Marines were ready. MacArthur immediately requested the Joint Chiefs of Staff assign the unit to his Korean command.

Six days later, the 1st Provisional Brigade, under the command of Brigadier General Edward Craig, was created. The 5th Marines, reinforced with tanks and an artillery battalion, were the core of the unit. Air support was to be provided by Marine Aircraft Group 33, which was comprised of three fighter-bomber squadrons and four experimental Sikorsky helicopters, the first to be formed into a combat unit. The brigade was ordered to ready for deployment with all possible speed. On July 12, only five days from its inception, the 1st Provisional Brigade sailed from San Diego. It headed toward Japan, where last-minute training was planned.

With the situation in Korea critical, MacArthur appealed for additional reinforcements—an entire Marine division. To provide those troops, General Cates requested the Marine Corps Reserve be activated. President Truman agreed. On July 25, the Joint Chiefs of Staff finally acquiesced to MacArthur, giving him the additional forces. General Cates informed the 1st Marine Division that it would depart in two weeks.

The task of assembling the required manpower was almost insurmountable, yet the Marine Corps managed. Subordinate units of the 2nd Marine Division were transferred from Camp Lejeune to the west coast. The strength of Marine forces guarding naval bases was reduced by some 50 percent, and those forces also moved west. All enlistments were extended. Reservists were absorbed. On August 22, the 1st Marines sailed for Korea. The 7th Marines departed California a week later.

On the flight to Japan, Major General O.P. Smith, new commander of the 1st Marine Division, learned of MacArthur's plan to launch an amphibious assault against the port city of Inchon. The 1st Marine Division was to spearhead the attack, scheduled for September 15. Those plans, however, would change. While the Provisional Brigade was en route to Japan and the 1st Marine Division prepared to sail, the fighting in Korea continued. The situation faced by U.N. forces was critical. The Eighth Army, comprised of all U.S. Army and ROK troops, had been unable to stop the North Korean advance. Lieutenant-General

Below: Marines snipe at enemy positions during street fighting in the South Korean capital of Seoul. The city was defended by more than 20,000 North Koreans.

Above: Marine Corps artist John Groth depicts U.S. Marines running through the streets of Seoul. Marines came under fire from enemy snipers positioned with the city's buildings.

Walton H. Walker, in command of the Eighth Army, had established a weak perimeter around the city of Pusan, but his forces were hammered. U.S. casualties were already numbering over 6,000; a total of 70,000 Koreans had been killed or wounded. Were Pusan to fall, the entire peninsula would be lost to NKPA forces. Walker's only hope at that point was reinforcement.

On July 25, Craig was informed that his Marines were to land at Pusan, and would serve in support of the Eighth Army. There would be no time available for training in Japan. Four days later, Lieutenant-General Walker addressed his many battle-weary troops with exhortations to loyalty and to determination: "A Marine unit and two regiments are expected in the next few days to reinforce us. … There is no line behind us to which we can retreat. … We must fight until the end."

On August 2, the Marines landed in Korea. They came ashore not under intense enemy fire, but rather aboard troop transports, casually standing at the rails and disembarking on the busy docks of Pusan. That night was a hectic one as the brigade's supplies were unloaded, but Marines travel light and were ready to move out the following morning. Despite the fear that permeated the city, the Marines stood as a strong, solid force fortified by training and the words of General Cates:

Right: From the initial perimeter around Inchon, the Marines and supporting forces moved rapidly on Seoul, where they were engaged in vicious streetfighting.

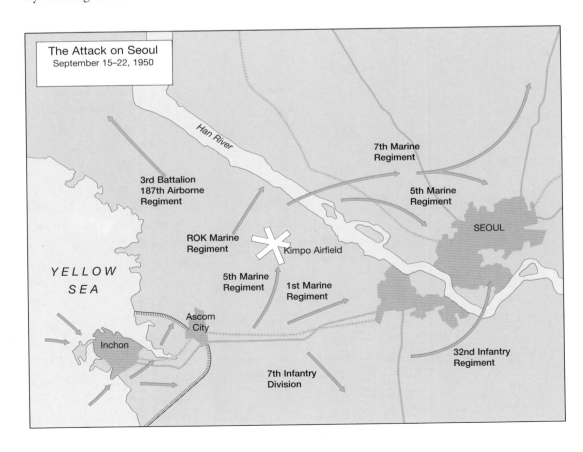

Left: Marines move through smoke and dust in the streets of Seoul. The numerous North Korean roadblocks which had been set up in the city required the Marines to call in artillery fire or Corsair strikes in order to help clear them.

"The proud battle streamers of our Corps go with you in combat. The pride and honor of many generations of Marines is entrusted to you today. You are the old breed. With you moves the heart and the soul and the spirit of all who ever bore the title 'United States Marine.' "

As the ground forces prepared to move to a staging area in Changwon, Marine aviators took to the skies. An eight-plane flight from VMF-214, "the Black Sheep squadron," pounded the city of Chinju with rockets and incendiary bombs. For the next several days, NKPA positions were the target of Marine aircraft.

The First Counteroffensive

The primary threat to the Pusan perimeter was in the south. The NKPA's 6th Division, reinforced by the 83rd Motorcycle Regiment, threatened to break through. General Walker decided he had enough manpower to launch the first counteroffensive of the war. The objective was the town of Chinju. The Marines were to take a southern route, clearing the ridges near Chindong-ni and advancing to Sachon. The Army's 25th Infantry Division and the 5th Regimental Combat Team (RCT) would advance on Chinju on the right flank.

On the morning of August 7 (the eighth anniversary of the Marine landing on Guadalcanal), Walker launched the offensive. In the meantime, the North Koreans had launched one of its own. Battle plans called for the 5th RCT to take a center route, but the soldiers ended up moving south, leaving the center vulnerable. A U.S. Army company had earlier moved up Hill 342, which overlooked a main supply route. As the North Koreans advanced, however, the hill was surrounded. The Marines received orders to relieve the

The pride and honor of many generations of Marines is entrusted to you today. You are the old breed. With you moves the heart and the soul and the spirit of all who ever bore the title "United States Marine."

beleaguered soldiers and hold the hill. The morning of August 7 had dawned clear. As the Marines advanced on the hill, the blinding sun and oppressive heat exacted a heavy toll. Leathernecks succumbed to heat exhaustion. Water was scarce. Enemy fire urged the Marines to the crest, but only 37 of the original 52 men made it to the summit. Second Lieutenant John J.H. Cahill called for artillery support—and air drops of water.

The next day, two rifle companies of the 2nd Battalion, 5th Marines advanced on Hill 342. The temperature was a scorching 112 °F (44 °C). Men collapsed from heat exhaustion, unable to go any further in the extreme heat. On the crest of the hill, the soldiers and Marines were without water and surrounded, but managed to hold on, fighting off the North Koreans in brutal, hand-to-hand combat.

By August 8, Company D crested the hill, but the struggle to hold it was no less easy. Enemy fire was concentrated on the position and North Koreans were slowly advancing up Hill 342's steep sides. The Marines were taking casualties, but they held on with the help of artillery and close air support. Fire from Marine Corsairs ripped through the NKPA, killing or wounding an estimated 400 North Koreans.

Above: This painting by combat artist Horace Avery Chenoweth depicts Marine helicopters approaching the front. Chenoweth served as an infantry platoon leader in the Korean war.

To the east, the 3rd Battalion, 5th Marines was given the mission of clearing enemy forces from Hill 255. First, they had to take a smaller hill, but the initial Marine assault was repelled. With heavy machine-gun fire and grenades, the Leathernecks cleared out the North Korean positions one by one. It was a grueling task, made worse by lack of water. By evening, however, Hill 255 loomed ahead. In the morning, artillery pounded the hill and the first napalm strike of the war was delivered. The Marines of Company H then reached the crest with little opposition. After two days of fighting, the Marines had opened the road to Chinju, and the North Korean Army, after easily sweeping across the peninsula, had finally been checked.

During the next few days, the Marine brigade advanced over 30 miles (48 km). Once again, Marine air played an important role, decimating a NKPA column of vehicles fleeing the town of Kosong. Corsairs ripped into elements of the 83rd Motorcycle Regiment.

"The slaughter began … the Corsairs swung low up and down the frantic NKPA column, raining death and destruction in a hail of fire from rockets and 20 mm [0.78 in] cannon. …The enemy regiment was trapped. It was a scene of wild chaos: vehicles crashing into each other, overturned in ditches, afire and exploding; troops fleeing for safety in every direction."

The Marines took Kosong with little opposition and were well on their way to completing the sweep to Chinju, but events elsewhere along the front halted the advance. North Korean troops had breached the lines along the Naktong River. Three Army artillery batteries had been overrun. The Marines were needed to shore up the Pusan perimeter.

On the night of August 5, the North Korean 4th Division crossed the Naktong and established a position on the east bank of the river. Army counterattacks against the bulge proved unsuccessful. The Marine brigade was to be part of a full-scale assault by the Army's 24th Division and 9th Infantry Regiment. The Marine objective was the Obong-ni Ridge, punctuated by deep

gullies and steep hills. The terrain to its left prohibited an assault from the flank, and the presence of the 9th Infantry on the right meant that a frontal assault was the only option.

The attack began at 08:00 hours on the morning of August 17. Both Marine artillery and air strikes proved ineffective, and as the Marines advanced on the ridge, there was little natural cover. The Leathernecks took withering enemy fire. Mortars, grenades, and machine-gun fire ripped through the Marine lines. The 2nd Battalion suffered some 60 percent casualties. The 1st Battalion, 5th Marines was committed to the fray. As the

Above: A Marine M4 Sherman tank with a bulldozer blade pushes two knocked-out North Korean T-34/85 tanks off a highway.

John Glenn

Although perhaps more widely recognized as an astronaut or U.S. Senator, John Glenn had a long and distinguished career as a Marine aviator. During World War II, Glenn served with Marine Fighter Squadron-155, flying 59 missions during the campaigns in the Marshalls and the Marianas. Promoted to the rank of major, Glenn was sent to Korea in early 1953. Assigned to Marine Fighter Squadron-311, he soon earned a reputation for seemingly reckless flying and the sobriquet "Magnet Ass" for his ability to attract large amounts of enemy flak. On more than one occasion Glenn returned from missions with his Grumman F9F-2 Panther riddled with holes. The photograph to the right shows the

smiling Glenn next to his damaged aircraft on one of these occasions: a Communist 2.95 in. (75 mm) shell had passed through the tail of the aircraft. Glenn flew 63 missions in Korea before joining the Air Force 25th Fighter Squadron in an exchange program. To this point in his career, he had accumulated four Distinguished Flying Crosses. Now with an Air Force squadron, flying the F-86 Sabre jet, Glenn was ready to engage enemy Mikoyan-Gurevich MiG-15s. By 1952, the Soviet-built aircraft had been provided to a number of Communist nations, including North Korea. With "MiG-Mad Marine" painted in bright red letters on the fuselage of his F-86, Major John Glenn shot down three of the enemy aircraft in a five-day period. He was subsequently awarded his fifth Distinguished Flying Cross.

Right: Exhausted Marines take advantage of a lull in the fighting, and find the time to grab a moment's rest during their retreat from Chosin Reservoir. Bitter cold and snow would constantly plague the Marines who were fighting their way from Yudam-ni to Hagaru-ri.

battalion advanced, fire from Marine aircraft, artillery, and the brigade's tank battalion pummeled the crest of the ridge, but the heavy fire from Obong-ni Ridge continued. On the left of the ridge, Company A attacked repeatedly, but could not advance against the Communist firestorm. On the right of the ridge, Company B faired better, making slow progress with the aid of an 3.19 in. (81 mm) mortar barrage. By late afternoon, the northernmost hills belonged to the Marines.

That night, the North Koreans launched a counterattack spearheaded by four T-34 tanks. Marine Corsairs roared into the fight, killing one tank and strafing the enemy infantry. The remaining tanks were slowed by fire from 2.95 in. (75 mm) recoiless rifles and 3.5 in. (90 mm) rocket launchers. The new M-26 Pershing tanks went into action; 3.54 in. (90 mm) armor-piercing rounds slammed into the Soviet-built tanks with deadly results.

At 02:30 hours, the North Koreans again hit the thin Marine lines. Machine-gun fire from higher positions along the ridgeline poured into the Marines and the enemy broke through Company A. Lieutenant-Colonel George R. Newton ordered the position held at all cost, and saturated the area with supporting mortar and artillery fire. The North Koreans withdrew. The Marines renewed the assault on Obong-ni Ridge in the morning. Four NKPA machine-gun positions proved troublesome until a Corsair dropped a 500 lb. (225 kg) bomb on the target. After this, North Korean resolve crumbled: the 1st Battalion, 5th Marines secured Obong-ni, the 3rd Battalion advanced to the crest of Hill 207. By the morning of August 19, the last objective (Hill 311) was seized and three bridges across the Naktong River were in Marine hands. The Naktong salient ceased to exist.

On September 1, the NKPA launched a massive attack in a effort to destroy the Pusan perimeter. Thirteen North Korean divisions—some 98,000 men—stormed five separate positions around the city. The Army's 25th Division in the southwest, and the 2nd Division at Naktong were hardest hit; four NKPA divisions smashed into the 2nd Division, slicing it in two. A new North Korean salient was created, 6 miles (9.6 km) wide, 8 miles (12.8 km) deep. Obong-ni Ridge, once again, belonged to the enemy. By 13:00 hours, the Marines were on the move, returning to the Naktong Bulge. Battle plans called for the Marines to relieve an Army regiment positioned on a ridge just to the west of the town of Yongsan. From there, they were to launch an attack into the center of the salient. By the morning of September 3, the situation had changed. The Army regiment had been swept off the ridge, its lines pushed back 1,000 yards (1,094 m). The Marines were forced to fight their way to the line of departure.

The attack continued throughout the day. Marines advanced, fighting their way up steep hills, calling in artillery and air support when enemy fire was too heavy. The coordination between air and ground elements was wondrous. Colonel Paul L. Freeman, commander of the 23rd Infantry, wrote:

> "The Marines on our left were a sight to behold. Not only was their equipment superior to ours, but they had squadrons of air in direct support. They used it like artillery. … They had it day and night … we just have to have air support like that, or we might as well disband the Infantry and join the Marines."

Within three days, the advance of the NKPA divisions had been stopped, the units smashed: North Korean casualties numbered almost 10,000. It was the second time the Marines saved the Pusan perimeter.

Just after midnight on September 6, the Marines boarded trucks and returned to the city of Pusan. Walker had relinquished command of the brigade to MacArthur, who was now busily making plans. Three weeks earlier, MacArthur had pointed to the western coast of Korea and intoned gravely, "We shall land at Inchon and I shall crush them." Although MacArthur's plan was bold, it offered great opportunity. Inchon was less than 20 miles (32 km) from the capital city of Seoul. An amphibious force could seize the port, and from

The Marines on our left were a sight to behold. Not only was their equipment superior to ours, but they had squadrons of air in direct support. They used it like artillery. …we just have to have air support like that, or we might as well disband the Infantry and join the Marines.

Left: The Marine Corps artist Charles Waterhouse captures the determination and defiance of the Marines against the Communist forces as they move down the narrow road to Hagaru-ri.

MacArthur's plan was bold, but offered great opportunity. The capture of Seoul and nearby Kimpo airport would put MacArthur's forces fully on the offensive, within striking distance of the North.

there then proceed to drive inland. The capture of Seoul and the nearby Kimpo airport would put MacArthur's forces fully on the offensive, and they would also be within striking distance of the North.

Landing at Inchon

An assault of Inchon was, however, fraught with danger. At first glance, the port city seemed impregnable: to reach it, a task force would have to navigate the narrow Flying Fish Channel. The tides in the area further complicated any landing. Among the highest in the world, tides could range as much as 32 ft. (9.75 m). At low tide, the channel could not be traversed and the city's harbor was turned to huge mud flats. There were no beaches upon which to land, and the port was protected by concrete seawalls. Moreover, the island of Wolmi-do offered fine positions for the defense of the city.

Before the Marines landed at Inchon, Wolmi-do would have to be secured. Pre-invasion bombardment began on September 10. The landing was scheduled for September 15. At 06:33 hours, the 3rd Battalion, 5th Marines stormed ashore on Wolmi-do and moved inland against sporadic resistance. Twenty-two minutes later, the American flag flew proudly over Radio Hill. By noon, the entire island was in Marine hands.

At 14:30 hours, the bombardment of Inchon resumed. The city was soon ablaze. Smoke mixed with rain and fog, obscuring the landing beaches. Units became confused and the scene soon turned to chaos. Fortunately for the 1st Marines, under the command of Colonel Lewis "Chesty" Puller, resistance was light on Blue Beach. The initial objectives were easily seized, and Puller commented disdainfully on his new foes. The 1st and 2nd Battalions, 5th Marines landed side-by-side on Red Beach, in the heart of the city. The going was tougher, but 13,000 Marines were in Inchon by midnight. Twenty-two Marines had been killed and 174 wounded; MacArthur's gamble had paid off. Major General O.P. Smith, commander of the 1st Marine Division, ordered the attack resumed in the morning.

Below: As the 1st Marine Division moves toward Hagaru, Marines guard the flanks of the main column in the company of an M26 Pershing tank.

Left: The Marine artist John Groth captures well the sense of brutal cold which was faced by the Marines during their breakout from the Chosin Reservoir in the depths of winter. The Marines pictured here are trying desperately to stay warm, despite the fact that temperatures were plummeting to as low as –4° Fahrenheit (–20° Centigrade.)

Just after dawn on September 17, the NKPA launched its first counterattack. A column of infantry and five tanks approached an outpost of the 5th Marines. Corporal Okey Douglas knocked out the lead tank and damaged another with a 2.36 in. (60 mm) rocket launcher. From the rear, Pershing tanks, recoiless rifles, and 3.5 in. (90 mm) bazookas blasted the rest. The North Korean infantry was cut to pieces.

While the 1st Marines advanced toward Seoul, the 5th Marines diverged to the northeast, moving toward Kimpo Airfield. By the night of the 17th, the southern half of the airfield was held by the Marines. A North Korean tank attack was launched during the night, but the Leathernecks held. By mid-morning, Kimpo Airfield belonged to the Marines. The following day, three squadrons from the 1st Marine Aircraft Wing landed, and were soon ready to begin operations.

Puller's 1st Marines took increasingly heavy casualties as they moved toward Seoul. On September 19, the 2nd Battalion encountered minefields covered by North Korean machine guns and mortars. Artillery and air support were called in. Later

Left: Colonel Lewis "Chesty" Puller (with pipe), the acerbic commander of the 1st Marine Regiment. His unit was involved in many of the key battles of the war.

that morning, the 32nd Infantry replaced the 1st Battalion, 1st Marines. That event created more problems for Puller. Rather than continuing the attack, the 32nd Infantry spent the day mopping up and consolidating the line formerly held by the 1st Battalion. As the 2nd Battalion continued to advance, a gap opened on their right flank. It widened to some 3 miles (4.8 km), and the Marines began taking flanking fire from North Korean forces. The enemy was becoming much more organized and even more determined than before, but by evening the 1st Marines had managed to reach the hills which overlooked the city of Yongdung-po. Beyond the city lay the Han River, as well as the heavily populated and sprawling capital city of Seoul.

Before dawn on September 20, the North Koreans launched two counterattacks. The unoccupied heights of Hills 80 and 85 were seized, and Communist forces now stood between the 1st Marines and the Kalchon River. Simultaneously, a battalion-size force, led by five T-34 tanks, moved down the Inchon/Seoul highway and rolled into an ambush. Blocking the road was Company F of the 2nd Battalion, while Companies D and E occupied positions on each side of the highway. As howitzer fire coming from the 11th Marines covered their line of retreat, Marine proceeded to pour enormous weights of fire onto the North Korean forces. Only a half-hour later, the 2nd Battalion was again on the move and, by 12:30 hours, it had secured the first of two bridges which spanned the Kalchon River.

On the left flank, the 1st Battalion, 1st Marines relieved the 1st Battalion, 5th Marines and went on to capture Hills 80 and 85. During that action, Lieutenant Henry A. Commiskey earned the Medal of Honor. Armed with a pistol, Commiskey charged ahead of his men and jumped into a North Korean machine-gun emplacement. He disposed of the five-man crew, then moved on to the next emplacement, where he killed two more enemy soldiers. The remaining North Korean troops rapidly fled, and by the time evening fell, the high ground was in the hands of the U.S. Marines.

Below: The frozen remains of both US and British Royal Marines await burial near Koto-ri. Conditions were appalling, but the Marines carried themselves with distinction.

That same day, the 5th Marines crossed the Han River. The first attempt did not go well. Before dawn, swimmers from the division Recon Company crossed the Han. Finding no evidence of an enemy presence, they signaled the company to cross the river. The sound of the LVTs brought concentrated enemy fire onto the Marines. Four of the tractors became stuck in the mud and the advancing Marines pulled back. A bombardment of the east bank was ordered. Tanks, Marine Corsairs, and artillery pounded the North Korean positions. The Leathernecks made an attempt at a second crossing. By evening, the 5th Marines were across the Han.

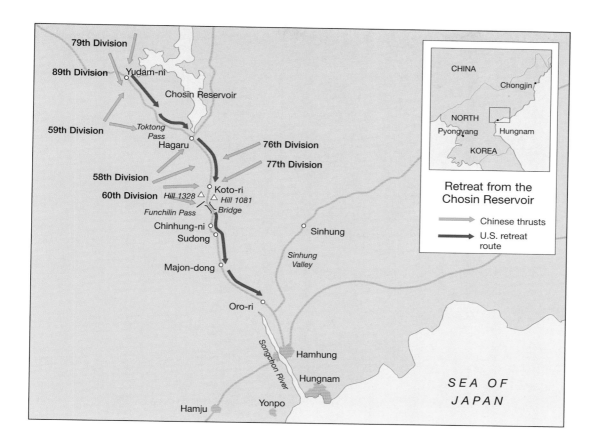

Retreat from the Chosin Reservoir

→ Chinese thrusts

→ U.S. retreat route

79th Division
89th Division
Yudam-ni
Chosin Reservoir
59th Division
Toktong Pass
Hagaru
76th Division
77th Division
58th Division
60th Division   Hill 1328
Koto-ri
Hill 1081
Funchilin Pass   Bridge
Chinhung-ni
Sudong
Sinhung
Sinhung Valley
Majon-dong
Oro-ri
Songchon River
Hamhung
Hungnam
SEA OF JAPAN
Hamju   Yonpo

CHINA
Chongjin
NORTH
Pyongyang   Hungnam
KOREA

Left: The fighting withdrawal which gathered pace on the way from Yudam-ni to the coast saw the Marines managing to beat off furious attacks from the Chinese forces on both flanks of their march.

That night, the city of Yongdung-po was smashed, set ablaze by a bombardment of rockets, incendiary bombs, and napalm. The following day, September 21, as the 5th Marines moved southeast toward Seoul, Puller's 1st Marines attacked the burning city. The 2nd Battalion continued to advance further along the Inchon-Seoul highway, while the 1st Battalion moved across country.

The 2nd Battalion crossed the bridge over the Kalchon and immediately came under heavy fire from an enemy-held ridgeline. Lieutenant-Colonel Allan Sutter ordered his 4.2 in. (107 mm) mortars to bombard the North Korean positions and sent Companies E and F to seize the high ground. Company D continued to move toward the second branch of the river. Both advances met heavy resistance and casualties mounted. Puller committed his 3rd Battalion, which had been held in reserve. For the 3rd Battalion, crossing the Kalchon was reminiscent of the trench warfare of World War I. As the Marines went over the dike, Maxim machine guns opened up. Lacking artillery support, Major Edwin H. Simmons, Weapons Company commander, called for six water-cooled Browning machine guns. The Brownings silenced the Maxims and the 3rd Battalion went on to cross the river.

While the rest of Puller's 1st Marines encountered heavy resistance, Captain Robert H. Barrow led Company A, 1st Battalion across a quiet rice paddy. Barrow's company slipped over the dike and entered Yongdung-po undetected, then advanced to the Kimpo–Seoul road. The Marines now held the main route of reinforcement or retreat. Scouting the immediate area, the Marines discovered a large building filled with weapons and supplies, protected by a group of North Koreans. A rifle grenade was fired and a massive explosion occurred as a well-camouflaged ammo dump blew skyward. The North Koreans were now without resources, but Company A was deep in enemy territory and on their own.

"In the moonlight I could see its turret with the long gun on it slowly circling back and forth, like some prehistoric steel-backed monster sniffing for prey."

Right: Marine aviators drop napalm onto Chinese positions during the breakout from Chosin. Marine air support was essential during this breakout, as it was heavy enough to clear the roadblocks which had been placed in front of the 1st Marine Division.

The Marines dug foxholes into the sides of a dike 25 ft. (7.6 m) high and had good fields of fire. As night fell, the North Koreans attacked. The rumble of tanks could be heard, moving down a dirt road that ran parallel to the Kimpo–Seoul highway. Private Morgan Brainard recalled the event,

"In the moonlight I could see its turret with the long gun on it slowly circling back and forth, like some prehistoric steel-backed monster sniffing for prey. I pressed tightly against the side of my hole and waited for the flash and fire of its gun."

The tanks began firing their 3.35 in. (85 mm) guns from a range of 30 ft. (9 m), making a total of five passes, but the Marines were well dug-in. They sustained only one casualty. Marine bazookas destroyed three of the T-34s. At 21:00 hours, a company-size force of North Korean infantry hit the Marine position, but the attack was repelled. Three more assaults also failed. In the morning, Barrow counted the bodies of some 275 dead North Koreans around the dike.

The 1st and 3rd Battalions advanced through Yongdung-po to relieve Company A. They encountered little resistance, for the North Koreans had withdrawn over the Han River. That same day, the 7th Marines arrived and moved into position north of Seoul. The 1st

Below: Marines move through a Korean village. After the Chinese offensive had been halted, the Marines were required to take part in General Ridgway's new push northwards towards the "Iron Triangle."

Marine Division was complete and ahead lay the capital city, defended by the 78th Independent Regiment and the 25th Brigade.

On September 22, the 5th Marines, under the command of Lieutenant-Colonel Raymond L. Murray, attacked from the northwest and met an enemy force 10,000 men strong. The 25th Brigade, comprised of men who had fought with the Communists in China, were dug into a hill complex that guarded the approaches to the capital city. It was four days of brutal combat, much of it hand-to-hand, a yard-by-yard advance supported by devastating air strikes and artillery and mortar barrages. Casualties were similar to the battlefields of the Pacific. Company D of the 2nd Battalion was virtually gone; only 26 men remained, the other 180 Marines having been killed or wounded. The 5th Marines, though, had battered their way through the North Korean main defensive line.

The Capture of Seoul

On the morning of September 25, the three Marine regiments were in position along a single front. The assault on Seoul began in earnest. At 07:00 hours, the 3rd Battalion, 1st Marines advanced up the broad Ma Po Boulevard. Enemy snipers fired from windows and threw Molotov cocktails onto the advancing Marines. What's more, the North Koreans had constructed roadblocks at major intersections; these were essentially small forts constructed out of filled rice bags. Despite the presence of mines, which destroyed two M-26 Pershing tanks, the remaining Pershings destroyed the first two roadblocks the Marines

Below: This Marine carries rifle grenades, which were used to take out Communist bunkers. By the summer of 1951, Marines were heavily engaged in brutal fighting near the "Punchbowl."

encountered. A third roadblock proved too heavily defended by mines and antitank guns. No support fire was available and the battalion assumed defensive positions. Major Edwin H. Simmons coordinated the defenses, bringing forward two rifle squads, Browning heavy machine guns, rockets, and 2.95 in. (75 mm) recoiless rifles.

In the early morning hours, the Marines heard the rumbling of tanks. The battalion's defenses were ready. The enemy fired the first shots, but the Marines responded immediately, pouring deadly fire onto the North Koreans. Five battalions of artillery, including an Army 6.1 in. (155 mm) howitzer unit, provided support. Just before dawn, the fighting subsided. Ma Po Boulevard was a scene of carnage. The hulks of seven T-34s littered the streets and some 475 enemy soldiers lay dead. The Marines called the area "Slaughterhouse Hill."

By September 26, the advance through Seoul continued, though at a very slow pace. Progress was, according to Chesty Puller, "agonizingly slow," for the process of eradicating the North Korean roadblocks was time-consuming. By the 27th, however, the resolve of the North Koreans was beginning to fail, and the Marine advance picked up speed. While Murray's 5th Marines fought for control of western Seoul, Puller's 1st Marines raised the flag over the U.S. Embassy, prompting one Army officer to comment that Marines would apparently rather carry a flag into battle than a weapon. Back came Puller's acerbic response: "A man with a flag in his pack and the desire to run it up on an enemy position isn't likely to bug out!"

The 7th Marines still battled north of the city. In its mission to protect the northern flank of the Marine Division, the regiment repelled an enemy counterattack at the Han River, then began to advance on Uijong-bu. It would be a bloody three-day battle for the 7th Marines. However, as September 28 dawned, the battle for the city of Seoul was over.

Below: Marines advance up a hill after clearing an enemy bunker. After their experiences in the Pacific in World War II, the Marines were experts in knocking out fortified enemy defenses.

Twelve days after the dangerous landing at Inchon, the ancient city was in U.N. hands and North Korean forces were in full retreat. The victory was not without cost: Marine casualties numbered 421 killed, another 2,029 wounded.

With the hope of reuniting the Korean peninsula, President Truman authorized MacArthur to push north of the 38th Parallel. Chou En-lai, Premier of Communist China, warned that his country would not tolerate "North Korea being savagely invaded by imperialists." Few took his warning seriously, and MacArthur ordered troops to advance up Korea's east coast and across the 38th Parallel. On October 15, the Marines set sail for Wonson. Initially, the plan called for an amphibious assault of the town, but this was made unnecessary by the rapid advance of the Eighth Army, which had broken out of the Pusan perimeter and moved north. By the time the Marines landed at the port, the ROK forces in the area had secured Wonson.

The 1st Marine Division was given a zone of action stretching 50 miles (80 km) wide and some 100 miles (160 km) north to south. While the 1st Marines remained in the vicinity of Wonson, the 5th and 7th Marines traveled north to relieve Korean troops near the Chosin Reservoir. It was a situation that worried Major General O.P. Smith. His Marines were scattered across the North Korean countryside, like Army forces in a land campaign. Unlike the Army command, Smith was not optimistic about the situation. The terrain where his Marines were heading to the north could only be described as forbidding. Winter, terribly cold in North Korea, was approaching. NKPA forces remained in the area and intelligence suggested that Chinese forces were crossing the Manuchurian border.

It was Puller's 1st Marines who initially entered combat in North Korea. The 1st Battalion was dispatched to the seaport of Kojo to relieve Korean troops. On the night of October 27, soldiers of the North Korean 5th Division hit the Marine lines. The battle raged throughout the night. As the day dawned, the 1st Battalion counted 74 casualties.

Chou En-lai, Premier of Communist China, warned that his country would not tolerate "North Korea being savagely invaded by imperialists." Few took his warning seriously.

Right: Marines of the legendary "Black Sheep" Squadron load a 5 in. (127 mm) rocket on a Vought F4U-4B Corsair. Beginning on August 7, 1950, four to ten of these veteran planes flew overhead continuously, providing close air support for the Leathernecks on the ground, whenever they needed it.

Below: A white phosphorous shell explodes in front of this Marine machine gunner. Phosphorous burns in contact with the air, and could start fires or inflict terrible burns on anyone it touched.

The 3rd Battalion was moved some 30 miles (48 km) west to occupy the village of Majon-ni. Nestled in a valley, Majon-ni sat astride an intersection of roads that connected Seoul, Wonson, and the North Korean capital of Pyongyang. On November 2, a Marine platoon was ambushed in a gorge south of the village by elements of the NKPA 15th Division. Over the course of the next two weeks, the Marines fought off attacks and fought through ambushes in the high mountain pass approaching the village. Then, relieved by an Army battalion, the 1st Marines moved north.

The route was a torturous one. The narrow gravel road ran north from Hungnam to Hamhung and into the forbidding Taebaek Mountains. For the first 43 miles (69 km), the road rose gently, then threaded its way through the towering heights of Funchilin Pass to Koto-ri. At the town of Hagaru-ri, the road divided; to the west lay the 4,000-ft. (1,220-m) Toktong Pass and Yadum-ni. This narrow road, frought with hazard, became the Marines' main supply route.

The 7th Marines led the way north. Almost immediately, they were attacked by elements of the 124th Chinese Division. While MacArthur denied first the presence of, then the tactical value of, Communist Chinese forces in North Korea, the Marines fought their way along the main supply route for the next five days. Lieutenant Joseph Owens described the first battle with the Chinese: "The eerie chant, 'M'line die! M'line die!' issuing from a chorus of Chinese voices, then the crash of mortars, the boom of concussion grenades, and the sharp sputter of burp guns [submachine guns.]

Marine Helicopters

Shortly after the outbreak of war in Korea, 7 pilots, 30 enlisted men and 4 Sikorsky HO3S-1 helicopters were ordered to service with the 1st Provisional Marine Brigade. As part of Marine Observation Squadron-6, they were the first helicopters in the fight.

Four years earlier General Roy Geiger had recommended a review of the Marine Corps' amphibious doctrine. After witnessing atomic testing at Bikini Atoll, Geiger was convinced new concepts were needed for the Corps to meet the challenges of warfare in the future. Geiger urged General A.A. Vandegrift, then Commandant of the Corps, to look for alternatives to traditional amphibious landings. One possible alternative was "vertical envelopment"—the use of helicopters.

In January 1948 the first experimental helicopter squadron, HMX-1 was formed at Quantico, VA. Four months later, the amphibious capabilities of the Sikorsky HO3S-1 were tested. During an exercise held at New River, North Carolina, helicopters lifted Marines from the escort carrier *Palau* to the beach. The first manual of amphibious helicopter doctrine, known as Phib-31, was created by Marine Colonels Merrill B. Twining and Victor H. Krulak.

When the Marines landed in Korea, the helicopters were quickly put to use. On August 3, 1950, brigade commander Brigadier-General Edward A. Craig climbed aboard to scout a location for his forward command post. During August alone, the HO3S-1s made 580 flights including reconnaissance, artillery spotting, evacuation of wounded and rescue missions. It was a harbinger of the future. One year later, Marine Helicopter Transport Squadron-161 arrived in Korea. Flying the larger Sikorsky HRS-1 (above), it was now possible for helicopters to transport troops and supplies. According to Marine Corps historian J. Robert Moskin, over the course of the next two years, Marine helicopter squadrons airlifted 60,000 men and 7.5 million pounds of cargo. Some 9,815 wounded were evacuated to rear echelon units for medical attention.

Seconds later, there was the deeper sound of answering Marine rifles and BARs, joined by the pound of our machine guns and the explosion of Marine grenades. The screams of wounded men soon added to the melange of sounds, along with profanities of rage in both languages. More rockets streaked above, splashing eerie tints of green and red. Enemy mortars walked the ridgeline, thundering … and raining clods of earth on my mortarmen."

The Chinese tactics employed during those five days would continue for weeks to come. They attacked at night, or established roadblocks along the narrow route, supported by positions on the surrounding heights. But on November 7, the Chinese simply disappeared.

The Chosin Reservoir

Over the next two weeks, the Marines continued to move north toward the Chosin Reservoir. A new enemy, however, rose to confront the Marines: the bitter cold of the North Korean winter. Temperatures plummeted and the wind blew unceasingly. The Marines descended into Yudam-ni on November 24. The following day, word came that the Eighth Army had been overrun by the Chinese, abandoning both equipment and

There were tracers from both sides, brilliant lines of red and orange, flashes of grenades, the flaming bursts of the machine guns, and burp guns and rifles winking like swarms of fireflies.

Above: Marine Corps artist John Degrasse depicts Marine helicopters landing near the front lines, providing immediate reinforcements for a hard-pressed sector. Helicopters gave the Marines the opportunity to respond quickly to new threats.

casualties. Worried, Smith slowed the advance of the 7th Marines to await the arrival of the 5th Marines.

By 18:30 hours on November 27, darkness and bitter cold engulfed Yudam-ni. The temperature plunged to –4 °F (–20 °C), and snow fell. Eight Chinese divisions, under the command of General Sung Shih-lun, moved through the night. Their mission was the complete destruction of the 1st Marine Division. Three divisions hit Marines at Yudam-ni. "… the Chinese threw everything they had at Yudam-ni. Their all-out attack started with a heavy barrage of mortar fire. Then came the red and green rockets and the flares and bugles, more than we had ever heard and seen before, and thousands of their soldiers poured through the mountains. … The sky filled with the arcing red streaks of the artillery shells, and the hills blossomed with their fiery explosions. Star shells popped high in the air, their stark blue light casting unearthly shadows across the snowy ground. There were tracers from both sides, brilliant lines of red and orange, flashes of grenades, the flaming bursts of the machine guns, and burp guns and rifles winking like swarms of fireflies."

Another Chinese force attacked Fox Company, which was holding Toktong Pass, and cut off the main supply route to Hagaru-ri. Hagaru-ri itself came under attack, as did the road south. Still another Chinese division smashed into Koto-ri.

As November 28 dawned, Smith took stock of the situation. The high ground east of Hagaru-ri was lost to the Chinese, as was the road south to Koto-ri; that supply route had to be opened. Smith also had the two regiments isolated at Yudam-ni; the attack on the Toktong Pass threatened their escape. The 5th and 7th Marines would have to fight their way south to Hagaru-ri. Smith arranged for parachute drops of supplies and ammunition to his embattled Marines at Yudam-ni, and ordered the 5th Marines to hold their ground. The 7th Marines were to reverse direction and clear the main supply route. He then ordered Puller's 1st Marines to open the road from Koto-ri to Hagaru.

On the morning of November 29, Puller dispatched Task Force Drysdale to break through to Hagaru-ri. Comprised of Company G of the 3rd Battalion, 1st Marines, Baker Company of the 31st Infantry, and the Royal Marines 41 Commando, the unit was under the command of Royal Marine Lieutenant-Colonel Douglas B. Drysdale. According to Marine Corps legend, in describing the tactical situation to the British commander, Puller commented, "They've got us surrounded. The bastards won't get away this time." As the task force advanced on Hagaru-ri, they encountered increasingly strong roadblocks and Chinese forces entrenched on the high ground. Two-and-a-half miles (4 km) north of

Koto-ri, Company G was hit with machine-gun and mortar fire. Drysdale decided to wait for the support of the two tank platoons Puller had sent to bolster the task force. When the advance was renewed, 17 tanks led the way, blasting enemy positions. Another 12 tanks followed. Corsairs flew overhead, providing close air support.

Halfway to Hagaru-ri, in a valley 1 mile (1.6 km) long, heavy enemy fire brought the column to a halt—Drysdale's task force had entered Hell Fire Valley. Men leapt from vehicles to return fire. A mortar shell struck an ammunition truck and blocked the narrow road, splitting the column into two. The units in front, the tanks, Company G, and most of the Royal Marines fought their way north to Hagaru-ri. The troops behind the burning truck attempted to turn around and return to Koto-ri, but the Chinese would not allow an escape. As darkness fell, the Corsairs could no longer provide air support, and many of the tanks to the rear of the column had been stopped by heavy fire. The enemy advanced and, by 02:00 hours, most of the men were out of ammunition. The Chinese demanded surrender. Marine Major John J. McLaughlin delayed the inevitable long enough for some men to escape over the mountains to Koto-ri.

To the north, the move to Hagaru-ri began. The 5th Marines withdrew from positions to the north and west of Yudam-ni, letting the 7th Marines fall back further south. Colonel Homer L. Litzenberg and Lieutenant-Colonel Murray, commanding the two regiments, realized that no breakout would occur unless Fox Company, still holding on at Toktong Pass, could be relieved. Litzenberg made four attempts to reach the beleaguered company, but each failed. Lieutenant-Colonel Raymond Davis, commanding the 1st Battalion, 7th Marines, offered up a plan: since Fox Company could not be reached by road, his battalion would move that night across the ridgetops. Litzenberg agreed.

As night fell on December 1, the remnants of the 1st Battalion, which had now been reinforced by Company H of the 3rd Battalion, began the 8-mile (13-km) trek to Toktong Pass. The temperature was down to –11 °F (–24 °C) and the wind howled around them mercilessly. Lieutenant Joseph Owen later recalled the horror of that night:

"The windborne cold attacked with terrible fury. When we stopped for bearings, we stood silent and motionless. Because we needed to maintain silence, we could not slap our hands against our sides or stomp our feet to maintain circulation. The cold gnawed at our toes and fingers and ate into our bodies. The sweat we generated while climbing froze to our skin. Time had no meaning. We labored through infinite darkness in ghostly clouds of snow over an icy path that rose and fell

The cold gnawed at our toes and fingers and ate into our bodies ... We saw only the back of the man ahead ... We carried on with the only strength that was left to us, Marine Corps discipline.

Below: A section of Marines take cover from enemy fire before launching an attack on the enemy's position.

Army commanders recommended a full retreat that left behind all weapons and equipment. Likewise, the Air Force offered to evacuate the Marines in an "aerial Dunkirk."

and seemed to lead nowhere. We saw only the back of the man ahead, a hunched figure in a shapeless parka, whose every tortured step was an act of will. We carried on with the only strength that was left to us, Marine Corps discipline."

By mid-morning, the battalion fought their way through Chinese forces and made radio contact with Fox Company. Captain William E. Barbar, commanding Company F, had been badly wounded, but offered to lead a patrol to guide Davis to their position. Davis declined, and at 11:25 hours on December 2, the 1st Battalion reached Company F.

"We were astonished by our first view of Fox Hill. The snowfield that led up to the embattled company's position was covered with hundreds of dead Chinese soldiers. … Men stood in wonder. Men bowed their heads in prayer. Some fell to their knees. … Tears came to the eyes of the raggedy Marines who had endured bitter cold and savage battle to reach this place of suffering and courage."

Both Davis and Barber were awarded the Medal of Honor. The defense of the Toktong Pass and the 1st Battalion's trek through North Korea's bitter cold to provide relief stand among the greatest acts of courage in Marine Corps history.

As the 1st Battalion left Yudam-ni, the 5th Marines began to fight their way down the main supply route. Seventy-nine hours later, a ragged column of Marines entered Hagaru-ri. During the period from November 30 to December 4, the 1st Marine Division had sustained horrific casualties: Marine dead numbered 219, and another 921 men had been wounded; severe frostbite and other non-battle related conditions claimed another 1,194 Marines.

Army commanders recommended a full retreat that left behind all weapons and equipment. Likewise, the Air Force offered to evacuate the Marines in an "aerial Dunkirk." Major General Smith declined, stating "We will fight our way out as Marines, bringing all our weapons and gear with us." He began to coordinate the next stage of the breakout. Marine fighters would give close air support, with Navy and Air Force fighters positioned further from the column. Air Force transports were to evacuate the wounded.

Above: Armed with a Browning automatic rifle, a squad support weapon which had seen widespread use in World War II, a Marine prepares to search a house for any sign of the enemy. Note the size of the pack he carries.

On December 6, the breakout south from Hagaru-ri began. With the aid of Marine Corsairs, the 5th Marines cleared East Hill, which dominated the road to Koto-ri. That night, the Chinese counterattacked in force. It was one of the fiercest engagements of the campaign. The Marines and reinforcing Army troops suffered heavy casualties, but inflicted severe losses on their enemy: some 800 Chinese soldiers lay dead; over 200 more had been taken prisoner.

By the morning of December 7, lead elements of the column entered Koto-ri. By midnight, the last elements of the 1st Marine Division arrived. Engineers had blown the

bridges behind them. Smith, however, was well aware he had to keep the column moving: aerial reconnaissance indicated that the Chinese were advancing across country, in an attempt to cut off the division's move south. As casualties were evacuated, Marine, Royal Marine, and Army dead were buried. A mass grave was dug out of the frozen earth. Each fallen man was wrapped in a sleeping bag or parachute, and covered over. Major General Smith attended, as did Litzenberg, Murray, and Puller.

As lead elements of the column set out from Koto-ri, heavy snow fell and visibility was reduced to nothing. Air support was grounded. Throughout the day, the 7th Marines fought southward, clearing the main supply route and seizing the dominating terrain to the west. Yet another problem, however, threatened to entrap the column, which had swelled to over 1,400 vehicles. The Chinese had blown a bridge over a sharp chasm, and there was no way around. Engineers called for sections of "Treadway Bridge." The following morning, the Air Force dropped eight of the large pieces by parachute, and the new bridge was quickly installed. By late afternoon, vehicles rumbled across the expanse, but a crossing bulldozer damaged the plywood decking. Once again, the engineers went to work. Repairing the bridge, they placed the treadways as far apart as possible. Tanks could pass with a few inches to spare, jeeps had less than a half-inch (1 cm). Throughout the night, the long column crossed the bridge.

At 02:45 hours on December 10, the lead elements of the 1st Marine Division reached Chinhung-ni. Later that afternoon, the rear guard departed Koto-ri. Chesty Puller was the last senior officer to depart. He left when the tanks did, his Jeep carrying dead and wounded Marines. Puller was on foot, encouraging his men, "You're the 1st Marine Division. ... We're the greatest military outfit that ever walked on this earth. Not all the Communists in hell can stop you."

During the long reaches of the night and in the snow storms many a Marine prayed for the coming of day or the clearing weather when he knew he would again hear the welcome roar of your planes as they dealt out destruction to the enemy.

Above: Marines move cautiously through a trench in Korea's rugged countryside. The war settled down to a stalemate. No more large offensives were launched, but small tactical battles continued to be waged along the front line.

By the morning of December 12, the 1st Marine Division reached Hungnam. It was a feat they could not have achieved without the aid of Marine aviators. The close air support they provided was instrumental to the breakout from the Chosin Reservoir. Major General Smith gratefully acknowledged the aviators in a message he sent to Major-General Field Harris, commander of the 1st Marine Aircraft Wing.

"During the long reaches of the night and in the snow storms many a Marine prayed for the coming of day or the clearing weather when he knew he would again hear the welcome roar of your planes as they dealt out destruction to the enemy … never in its history has Marine aviation given more convincing proof of its indispensible value to ground Marines."

The 1st Marine Division suffered 4,400 casualties during the breakout and thousands more cases of frostbite and pneumonia, but the Chosin Reservoir campaign remains one of the greatest moments in Marine Corps history. It was a tactical masterpiece, a campaign since synonymous with the words "courage" and "valor." Major-General Smith stated "No division commander has ever been privileged to command a finer body of men."

By December 15, the Marines were aboard transports bound for Pusan. There, they would recuperate from the hardships of Chosin and absorb replacements.

Ridgway Takes Command

With the new year came changes in the command structure. Lieutenant-General Walton Walker perished after his jeep was struck by an ROK truck. General Matthew B. Ridgway took command of the Eighth Army. His first priority was to rebuild the confidence of American fighting forces in Korea. On New Year's Eve, a Chinese-North Korean attack pushed the U.N. front back. Seoul, Inchon, and Wonju once again belonged to the enemy. Ridgway assigned the 1st Marine Division a sector stretching from Pohang on Korea's east coast to Andong. Their mission was to hunt down Communist guerrillas and to serve as a roadblock in the event of a renewed enemy assault on the port cities of Pohang and Pusan. The U.S. 24th Infantry Division recaptured Inchon and Kimpo Airfield on February 10. The Chinese immediately launched a counterattack. As their offensive died out, Ridgway planned a counteroffensive of his own. Named "Operation Killer," it would begin at 08:00 hours on February 21.

The 1st Marine Division jumped off from Wonju with the 1st Marines on the left, the 5th Marines positioned on the right. The objective was a ridgeline south of Hoengsong, situated 8 miles (12.8 km) to the north. The Marines advanced through drenching rains, melting snow, and mud. There was little resistance until February 23, when the 1st Marines encountered a battalion of enemy forces which was entrenched on a hill. However, air strikes destroyed the enemy positions, with the effect that the ridgeline was in Marine hands by the following day.

Left: Marine 3.5 in. (90 mm) rockets are fired at enemy positions in a blaze of light. The Marines as well as the other U.N. forces relied on their firepower and aerial superiority during the three years that the Korean war lasted in order to counteract the sheer numerical advantage enjoyed by their Communist opponents.

General Ridgway continued to pressure the enemy, moving his troops northward. The Marines encountered increasingly stiff resistance and were hampered by lack of air support. Although MacArthur had made an unofficial promise to General Lemuel Shepherd that Marine ground forces would not be separated from their close air support, after Chosin, however, he let the Air Force establish a Joint Operations Center (JOC). All air assets in Korea, including the 1st Marine Air Wing (MAW), were controlled through Eighth Army headquarters. Any request for air support was evaluated by the JOC, which did not consider close air support for ground troops a high priority. Indeed, requests to the JOC often got no response. General Shepherd pressured the Air Force, which finally agreed that Marine aircraft on *reconnaissance* missions could be diverted to support Marine ground forces.

Left: An F9F Panther laden with iron bombs prepares to take off for another sortie against the Communists. The Korean war saw Marine Corps aviation move into the jet age, although World War II-vintage planes such as the F4 Corsair continued to do sterling work.

With artillery support and a company of tanks, the Marines moved north of Hoengsong on March 4. Three days later, Ridgeway launched "Operation Ripper." The objective was to disrupt any preparations for a Communist offensive and to recapture the city of Seoul. A week later, ROK forces discovered Seoul had been deserted. The push north continued. Heavy spring rains and mud hampered progress almost as much as enemy fire, but on April 4, the 7th Marines crossed the 38th Parallel. Ahead, in an area the Marines called the "Iron Triangle," the Chinese were fortifying their position.

The Firing of MacArthur

One week later, President Truman announced that MacArthur was relieved of his command. Said Truman, "I could no longer tolerate his insubordination." By April 22, the 1st Marine Division had advanced to Hwachon Reservoir. Although there had been short, fierce battles with pockets of Chinese forces, resistance was generally light. That night, however, the Chinese launched their spring offensive. An estimated half-million Chinese troops rushed out of the Iron Triangle. The brunt of the attack fell upon the 6th ROK Division on the Marines' right flank. The forces crumbled under the onslaught and a gap opened in the line. Smith ordered the 1st Marines, his reserve, into position to protect his flank. The heaviest fighting was on the left of the division line, where the 1st Battalion, 7th Marines battled more than 2,000 Chinese soldiers. In three hours of fighting, much of it hand-to-hand, the Leathernecks beat back the enemy. With the entire Eighth Army front under heavy attack, Smith received orders to fall back. By the end of April, the 1st Marine Division was in a defensive position near Hongchon.

On May 16, the Chinese launched the second phase of the offensive. The blow fell to the Marines' right, crushing two ROK divisions and opening a hole 20 miles (32 km) wide and 30 miles (48 km) deep. The Marines repelled two substantial thrusts, then shifted to cover the 2nd US Infantry Division. By May 20, the Chinese, weakened by very heavy losses, withdrew to the north. The Eighth Army, now commanded by Lieutenant-General James Van Fleet, took the offensive. The Marines advanced northward, passing the Hwachon Reservoir. For the Leathernecks, the move through rugged, mountainous country became a series of battles over hill after endless hill. By late June, however, two months of brutal fighting came to an end after the Marines succeeded in seizing the series of ridges overlooking a deep circular valley known as "the Punchbowl." At Kaesong, peace talks began.

By late August, the Communists left the talks and the Marines were ordered to take two strongly defended ridges on the northern rim of the Punchbowl. The next 20 days were ones of bitter

Below: A Marine sniper team in Korea. With the front stabilized, targets of opportunity were few and far between, but Marine snipers took a steady toll on the enemy.

fighting. The Communists forces fought with great determination and with strong artillery support. Mines and mortars took a vicious toll. Once again, lack of close air support contributed to the heavy casualties sustained by the Marines—it was, in the understated words of Major-General Gerald Thomas, who had assumed command of the division, "unsatisfactory." In four particularly brutal days, the 1st and 7th Marines sustained over 800 casualties as they fought wave after wave of Communist troops on Hill 749. On September 20, 1951, General Van Fleet ended the offensive, and this date also marked the end of the war of movement in Korea.

Above: A Marine fires a 3.5 in. (90 mm) rocket launcher. Introduced in 1950, the "Super Bazooka" was designed for use as an antitank weapon, but was also used against enemy bunkers and other defensive positions.

It was not, however, to be the end of the fighting. In late March, the Marines were moved 180 miles (290 km) west, and positioned to the left flank of the U.N. front. Here, they assumed responsibility for 32 miles (52 km) of the Jamestown Line overlooking Panmunjom (site of the ongoing peace talks) and for the defense of the Pyongyang–Seoul corridor. This large sector was defended by a series of outposts, often lightly manned, and there were an estimated 50,000 Chinese troops in this area. There were no more major offensives, but the Marines would sustain 40 percent of their total casualties during this period alone, which would later be known as "the Outpost War."

Localized battles were fought at "Bunker Hill" and the "Hook." Then, between March 26 and 29, 1953, the Chinese launched a desperate offensive. Ten miles (16 km) northeast of Panmunjom, the 5th Marines occupied outposts "Reno", "Vegas," and "Carson." The Chinese hit in strength, enemy forces outnumbering the Marines almost twenty-to-one. Reno fell first. The defenders of Vegas and Carson managed to hold on for four days, often fighting the attacking Chinese hand-to-hand at this point with bayonets and knives. Marine casualties for those four days numbered a total of 1,015.

The fighting continued until 22:00 hours on July 27, when the armistice signed at Panmunjom went into effect and thousands of white star cluster shells illuminated the front. During the three years that the Korean War had raged, Marine casualties were substantial: 4,267 Marines had been killed, another 23,744 wounded. General Smith had delivered the most fitting epitaph for these men some months before the war's end: "Wherever they lie, the memory of what they did, and their sacrifice, will be remembered by their brothers-in-arms." The outstanding performance of the 1st Marine Division prompted President Truman to sign into law a statute that defined the Corps as "a separate service with the Department of the Navy, sized at a minimum of three divisions and three air wings and awarded primacy in amphibious warfare." The Marine Corps had achieved yet another unparalleled victory.

CHAPTER SIX

VIETNAM

As the Korean War drew to a close,
many Marines wondered whether they
would be deployed to southeast Asia,
to aid the French fighting in Vietnam.
If nothing else, to the men of the
1st Marine Division, who had survived
the Chosin Reservoir campaign,
Vietnam offered warmth.
American involvement in southeast Asia,
however, was still at a very early stage.

Left: Marines move through a Vietnamese village during Operation Red
Snapper, a search and destroy mission, on October 22, 1965.

Throughout the late 1950s and early 1960s, Marine attention was often focused elsewhere. In 1958, four battalions of Marines deployed to Lebanon. In 1962, the Cuban missile crisis loomed; Marines reinforced Guantanamo Bay and prepared for war. By 1965, civil war had come to the Dominican Republic. Fearing Cuban intervention, President Johnson ordered 6,000 Marines ashore, their mission to evacuate American citizens from Santo Domingo. As order was restored and security forces from the Organization of American States arrived in the Dominican Republic, the Marines were withdrawn.

During this time, however, American involvement in southeast Asia continued to grow. Soon, large numbers of Marines were committed to service in Vietnam. There, they fought a very different kind of war—there was no Guadalcanal, no Peleliu, no Iwo Jima or Inchon. General Raymond G. Davis said,

> "In my previous wars … my men and I fought for clearly defined objectives. We had to secure that beachhead, take that island, capture that hill. We met the enemy on the battlefield, defeated him, and claimed victory. Unfortunately, it wasn't that way in Vietnam."

Instead, it was a war of endless patrols; of ambushes and booby traps; of fierce firefights against a silent, swift, elusive enemy; of capturing a hill only to leave it behind to seek the enemy elsewhere. In this war, 14,691 Marines would die, and another 88,633 be wounded.

The Geneva Accords of 1954 divided Vietnam. To the north, Ho Chi Minh and the Lao Dong party were at the head of a Marxist government. The south, ostensibly democratic but undoubtedly corrupt and with little support from the populace, was under the leadership of Ngo Dihn Diem. In 1954, President Eisenhower offered economic aid to the embattled Diem and established the Military Assistance and Advisory Group. Initially MAAG's role was the demonstration of U.S. military equipment. By late 1954, however, its role was one of training and organization: the United States committed to providing weapons and training for 90,000 Vietnamese troops. Less than six months after the defeat of French forces at Dien Bien Phu in 1954, the first U.S. Marine arrived in Vietnam.

Below: Marines of the 3rd Battalion, 3rd Marines board a Sea Knight helicopter via its rear ramp near the DeMilitarized Zone (DMZ).

Lieutenant-Colonel Victor Croizat was assigned as an advisor to the Vietnamese Marine Corps. His mission was to train, to motivate, to turn the Vietnamese Marines into an effective fighting force.

It was not until 1962, however, that the first Marine units deployed to Vietnam. Forty-two Marines of the 1st Radio Company were dispatched to Pleiku, in the mountainous Central Highlands. On April 9, Marine Medium Helicopter Squadron 362 (HMM-362), landed at Soc Trang to begin Operation Shu-Fly. The squadron provided support for ARVN combat troops, flying over 50 missions before being relieved by HMM-163.

Left: In the vivid colors of battle, Marine Corps combat artist J.T. Dyer, Jr. captures two Marines engaged in a firefight with the enemy along the DeMilitarized Zone.

Below: The primary area of Marine operations in Vietnam was the I Corps Tactical Zone in the very north of the country.

By September, operations moved to the airbase at Da Nang. In April 1963, a platoon from the 3rd Marine Division, based in Okinawa, arrived. Its mission was to strengthen security at the airfield.

U.S. involvement in Vietnam now escalated at an alarming rate. In 1964, in the Gulf of Tonkin off the coast of North Vietnam, the American vessels *Maddox* and *C. Turner Joy* came under attack from North Vietnamese torpedo-boats. In response, President Lyndon B. Johnson ordered air attacks against North Vietnamese targets, and Congress overwhelmingly passed the "Gulf of Tonkin Resolution," which authorized Johnson to use whatever means necessary to prevent further aggression against the United States.

On March 8, 1965, the seas off Da Nang were heavy. Aboard the vessels USS *Henrico*, *Union*, and *Vancouver* was the 9th Marine Expeditionary Brigade, under the command of Brigadier-General Frederick J. Karch. The Marines had been warned of Viet Cong infiltrators in Da Nang and told that opposing fire could come from any quarter. At 09:02 hours, the first American ground combat forces committed to Vietnam waded ashore. Battalion Landing Team 3/9 were

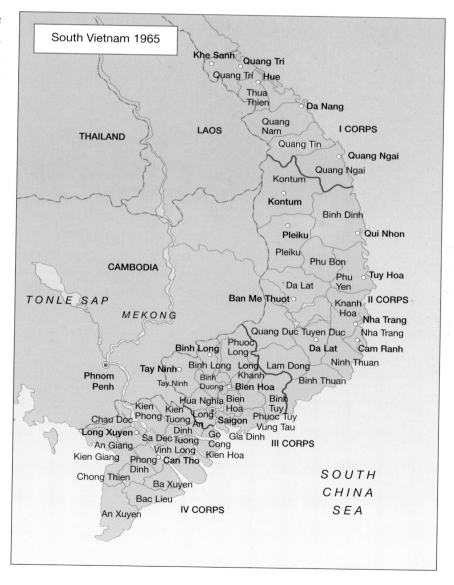

South Vietnam 1965

met not by fire from the guns of the Viet Cong, but by local dignitaries and Vietnamese girls, who were waiting to present them with garlands of flowers.

The primary mission of the 9th MEB was to strengthen the defenses of Da Nang Air Base. The 1st Battalion, 3rd Marines provided perimeter security. Company I, 3rd Battalion, 9th Marines moved immediately to the ridgeline west of the field, and took up its positions on Hill 327. Company K dug in on Hill 268 to the north. Shortly after that point, a Hawk missile battery belonging to the 1st Light Anti-Aircraft Battalion was ready and set up in firing position.

The Marine build-up in Vietnam continued. On April 11, the first fixed-wing Marine squadron arrived when VMFA-531 flew its F4B Phantom IIs into Da Nang. The same day, the 2nd Battalion, 3rd Marines arrived. Three days later, the 3rd Battalion, 4th Marines moved up the Perfume River to Phu Bai, 7 miles (11 km) southeast of the ancient city of Hue. On May 6, 1965, 6,000 Marines of the 3rd Amphibious Brigade came ashore on a sandy, barren beach 57 miles (92 km) south of Da Nang. The area was called Chu Lai. Lieutenant-General Victor "Brute" Krulak, commander of the Fleet Marine Force, Pacific, had chosen it for a new air base. Seabees and Marine Engineers completed runway construction 25 days later. Eight A-4 Skyhawks of Marine Air Group-12 came from the Philippines to give air support.

By late summer, four Marine regiments were in Vietnam, as were four Marine air groups. Their primary area of operation was the I Corps' Tactical Zone. Comprised of the five northern provinces of Quang Tri, Thua Thien, Quang Nam, Quang Tin, and Quang Ngai, "I Corps" stretched from the DeMilitarized Zone (DMZ) along the North Vietnamese border to the Annimite Mountains at Sa Huynh. It was an area 265 miles (427 km) long, and though South Vietnamese Government forces controlled the towns, the Viet Cong controlled the countryside. Marine patrols uncovered anti-personnel mines, booby traps, and hundreds of deadly *punji* stake traps—sharpened bamboo stakes dipped in excrement and embedded in camouflaged holes. With increasing regularity, firefights erupted between the Marines and the Viet Cong. Ninety days after their arrival, the Marines had suffered 209 casualties, including 29 men killed in action. At that point, Commandant Wallace M. Greene, Jr told the press that Marines were in Vietnam in order to "kill Viet Cong."

Above: Most Marines in 1965 were armed with the M14 rifle, an updated version of the M1 Garand used by their predecessors in World War II. Only this soldier's M1 helmet cover is camouflaged.

The Marines Go on the Offensive

The course of the war changed forever on August 6, when Major-General Lew Walt, commanding the newly created III Marine Amphibious Force, received official permission to go on the offensive. Intelligence reports indicated that the 1st VC Regiment was concentrated in the Van Thuong Peninsula and planned to attack Chu Lai, some 15 miles (24 km) to the north. Walt decided to strike the Viet Cong before they moved against Chu Lai. Three companies of the 3rd Battalion, 3rd Marines were to approach from the sea, land to the south and east of Van Thuong, and prevent any Viet Cong from escaping to the south. The 2nd Battalion, 4th Marines was to be inserted by helicopter; three different landing zones formed an arc to the southwest of Van Thuong. Finally, a company of Marines was to move south from Chu Lai and establish a blocking position northwest of the peninsula. The Marines would then sweep across Van Thuong to the sea, with artillery batteries at Chu Lai providing support, along with two U.S. destroyers and a cruiser.

On August 18, the Marines launched Operation Starlite, the first offensive of the war. Led by Colonel Oscar Peatross, the reinforced 7th Marines executed the three-pronged assault. Van Thuong was a VC stronghold, and the enemy was holed up in caves, tunnels, and spiderholes, while the small villages were fortified with barbed wire and *punji* traps. During six days of bitter, localized fighting, the Marines called in support from artillery, naval gunfire, and aircraft. At times, the Skyhawks and Phantoms dropped ordnance within 164 ft. (50 m) of Marine positions. At the end of the six days of combat, more than 600 Viet Cong bodies were counted. Never again did the enemy willingly engage the Marines in a pitched battle. Instead, they reverted to the tactics of guerrilla warfare.

On the night of October 27, enemy sappers struck. These were the *dac cong*, highly trained combat engineers who slipped silently through the night, clearing passages through the perimeter defenses. At the Chu Lai airfield, 20 penetrated the Marine lines. Machine-gun fire and satchel charges destroyed two of MAG-12's A-4 Skyhawks and severely damaged six more. The simultaneous attack on the helicopter facility at Marble Mountain,

Below: A Marine of Company M, 3rd Battalion, 4th Marines moves forward with a 3.5 in. (90 mm) round. This photograph was taken near the DMZ during Operation Prairie (August 3, 1966–January 31, 1967.)

Above: Marine Private First Class Robert H. Murray moves cautiously through Vietnam's thick jungle. The Viet Cong enemy were experts at concealment and ambush.

south of Da Nang, was much more destructive. Under a heavy mortar barrage, the *dac cong* entered the base, six reaching the flight line. Setting off Bangalore torpedoes and satchel charges, they destroyed 24 helicopters and damaged 23 more. Brigadier General Edwin Simmons stated, "Later, as the war wore on, it would come to be accepted that no number of American defenders could guarantee an absolute defense against rockets or mortars or even determined sappers."

By late fall, Viet Cong forces were on the move. Hiep Duc, district headquarters in Quang Tri Province, was overrun by a revitalized 1st Viet Cong Regiment. Marine helicopters lifted two ARVN battalions into an area west of the town. The first wave of helicopters landed unopposed but the second wave took heavy fire from a North Vietnamese Army antiaircraft battalion entrenched on a ridgeline. Twenty-one helicopters were hit. Within minutes, Skyhawks and Phantoms began the systematic pounding of the enemy-held positions. In several hours of hard fighting, aided by Marine air support, the South Vietnamese recaptured Hiep Duc. Surviving VC slipped into the Que Son Mountains. General Nguyen Chanh Thi, commander of the South Vietnamese forces and short of manpower, ordered the town abandoned.

On December 8, Operation Harvest Moon began. Its purpose was to clear Viet Cong forces from the Que Son Valley. The plan was simple. Two battalions of the 5th ARVN Regiment were to move southwest along one of the roads entering the valley. After contact with the enemy was made, the 2nd Battalion, 7th Marines (2/7) was to be inserted behind the Viet Cong to force them into the advancing ARVN troops. The 3rd Battalion, 3rd Marines was to be used to reinforce the 2/7 as needed.

The 5th ARVN Regiment moved out of Thang Binh. Halfway to Que Son, the men were ambushed by the 70th VC Battalion. The enemy let the ARVN close to within 66 ft. (20 m), then opened fire. Within 15 minutes, one-third of the ARVN force was destroyed. Marine helicopters evacuated the wounded and, later that night, inserted another ARVN battalion. In the morning, however, South Vietnamese forces again came under heavy attack. The 60th and 80th VC Battalions struck, killing the ARVN regimental commander and scattering what remained of his force.

General Walt committed the two Marine battalions. The 2nd Battalion, 7th Marines was to push east, while the 3rd Battalion, 3rd Marines was to drive to the northwest, squeezing the enemy between the two forces. On December 10, the 2nd Battalion, 1st Marines landed between them, to block any avenue of escape to the south. After a day of heavy fighting, the enemy vanished, apparently into the Phuoc Ha Valley, a known VC stronghold. B-52s, flying out of Guam, made their first strikes in Vietnam when they hit the Phuoc Ha Valley just before the Marines entered it. Over the next few days, the Marines were to uncover large caches of supplies and equipment which belonged to the enemy, but by this point, the Viet Cong had faded away.

By the end of 1965, 454 Marines had been killed, another 2,093 wounded. The escalation of the war, however, continued. General Westmoreland saw victory in a war of attrition. Territorial gains were unimportant; what mattered was the body count: the goal was to kill more Viet Cong and North Vietnamese Army troops than could be replaced. To "fix, find, and destroy" enemy forces, large-scale "search and destroy" operations were required.

Above: Marine Corps combat artist L.H. Dermott's depiction of five Marines moving quietly along a river near Hoi An.

Left: "Golf" Company, 2nd Battalion, 9th Marines approach the hamlet of Ha Chou on a patrol. Stealth was vital, as wooden boats such as these were extremely vulnerable to enemy fire.

Below: Marines of the 1st
Battalion, 4th Marines
wade ashore near Sa
Huynh during Operation
Deckhouse IV in January
1967. The Marines were
to destroy enemy forces in
the area prior to the
construction of a U.S.
Army Special Forces camp.

Unfortunately, these contradicted Marine tactics, which emphasized the importance of countering the guerrillas. Though Westmoreland was scornful, General Walt was convinced that the objective of the war was to win the loyalty of the populace to the government in Saigon. The only way to accomplish that was to counter the Viet Cong presence, and to that end, the Marines undertook the development of the combined-action platoons. These were typically a squad of Marines assigned to a village to provide security. With near-constant patrolling, the Marines maintained a highly visible presence, which was gradually to be extended as manpower became available. General Westmoreland later wrote:

> "I believed the Marines should have been trying to find the enemy's main forces and bring them to battle, thereby putting them on the run and reducing the threat they posed to the population. ... Rather than start a controversy, I chose to

issue orders for specific projects that as time passed would gradually get the Marines out of their beachheads."

By December 1965, intelligence reports indicated the 325A NVA Division was operating along the southern boundary of I Corps. In a coordinated attack, the Marines, with the support of the 2nd ARVN Division, were to strike enemy forces within the Quang Ngai province. To the south, in II Corps Tactical Zone, the U.S. Army's 1st Cavalry Division and elements of the 22nd ARVN Division were to find and destroy the enemy base. Operation Double Eagle was planned to begin early the following year, in January 1966.

In the largest amphibious operation of the war to date, the 3rd Battalion, 1st Marines and 2nd Battalion, 4th Marines landed near Thach Tru. Before the operation was over, two more battalions were committed. Over the course of the next few weeks, the Marines had only intermittent contact with the Viet Cong. Said one company commander, "The VC would hit us, then pull out. They wouldn't stick around." The Marines swept the area, but it soon became apparent that the Viet Cong had moved south into Binh Dinh province.

Above: A Marine F-8A flies close air support near the Khe Sanh Combat Base, dropping napalm canisters on the enemy. This painting is the work of Marine Corps artist Ned Conlon.

Throughout February and March, however, the Marines engaged in some very heavy fighting. In late February, the 2nd Battalion, 1st Marines went to the aid of an ARVN regiment near Phu Bai. By March 3, intelligence reported that the 21st NVA Regiment was northwest of Quang Ngai City. The 7th Marines, together with the 2nd ARVN Division, were ordered to attack. The plan involved a battalion of ARVN airborne troops landing first to secure the landing zone. A Marine battalion would then follow, and together the force was to sweep the area to the southeast along Highway 527.

Early on the morning of March 4, Marine Skyhawks and Phantoms bombed the area around the selected landing zone. Despite the preparatory bombardment, Marine helicopters carrying the ARVN forces took very heavy 0.5 in. (12.7 mm) antiaircraft fire. All four of the UH-1Es Huey gunships that accompanied the force were hit. Marine air dropped napalm on the enemy positions. The airlift continued, as did enemy fire. By afternoon, both battalions were on the ground. Lieutenant-Colonel Leon N. Utter

There we were, taking it from three sides, the front and both flanks, and from an enemy who was literally hugging us so we wouldn't use our supporting arms.

ordered his Marines to secure the area, including the important terrain of Hills 85 and 97. They encountered only light resistance. The ARVN battalion to the north was not so fortunate. As they approached Hill 50, they ran into a firestorm. The ARVN commander requested the aid of the Marines. Utter moved his Marines to the north, where he planned to tie in to the right flank of the ARVN battalion. The Marines had advanced only a few hundred yards when two battalions of the 21st NVA Regiment opened fire. With his Marines simply too close to the NVA positions, Utter was unable to call for artillery or air support. The Marines took cover behind rice paddy dikes but "NVA heavy machine-gun fire was delivered at so close a range that it actually destroyed sections of the dikes."

Utter's situation deteriorated. Company H occupied the right flank of the Marine lines. Although they had battled forward and were approaching the NVA positions, an NVA company had maneuvered south and hit Company H on its right rear flank. To the left, the ARVN battalion failed to advance, creating a gap and leaving Company F vulnerable. Utter radioed the ARVN battalion commander, requesting the gap be closed. His request was refused. The NVA seized the opportunity and struck the exposed flank. Utter later complained:

> "Our left flank was wide open, with nothing to put there. But the PAVNs [People's Army of Vietnam] had plenty of people so they poured through ... and back to the south the enemy was going at it again with 'H' Company. And there we were, taking it from three sides, the front and both flanks, and from an enemy who was literally hugging us so we wouldn't use our supporting arms."

Fighting raged late into the afternoon. Utter faced a desperate situation:

> "... darkness coming ... up against superior numbers ... no reserve, the enemy increasing his fire and his movement around us; wounded and dead on our hands; and fast running out of ammunition."

Right: Marines carry a buddy killed in action near Tam Ky. The 1st and 3rd battalions, 5th Marines engaged in heavy fighting during Operation Union II in May/June 1967.

The M60 Machine Gun

After World War II, the search began for a lighter weapon to replace the M1917 and M1919. Borrowing heavily from German designs, the M60 was a general purpose machine gun. Weighing 23 lb. (10.4 kg), the M60 fired 0.3 in. (7.62 mm) rounds at a maximum rate of 550 rounds per minute (rpm) from a disintegrating link belt. The M60 had a rapid rate of fire of 200 rpm and a sustained rate of fire of 100 rpm. The machine gun could be fired from a handheld position, with a pistol grip and sling hooked to swivels, from bipod or mounted on a tripod. The M60 had a removable barrel which could be quickly changed. Design specification recommended the barrel be changed every 500 rounds to prevent overheating. The Marine Corps tested the M60 in 1961 and adopted it the following year.

In 1964, the decision was made to arm the UH-34 Sea Horse helicopters. Initially, it was felt that machine gun mounts in doorways would obstruct the movement of troops. Marine helicopters operating in Vietnam, however, were coming under increasingly heavy fire. By the spring of 1964, the UH-34s carried two to four M60D machine guns, a flexible, gas-operated, air-cooled weapon. By 1965 Marine UH-1Es were in Vietnam fitted with four M60Ds.

A later model of the M60 was the M60E3, adopted by the Marine Corps during the 1980s. Also designed for ground operations, the M60E3 is a lightweight, air-cooled, portable or tripod-mounted machine gun. The M60E3 was modified from the parent model to make it easier to employ and reduce the load carried by the machine gunner. Like its predecessor, it was the standard machine gun for infantry and supporting units but it still suffered from reliability problems. Consequently, the M60E3 was replaced during the 1990s.

He ordered a withdrawal. Once complete, the enemy troops became the target of air attacks. They were engulfed by bombs and napalm.

During the long night of March 4/5, the Marines fought the NVA. As ammunition shortages became critical, Marine helicopters faced heavy fire to drop supplies to Utter's embattled men. The decision was made to commit reinforcements. The 3rd Battalion, 1st Marines and the 2nd Battalion, 4th Marines landed the next morning. It would take two more days of heavy fighting before the surviving NVA forces fled.

Throughout the first half of 1966, the 3rd Marine Division, now under the command of Major-General Wood B. Kyle, pushed southward from Da Nang. Kyle committed the 1st, 3rd, and 9th Marines to a systematic advance toward Hoi An, through territory long controlled by the Viet Cong. Within a three-month period, the Marines engaged the well-trained Doc Lap Battalion, and opened up Highway One. By June, intelligence reported the 324B NVA Division had crossed the DeMilitarized Zone and entered Quang Tri province. Marine reconnaissance patrols confirmed a large North Vietnamese force operating south of the DMZ. Well-camouflaged enemy positions were observed in an area near the "Rockpile," a 700 ft. (213 m) spire some 16 miles (26 km) west of Dong Ha. A new phase of the war was about to begin.

Four infantry battalions and an artillery battalion were committed to Operation Hastings, which opened on July 15 near Cam Lo. The objective was to drive the NVA forces out of

Utter ordered a withdrawal. Once complete, the enemy troops became the target of air attacks. They were engulfed by bombs and napalm.

Quang Tri province. Some of the heaviest fighting took place in the Song Ngan Valley. Plans called for a two-battalion helicopter assault into the valley. In preparation, Skyhawks and Phantoms unleashed a lethal combination of bombs and napalm canisters. Once the Marine aircraft completed their bombing runs, the artillery battalion at Cam Lo—the 3rd Battalion, 12th Marines—opened fire. Twenty minutes later, the first wave of Marines flew into the Ngan valley. The landing was unopposed. As the second wave of CH-46 Sea Knight helicopters approached, the air was filled with enemy small-arms fire. The landing zone was small, and as the helicopters took evasive action, two collided, falling to earth. A third helicopter crashed into a tree. Later that day, another took enemy fire, and smoke and flames billowed from the helicopter as it hit the ground. The Ngan Valley soon became known as "Helicopter Valley."

Over the course of the next two weeks, the Marines faced well-trained, well-equipped NVA forces. The fighting was very heavy. On July 18, Staff Sergeant John J. McGinty's platoon came under enemy attack:

Below: E Company, 2nd Battalion, 7th Marines moves through heavy brush on patrol southeast of Da Nang. The lead Marine is the M60 gunner; he and his loader carry belts of M60 ammunition around them.

"…we started getting mortar fire, followed by automatic weapons fire from all sides … they were blowing bugles, and we could see them waving flags. … "Charlie" moved in waves with small arms right behind the mortars, and we estimated we were being attacked by a thousand men. We just couldn't kill them fast enough."

For the most part, the remainder of Operation Hastings was characterized by brief but fierce firefights. On July 28, some 250 North Vietnamese troops were sighted near the "Rockpile." It was the last significant sighting of NVA troops during Operation Hastings; the 324B Division either crossed over the DMZ or fled into the jungle to the west. Ultimately, 8,000 Marines and another 3,000 South Vietnamese troops participated in Operation Hastings, making it the largest and most violent operation of the war thus far—but only a prelude to what was to come.

By August, intelligence led Westmoreland to believe that elements of the 324B Division remained south of the DMZ. Furthermore, there were indications that the North Vietnamese had amassed both the 304th and 341st Divisions just north of the DeMilitarized Zone. This led to Operation Prairie I, conducted by the 4th Marines. Beginning on August 3, Prairie initially relied heavily upon the 1st Force Recon Company. By the time it ended 182 days later, Operation Prairie I eclipsed Hastings as the longest and bloodiest battle of the war.

On September 26, intelligence reported enemy troops concentrations near Khe Sanh. The 1st Battalion, 3rd Marines, with a supporting artillery battery, boarded KC-130 transports bound for the remote area. Its mission was to determine enemy strength around Khe Sanh. To this end, the Marines conducted extensive patrols, but had little contact with the elusive enemy forces.

Above: This Marine grenadier watches intently as he moves through the undergrowth of the jungle. As the war gradually progressed and became more intense, increasing numbers of Marines began to carry the M16 rifle, but this weapon was not popular, due to its tendency to jam.

Two Separate Wars

Throughout 1966, the Marines in effect fought two separate wars in Vietnam. The 3rd Marine Division in the north was engaged in action that more closely resembled a traditional ground campaign. To the south, the 1st Marine Division continued to fight a guerrilla war in the provinces of Quang Nam, Quang Tim, and Quang Ngai.

General Westmoreland planned that 1967 would be the year in which American forces would engage the Viet Cong and North Vietnamese in large-scale operations, inevitably leading to victory for the U.S. To this end, U.S. forces were assigned the bulk of offensive operations, while the ARVN concentrated on pacification efforts. In the southern portion

Above: A drawing of a wounded Marine who is being helped along by his buddies in the I Corps Tactical Zone. This is the work of artist Isa Barnett, and is evidence of how the Marines would form close bonds with each other in Vietnam, encouraged by the isolation of the jungle and the constant threat of the enemy.

of I Corps, the 1st Marine Division began 1967 with extensive patrolling. No fewer than 36,000 company-sized operations were conducted between January and March. The main objective of these operations was the protection of the civil population as well as allied installations in the area. Larger operations, each utilizing at least a battalion, were launched with the purpose of ferreting out any entrenched enemy forces.

Duc Pho, in Quang Ngai province, had long been a VC sanctuary. By early 1967, it was suspected that NVA units had moved north from II Corps into Duc Pho. While the South Vietnamese had outposts on two predominant hills, the enemy had constructed extensive fortifications in the region. In an effort to eliminate those fortifications, Operation Desoto was conducted by the 3rd Battalion, 7th Marines. Particularly heavy fighting occurred near the villages of Tan Tu and Hai Mon. On February 5, advancing toward Hai Mon, the Marines encountered intense small-arms fire. Close air support was called for and Marine air pounded the area with napalm and 500 lb. (226 kg) bombs.

As the day wore on, the situation worsened. Hai Mon was highly fortified, and the Marines took deadly crossfire from VC positions dug into the rice-paddy dikes. Once again, supporting arms were called for: a total of 325 5 in. (127 mm) naval shells, 125 5 in. (127 mm) shells, 590 4.13 in. (105mm) rounds, and 50 tons (45.3 tonnes) of aviation ordnance were poured onto Hai Mon. After Hai Mon was secured, a vast tunnel and cave system was discovered and subsequently destroyed. The operation continued into February, as other villages were cleared of Viet Cong. But for the Marines on the ground, each one was just another 'ville' that had to be seized and cleared, a dirty and often painful task.

By April 1967, elements of the 1st Marine Division engaged the 2nd NVA Division in the Que Son Valley in two phases of Operation Union. In the early morning hours of April 21, Company F, 2nd Battalion, 1st Marines moved out of the hill complex of Nui Loc Son. After brief encounters with NVA forces, the Marines came under heavy fire as they approached the village of Binh Son. The 3rd Battalion, 1st Marines entered the fight, landing under intense enemy fire. By evening, both the 1st Battalion (1/1), and the 3rd Battalion, 5th Marines (3/5) were committed to the battle. Once again, Marine air and artillery provided support. The NVA fled north. Over the course of the next 27 days, the Marines pursued the enemy through the Que Son Valley. By the end of Union I, enemy casualties were listed at 865 killed, another 777 "probable."

Despite such heavy losses, the 3rd and 21st NVA Regiments soon moved back into the Que Son Valley. Operation Union II was launched. This was a coordinated assault of the Que Son Valley by two Marine battalions, the 6th ARVN Regiment, and the 1st ARVN Ranger Group. On May 26, the 3rd Battalion, 5th Marines landed east of the Nui Loc Son outpost and immediately came under intense enemy fire. After a day-long firefight, the entrenched NVA forces were overrun. For the next few days, contact with the enemy was sporadic. The ARVN pulled out of Union II on May 29.

The Marines, however, did not give up so easily. Both the 3/5 and the 1/5 moved to the southern rim of the valley and began a sweep to the northwest. On the morning of June 2, near the village of Vinh Huy, some 200 entrenched NVA soldiers fired on the 3/5. In response, the 1/5 then attempted to flank the enemy positions, but machine-gun fire ripped into the Marines. Captain James A. Graham led a small group to wipe out one of the enemy machine-gun positions. That accomplished, he went after the second position. He was wounded twice and, with ammunition running low, ordered his Marines to pull back. He stayed behind to protect a Marine too badly wounded to be moved. Graham's last message over the radio was that he was under attack. The citation that accompanied his posthumous Medal of Honor read, "... he died while protecting himself and the wounded man he chose

Below: The battle for Khe Sanh was one of the bloodiest of the war for the Marine Corps. After a successful defence of the post, it was ordered abandoned in June 1968.

not to abandon. His outstanding courage, superb leadership, and indomitable fighting spirit undoubtedly saved the second platoon from annihilation. ... He gallantly gave his life for his country." With both battalions under heavy fire, the division reserve, the 2nd Battalion, 5th Marines, landed. The NVA fled. Operation Union II drew to a close. The enemy, however, did not fail to return. By September, the Marines were engaged in Operation Swift. Once again, after heavy fighting, the NVA would flee the Que Son Valley.

In the northern sector of I Corps, Operation Prairie wrapped up and Prairie II began. Initially, enemy activity in the area was limited to reconnaissance patrols. The situation changed drastically after the Tet holiday: reconnaissance revealed the NVA was massing troops inside the DMZ. Brigadier-General Michael P. Ryan, commanding the 3rd Marine Division, requested permission to fire artillery into and north of the DeMilitarized Zone. It was given, and thousands of artillery rounds slammed into the DMZ.

The North Vietnamese response began on February 27, when mortars,

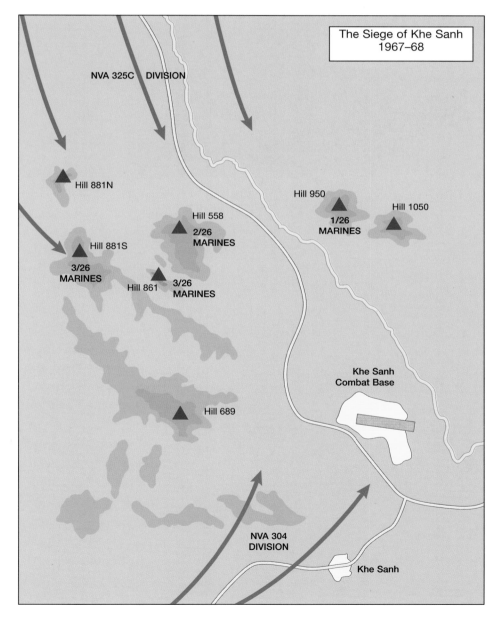

The Siege of Khe Sanh
1967–68

NVA 325C   DIVISION

Hill 881N

Hill 950

Hill 558
2/26
MARINES

Hill 1050

1/26
MARINES

Hill 881S

3/26
MARINES

Hill 861   3/26
MARINES

Khe Sanh
Combat Base

Hill 689

NVA 304
DIVISION

Khe Sanh

Right: Men of the 9th Marines take cover amongst the earth and rocks as the North Vietnamese launch an artillery and rocket attack against the outpost at Con Thien.

Below: Khe Sanh base was defended by the 26th Marines, 1st Battalion of the 9th Marines, and the 37th ARVN Ranger Battalion. It was dependent on the airstrip for its resupply.

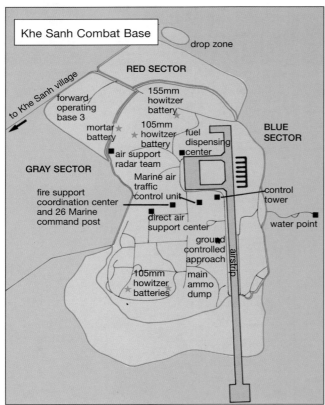

Khe Sanh Combat Base

drop zone

RED SECTOR

to Khe Sanh village

forward operating base 3

155mm howitzer battery

mortar battery

105mm howitzer battery

fuel dispensing center

air support radar team

BLUE SECTOR

GRAY SECTOR

Marine air traffic control unit

fire support coordination center and 26 Marine command post

control tower

direct air support center

water point

ground controlled approach

airstrip

105mm howitzer batteries

main ammo dump

rockets, and artillery hit the Marine strongholds at Con Thien and Gio Linh. Northwest of Cam Lo, a Marine reconnaissance team engaged the lead elements of the 812th Regiment, 324B NVA Division. Reinforcements were sent to relieve the embattled Marines, but heavy fighting continued for the next two days. Major Robert F. Sheridan recalled the action:

"We were ordered to proceed … knowing full well we were walking into a hornet's nest. Based on the number of enemy forces we had already encountered and the vast amounts of equipment, new weapons, and ammunition, we knew we were outmanned and outgunned. … One could almost smell the enemy forces … casualties continued to mount. Moving the dead and the wounded out of the killing zone required feats of bravery beyond comprehension. The NVA were everywhere."

Once again, the NVA fled to the north. And once again, it quickly became clear that not all enemy forces had withdrawn. Prairie II drew to a close, to be followed by two more phases of the same operation. Five infantry battalions and four artillery battalions were committed to the area. Throughout the spring, the Marines continued to engage elements of the 324B and 341st NVA Divisions. Intelligence also reported that elements of the 808th VC and 814th NVA Battalions were operating near Quang Tri City. Both Con Thien and Gio Linh continued to come under heavy attack.

On April 24, heavy fighting broke out in western Quang Tri province when a patrol from Company B, 1st Battalion, 9th Marines was ambushed near Hill 861. It was the opening of the First Battle of Khe Sanh. For the next 18 days, the Marines fought the 325C NVA Division, which was attempting to capture the Khe Sanh Combat Base. It proved to be one of the bloodiest battles of the war. While 940 enemy troops were killed, some 155 Marines also lost their lives, and another 425 were wounded. Captain Michael W. Sayers recalled the effort to evacuate the dead and wounded from Hill 861:

> "We were carrying KIAs [Killed In Action] and WIAs [Wounded in Action] in ponchos [borne by] four men to a litter. The heat deteriorated the bodies rapidly and they bloated fast. Almost impossible to carry in the dark, the mud, and the rain. Many times we stopped our march to retrieve a body that had fallen out of a poncho and rolled down a hill. Identification was difficult as KIA tags were lost. ...not until we arrived back at Khe Sanh and matched our company roster with the evacuation list was I convinced that we had not left a fellow Marine in the hills."

Above: A Marine of the 1st Battalion, 26th Marines, silhouetted against a setting sun, keeps watch at Khe Sahn Combat Base. At one stage the enemy's trenches were within 133 ft. (35 m) of the Marines.

On May 8, while fighting in the hills near Khe Sanh raged, the enemy launched a major attack on Con Thien. Under the cover of a devastating artillery barrage, two NVA battalions moved against the Marine stronghold, breaching the perimeter in front of Company D. In the hand-to-hand combat that ensued, more than 200 NVA troops were killed. By 09:00 hours, the enemy withdrew. They would return—Con Thien again became the scene of battle in July and also in September.

During 1967, Marine casualties numbered 3,452 killed, and another 25,994 wounded. No-one assumed the year 1968 would be any better. General Westmoreland stated, "I believe the enemy has already made a crucial decision to make a maximum effort." Said President Johnson, "We face dark days ahead."

Throughout early January, it became clear that the North Vietnamese were massing for an attack in Quang Tri province. Intelligence reported the 325C NVA Division operating near the Khe Sahn Combat Base. To the northeast were two regiments of the 320th Division. A third division, the 304th, was across the border in Laos. Marine reconnaissance patrols moving through western Quang Tri province, however, discovered little. Then, on January 18 and 19, contact was made with the enemy. Captain William Dabney, commanding Company I, 3rd Battalion, 26th Marines, on Hill 881S requested permission to conduct a sweep to the north. At 0:500 hours on January 20, Dabney led his company out of their fortified positions toward Hill 881N. The company was split into two columns, which moved along parallel ridgelines.

"A thick layer of milky-white fog covered the area like a taut blanket. The swirling mist cut visibility to mere feet. Though the men had walked this land many times before, they inched forward cautiously, all their muscles tight in anticipation of a burst of enemy fire. ... In four hours, Company I had moved but five hundred meters [1,640 ft.]."

As the fog lifted, Company I began the ascent toward Hill 881N. Thirty minutes later, enemy machine-gun fire ripped into the Marines. As artillery fell on the enemy-held positions, the 3rd Platoon, under the command of Second Lieutenant Thomas D. Brindley, surged ahead, storming the NVA positions. Brindley was killed by sniper fire, but the Marines were atop the hill. Dabney ordered his reserve platoon to reinforce Brindley's embattled men. Supporting fire tore into the NVA positions. Marine air dropped bombs and canisters of napalm within 328 ft. (100 m) of 3rd Platoon. Mortars and recoilless rifles situated atop Hill 881S added their destructive power. Reinforcements were requested, but denied. Company I was ordered to break contact and withdraw back to Hill 881S. With 7 Marines already killed and another 35 wounded, the second battle of Khe Sanh began.

While the fighting around Hill 881N raged, a North Vietnamese officer surrendered at the perimeter of the Khe Sanh Combat Base. Lieutenant La Thanh Tonc confirmed the presence of three NVA Divisions in Quang Tri province, and also revealed that an attack

Below: An A-4E Skyhawk of Marine Attack Squadron-211 on the runway, armed with a payload of "iron" bombs. Skyhawks operating out of Chu Lai flew almost constantly in support of Marines on the ground.

on the combat base was scheduled to come that same night.

Shortly after midnight on January 21, the night sky above Hill 861 was lit by signal flares as 300 North Vietnamese soldiers hit the Marine lines. Supported by mortar fire, the enemy blasted through the perimeter with Bangalore torpedoes. As hundreds of NVA rockets and rocket-propelled grenades (RPGs) pounded Hill 861, the Marines of Company K engaged the enemy in

Left: A study of a Marine F-4 Phantom from VMFA-542 shown overflying secondary explosions at Khe Sanh. This picture is by the artist Larry Zabel.

hand-to-hand combat. To the west, the Marines on Hill 881S began firing in support of Hill 861. The battalion's 3.2 in. (81 mm) mortars fired 680 rounds into the advancing NVA. The mortars' tubes became dangerously hot, forcing the Marines to use precious drinking water, then cans of fruit juice, and finally, as a measure of their desperation, their own urine in order to cool them down.

By 05:30 hours, the Marines on Hill 861 launched a counterattack, and the NVA was driven from the hilltop. Almost simultaneously, the Marines atop Hill 881S watched as the NVA to the north let loose a monstrous barrage of mortars, 4.72 in. (120 mm) rockets, and artillery. Sergeant Frank Jones recalled the chaos:

> "The next thing I saw was what appeared to be gigantic orange beach balls—five or six of them—bounce in front of me, about 50 or 60 yards [54–65 m] away. It was incoming rockets or artillery rounds exploding. I hadn't even heard them coming in. They started getting closer. I was terrified. The rounds were hitting all around us. It seemed like the whole Earth had exploded."

Khe Sanh Combat Base erupted in flames as enemy rounds struck the main ammunition dump, destroying more than 90 percent of the Marines' ammunition stores. Drums of aviation fuel ignited. Khe Sanh's airstrip was torn to shreds, and helicopters damaged or destroyed. Clouds of teargas spread, adding to the misery and confusion. Large quantities of C-4 explosive detonated, sending shock waves across the base. Despite the confusion which reigned, the Marines managed to guard the perimeter against any incoming NVA attacks.

To the south of the combat base, the NVA struck Khe Sanh village. Colonel David Lownds, commanding the 26th Marines, ordered the village evacuated. By January 22, many of the Marines wondered why the NVA hadn't launched a ground attack against the combat base. First Lieutenant Nick Romanetz recalled:

Below: Marines on moonlight patrol enter Elephant Valley. This evocative painting is the work of combat artist Horace Avery Chenoweth.

Right: Marine artillery lets fire at the enemy positions. The M101—as it is now known—originally served during World War II, and then went on to see action in Korea. It was used at Khe Sanh, and it is still listed in the Marine Corps inventory today.

"My sector was very, very vulnerable to ground attack. We did not have real good defensive positions; we did not have good, deep trenchlines; we did not have enough barbed wire or minefields or interlocking fields of fire; we did not have covered fighting positions for all of our men. If the enemy had decided to attack the combat base in force with a ground attack during those first few days, there is no doubt in my mind that they would have penetrated our defenses and caused quite a bit of havoc."

My sector was very, very vulnerable to ground attack ... If the enemy had decided to attack the combat base in force with a ground attack during those first few days, there is no doubt in my mind that they would have penetrated our defenses and caused quite a bit of havoc.

Marine Lieutenant-General Robert Cushman ordered the 1st Battalion, 9th Marines to reinforce Khe Sanh. The 37th ARVN Ranger Battalion was also committed to the defense of the combat base, as were two additional 4.13 in. (105 mm) howitzer batteries. Because all resupply had to be done by air, it was not possible to send a greater number of reinforcements to Khe Sanh.

The Tet Offensive

In late January 1968, with the approach of the Tet holiday, the Viet Cong announced a truce. A cease-fire was to be observed between January 27 and February 3. That cease-fire was violated on January 29–30 with the beginning of the Tet Offensive. Mortars and rockets slammed into the Marine air facilities at Da Nang, Marble Mountain, and Chu Lai, while Viet Cong and NVA forces struck simultaneously in large-scale attacks throughout South Vietnam. Most major cities throughout the five provinces of I Corps were hit. Quang Ngai City, Tam Ky, Hoi An, Phu Loc, Cam Lo, and Quang Tri City came under Communist attack. The major assaults were against Da Nang and the ancient capital, Hue.

At Da Nang, the enemy struck I Corps headquarters. Viet Cong sappers penetrated the perimeter and attacked the 7th Communication Battalion. Shortly thereafter, another sapper unit, using satchel charges, Bangalore torpedoes, and RPGs, broke through Marine lines to hit a combat operations center and communications facility; its purpose was to disrupt command and control, to sever lines of communications while the NVA 2nd Division attacked. The lead elements of the NVA Division had earlier been spotted near An Hoa and Marine artillery began firing on suspected avenues of approach. Overhead, circling Da Nang in a Marine helicopter, Lieutenant-General Cushman saw enemy forces advancing toward the river south of the airfield. The 3rd Battalion, 5th Marines, was dispatched to reinforce an ARVN battalion. With the support of Marine air, artillery, and mortar fire, the enemy was stopped. On the western approaches to the airfield, elements of the 2nd Battalion, 3rd Marines came under attack, either from two companies or a reinforced company of the 31st NVA Regiment. The Marines took heavy casualties. Under intense fire from Marine aircraft and artillery, however, the NVA forces began to withdraw.

In the old city of Hue, the situation was in doubt. More than 60 percent of the Imperial Citadel was under the control of the 6th NVA Regiment, and a Viet Cong flag flew over its heights. What's more, the 4th NVA Regiment, supported by the Hue City Sapper Battalion, had launched an attack against the southern portion of Hue. By 06:00 hours on January 30, all of modern Hue except the MACV compound, the prison, and some isolated pockets of resistance, were under NVA control. Two companies of the 1st Battalion, 1st Marines moved out from Phu Bai en route to Hue. They fought through scattered resistance and, by mid-afternoon on January 31, reached the MACV compound. The Marines then advanced across the Perfume River toward the 1st ARVN Division Headquarters. Fighting across the bridge was very heavy and casualties mounted. The

Below: Marines from E Company, 2nd Battalion, 3rd Marines in action on Mutter's Ridge, north of Dong Ha. The two standing Marines are throwing grenades.

embattled Marines reached the Citadel wall, but could not penetrate it. They withdrew to the MACV compound, where they were ordered to await reinforcements.

By February 4, the 2nd Battalion, 5th Marines arrived in Hue. Lieutenant-Colonel Ernest C. Cheatham, commanding the 2nd Battalion, was given the order, "… attack through the city and clean the NVA out." While the 1st ARVN Division concentrated on clearing the Citadel, the Marines secured the city south of the Perfume River. In a point-blank, house-to-house sweep, the Marines relied upon recoilless rifles, rockets, and tank guns. Clearing the southern portion of Hue took five bloody days.

North of the river, the ARVN troops were less successful. On February 12, the 1st Battalion, 5th Marines moved into Hue from the north. It took another ten days for the Marines and ARVN forces to reach the southeast wall of the Citadel. South Vietnamese forces recaptured the Imperial Palace and, on February 24, removed the Viet Cong banner that flew over the Citadel. By March 2, the battle for Hue was over, the ancient capital lying in ruins. Some 142 Marines were killed in the battle, another 857 wounded.

Khe Sanh and Lang Vei

To the north, Khe Sanh Combat Base was the only major military installation not to come under attack during the Tet Offensive. Early on February 5, however, electronic sensors alerted the Marines that the enemy was approaching. NVA mortars and artillery pummeled Hills 881S and 861; Viet Cong sappers overran elements of the 2nd Battalion, 26th Marines. The Marines, under the command of Captain Earle G. Breeding, flooded the hilltop with teargas and counterattacked. In bitter, hand-to-hand fighting, the NVA assault was thrown back. The following night, the enemy struck again. The Special Forces Camp at Lang Vei was overrun by the 66th NVA Regiment accompanied by nine Soviet-built PT-76 tanks.

Above: The enemy. A Viet Cong guerrilla armed with an AK-47 rifle and wearing the trademark black pants. The soles and straps of his sandals are made out of vehicle tires.

Right: Marines carry a wounded buddy through the rubble. The Tet Offensive brought the NVA into open conflict with the Marines for the first time since their arrival three years before.

Marine artillery fired in support of the camp, but Colonel Lownds could not send reinforcements, fearing an attack on the combat base was imminent. Moreover, to send a relief column, at night, into enemy-held territory with enemy tanks holding the main avenue of approach was "suicidal." At dawn, Marine helicopters evacuated the surviving Green Berets and allied forces.

Hundreds of enemy mortars, rockets, and artillery shells slammed into the base at Khe Sanh. Simultaneously, three companies of the 101st Regiment struck Hill 64. The outpost was protected only by a platoon from the 1st Battalion, 9th

Above: A Marine discovers an enemy tunnel complex. The Viet Cong relied on tunnels to shelter them from bombing and provide them with a secure base. The painting is the work of Marine Corps artist James Fairfax.

Marines. Under the cover of a heavy mortar barrage, the advancing NVA troops threw canvas over the perimeter wire and overran the Marines. Survivors of the platoon attempted to regroup, but ammunition was low and many of the Marines were wounded. At sunrise, a relief force fought its way to the base of Hill 64 and, in a frontal assault, drove the NVA off the hill. Of the original Marine defenders, all but one had been killed or wounded.

As February progressed, the circle of NVA forces tightened around the Khe Sanh Combat Base. NVA trenches encroached on the Marines' perimeter. Said one Marine, "We watched with some fascination and no small apprehension, day by day, as the trenches crept closer and closer to our perimeter." Often these trenches came within 133 ft. (35 m) of the Marine lines. Life for the Marines at Khe Sanh became very tense; the base was under a constant barrage of rocket, artillery, and 3.2 in. (82 mm) mortar fire. Through that fire, supplies had to be flown in and casualties evacuated. The persistent heavy fog made those tasks even more difficult: in conditions of zero ceiling and zero visibility, cargo planes had to make instrument landings along a very precise path. Meanwhile, NVA gunners simply positioned their weapons and fired upon the approaching aircraft. Those planes that did land became instant targets for enemy mortars and artillery. Said USAF Sergeant David Mach,

> "On the first mission we brought in five pallets in ammunition. I'll always remember them telling us we had five minutes total on the ground. We landed, combat-offloaded the five pallets, taxied ahead, stopped to pick up ten wounded Marines, taxied to the runway, and took off just as the mortars started to hit the base. My second mission was a couple of days later. Same as before—five pallets of supplies—but this time we had to be gone in three minutes."

During the latter part of February, only 50 planes managed to land at Khe Sanh. The rest of the supplies were dropped by parachute.

Cargo planes were by no means the only aircraft flying above the Khe Sanh Combat Base. Marine aircraft delivered massive amounts of rockets and bombs on NVA positions. On February 13, General Westmoreland recommended that B-52s mount "Arc Light"

Above: Two A6A Intruders burn on the runway after being hit by enemy fire. The Viet Cong used mortars to attack U.S. bases without warning, before quickly melting back into the jungle.

strikes in close proximity to the Marine positions. Said one Marine historian, "Anyone who ever witnessed a B-52 'Arc Light' mission in Nam knew this to be one of the most awesome conventional weapons in the nation's arsenal." The ground rocked with the concussive force. Entire ridgelines disappeared, at times swallowing entire NVA battalions. Still the enemy fought back. On February 23, Khe Sanh was hit with 1,307 rounds of artillery, rocket, and mortar fire.

On February 25, men from Company B, 1st Battalion, 26th Marines moved through the perimeter and headed south into a deadly ambush. The NVA opened fire at point-blank range and automatic weapons ripped into the 29-man patrol. A relief column was dispatched, but they too were ambushed. First Lieutenant Ernie Spencer later stated,

> "Bravo sent out another platoon. It got chewed up by concentrated fire from [the NVA]. Marines died trying to save Marines. That is our way. That is what separates us from everyone else."

Airstrikes and artillery were ordered to hit the NVA positions and the Marines withdrew. The bodies of 25 Marines remained outside the perimeter, and would not be recovered until April 6.

On February 29, the NVA launched the last major assault on Khe Sanh. The Marines unleashed every weapon at their disposal. B-52s delivered Arc Light strikes with spectacular results, destroying two NVA battalions. Not to be outdone by the Air Force, the Marines pounded the NVA forces with "Mini Arc Lights," a combined strike of Marine artillery, the Army's 6.9 in. (175 mm) guns located at Camp Carroll, and A-6 Intruders. The siege of Khe Sanh continued for several more weeks. North Vietnamese sappers hit the ARVN 37th Ranger Battalion several times and artillery continued to fall. The end, however, was in sight. In early March, intelligence reported the 325C NVA Division was moving toward Laos, while the 304th Division was withdrawing to the southwest. Marine patrols began moving out of the perimeter. Finally, on March 30, behind a rolling artillery barrage, Company B moved toward the site where its platoon had been ambushed. Utilizing flamethrowers, bayonets, satchel charges, and grenades, the Marines advanced "killing all the NVA in sight." As Lieutenant-General Victor H. Krulak later wrote, the attack served to signal "that the siege was ended."

On April 1, Operation Pegasus began. Its purpose was the relief of the embattled Khe Sanh Combat Base. The 1st Marines and three ARVN battalions advanced westward along Route 9 from Cam Lo. The 1st Air Cavalry Division and an ARVN airborne division leapfrogged toward the base. At 08:00 hours on April 8, the 2nd Battalion, 7th Cavalry entered Khe Sahn. The Marines, however, were adamant that this was no rescue. Though fighting continued, the threat of a massive attack on Khe Sanh no longer existed. Three days later, on a foggy Easter Sunday morning, the 3rd Battalion, 26th Marines attacked NVA positions on Hill 881N. Following a massive bombardment by Marine artillery and close air support, three companies advanced abreast through a barren landscape of charred trees and huge bomb craters. Colonel Bruce Meyers, the new commander of the 26th Marines, later recalled,

> "As the advancing elements of the 3/26 approached the hated crest of 881N, some of the NVA defenders broke and ran. … with the exhilaration of nearly regaining what had once been theirs, the lead elements fixed bayonets and broke over the crest in a bayonet charge."

By 14:30 hours, Hill 881N belonged to the Marines. The battle for Khe Sanh ended where it had begun 77 days before. The cost of defending the combat base had not been insignificant: 205 Marines had died, another 1,668 were wounded. NVA casualty figures, though, were much higher. It is estimated that anywhere from 10,000 to 15,000 NVA troops were killed in the battle for Khe Sanh. Marine Corps historian Colonel Joseph Alexander wrote, "The disproportionate figures beg the question, 'Who was besieging whom?'" By the end of June, Khe Sanh was abandoned, the continued operation of the base no longer considered necessary. Said one Marine,

> "We had held Khe Sanh, which earned us a Presidential Unit Citation, but we also just abandoned Khe Sanh. … We had risked our lives to hold this place, and then we just walked off and left it."

In late spring, intelligence indicated that the 320th NVA Division had moved into the eastern DMZ, near Dong Ha. On April 29, an ARVN battalion engaged NVA forces 4 miles (6 km) north of the base. Meeting very heavy resistance, the ARVN asked for reinforcements. The following day,

Some of the NVA defenders broke and ran … with the exhilaration of nearly regaining what had once been theirs, the lead elements fixed bayonets and broke over the crest in a bayonet charge.

Below: This Marine, on patrol with 1st Recon, 2nd Battalion, 1st Marines, moves cautiously through the water. As well as the enemy, Marines had to contend with the insect life of Southeast Asia.

Marine helicopters inserted the 2nd Battalion, 4th Marines just north of the Dong Ha bridge. In a fierce three-day battle, the Marines fought the NVA in a cluster of hamlets known as Dai Do. The 2/4 suffered 81 dead, 397 wounded, but Dong Ha combat base remained secure. Despite reports that the 320th NVA Division had fled north across the DMZ, heavy fighting continued throughout much of May.

Shortly after the battle for Dong Ha, Major-General Raymond G. Davis assumed command of the 3rd Marine Division. One of his principal concerns was the mobility of his ground forces. He was committed to the "mobile concept" of offensive operations: the way to fight the war was to rely upon forward artillery positions and the use of helicopters to "carry the war to the enemy throughout the division's area of operations."

In late May, Davis put his tactics into practice. Intelligence reported the 308th NVA Division was south of Khe Sanh. Two Fire Support Bases were blasted out of the thick jungle. Following five days of preparatory bombardment, including B-52 strikes, the 1st Battalion, 1st Marines and 2nd Battalion, 4th Marines were inserted into Fire Support Bases Robin and Loon. The Marines fanned out and spent several days patrolling but found little. Then, on June 6, the NVA struck FSB Loon. The attack was easily thrown back. Over the next several days, the enemy made repeated attempts against the base. Finally, on June 19, the 308th NVA Division withdrew across the border to Laos, leaving 650 dead behind. Four of its six battalions had been decimated. By late August, the 320th NVA Division once again crossed the DMZ, moving through the mountainous terrain between the "Rockpile" and Cam Lo. Throughout August and September, the 3rd and 9th Marines battled the NVA. By October, with its ammunition stockpiles destroyed and 1,585 men killed, the 320th NVA Division moved back across the DMZ.

As 1969 began, the 3rd Marine Division continued operations in northern I Corps. To the west, the mountainous territory near the Laotian border was an NVA stronghold. There, the enemy had established several staging bases, stockpiling weapons, ammunition, and support facilities. From this area, two NVA regiments and an artillery regiment were reported to be moving eastward toward the Da Krong and A Shau valleys. To meet this threat, Operation Dewey Canyon was launched in the southwestern corner of Quang Tri province. It was later described by Brigadier-General Edwin Simmons as "perhaps the most successful high mobility regimental-size action of the war."

Beginning on January 22, 1969, the 9th Marines moved into the Da Krong Valley. Fire Support Bases were hacked out of the thick, nearly impenetrable jungle. Howitzer battalions were flown in, followed by three infantry battalions. Relying solely on

Below: This painting by Richard Yaco is entitled "Green Hell." It depicts the 9th Marines during Operation Dewey Canyon (January 22–March 18, 1969). The terrain in the area was as rugged and impenetrable as any experienced by the Marines in the war.

helicopter support, the Marines leapfrogged across the series of bases, engaging the enemy and destroying huge stockpiles of weapons and ammunition. By February 20, elements of the 2nd Battalion had reached a position overlooking the Laotian border. Below them, the Marines observed NVA convoys moving down Route 922. Colonel Barrow, commanding the 9th Marines, requested permission to carry operations across the border. It was given. Captain David F. Winecoff, leading Company H, 2nd Battalion, 9th Marines successfully ambushed an NVA convoy. The Marines then faded back into the jungle and across the border. Operation Dewey Canyon concluded on March 18, and by the time the last elements of the 1st Battalion, 9th Marines departed FSB Cunningham, 1,617 NVA troops had been killed.

To the south, the 1st Marine Division, operating near Da Nang, still fought an almost invisible enemy. Mines, booby traps, and ambushes accounted for half the casualties sustained by the Marines in southern I Corps.

In the early months of 1969, the Marines continued Operation Taylor Common in the mountains southwest of An Hoa. Its purpose was the destruction of an NVA staging area known as Base Area 112. Once the NVA base was destroyed, the Marines were to move farther west to intercept enemy forces crossing the border from Laos. This was the first high-mobility operation for the 1st Marine Division. Utilizing a series of Fire Support Bases, the Marines moved toward the southwest, and by mid-February, the NVA base area was neutralized. Base camps, supply dumps, and hospitals were destroyed as the enemy fled to the west. They would return. Throughout the remainder of February and into March, the Marines continued to battle in the An Hoa region. On March 8, Taylor Common concluded. Enemy casualties exceeded 500 dead, and huge caches of weapons, ammunition, and supplies had been destroyed. As soon as the Marines departed, however, enemy forces began to return—this was the way of war in Vietnam.

The Marines continued to engage the enemy, in battles fought and refought, near Da Nang, Charlie Ridge, Happy Valley, and the Arizona Territory. In late May, the Marines were given the mission of clearing two staging areas known as Dodge City and Go Noi Island. Operation Pipestone began on May 26 with a blistering bombardment. As elements of the 1st Battalion, 26th Marines and 3rd Battalion, 5th Marines moved to the east, enemy resistance increased. So did the number of mines and booby traps encountered by the Marines. By June 13, Marine air had pounded Go Noi Island, and enemy forces in the area

Above: Reconnaissance Marines patrol an area just below the DeMilitarized Zone. Note their unusual camouflage, and use of berets or jungle hats, rather than the trusty M1 helmet.

Right: Marines march wearily up a hill during a "Search and Clear" operation near Da Nang. The amount of equipment these men are carrying indicates that they can expect to spend a considerable length of time on patrol.

moved toward the Que Son mountains. Two days later, ten Marine Eimco M64 tractors and eight Army D7E caterpillars began clearing the area. Stripping 250 acres (101 hectares) of land at a time, they quickly turned Go Noi Island into 8,000 acres (3,238 hectares) of bare earth. The enemy had lost a staging area. However, by July, intelligence reports indicated they had simply moved into Dodge City.

Throughout the summer, heavy fighting continued in the Arizona Territory, where elements of the 5th and 7th Marines tangled with the 90th NVA Regiment. Then, on August 20, 1969, the 7th Marines were given responsibility for the Que Son Valley. Bitter fighting in August faded as enemy forces fled west. The remainder of the year was spent in endless patrols and numerous small, bloody engagements with North Vietnamese forces.

By the end of 1969, "Vietnamization" of the war was well underway, American forces being withdrawn. The last elements of the 3rd Marine Division departed on November 24. In August 1970, the Marines launched Operation Imperial Lake. This move into the Que Son area proved to be the final Marine offensive of the war. By spring 1971, only 500 Marines remained in South Vietnam. These were embassy guards and advisors to the South Vietnamese Marines. At the end of March 1972, the North Vietnamese launched the Easter Offensive, four NVA divisions pouring across the DMZ. Vietnamese Marines were positioned

Right: A CH-46 Sea Knight lands between rocks and trees to resupply Marines on Hill 381 in the Que Son Mountains. Marines on operations in Vietnam depended heavily on helicopters, both to resupply them, and to evacuate any casualties.

to block the thrust. Captain John W. Ripley, advisor to the 3rd Vietnamese Battalion, blew the bridge at Dong Ha and slowed the enemy advance. Marine aircraft and naval gunfire provided support. The North Vietnamese advance was stopped at My Chanh, north of Hue.

By 1975, North Vietnamese forces were on the move throughout South Vietnam. Phuoc Long province fell first, then the central Highlands. On March 30, the NVA moved into Da Nang. By late April, 18 NVA Divisions advanced on Saigon. On the morning of the 29th, Tan Son Nhut airbase came under rocket fire. The United States Marines began the evacuation of those Americans remaining in South Vietnam, as well as South Vietnamese civilians. On April 30, 1975, North Vietnamese forces entered Saigon. The war was over. Historian Edward F. Murphy wrote:

> "Whatever task the Marines were given—from securing Chu Lai to defending Khe Sanh to recapturing Hue to evacuating thousands of helpless refugees from Saigon—those who fought in Vietnam continued the proud tradition of their brethren who have fought America's wars from the Revolution to Korea."

Twelve years later, on a chilly November weekend, the Vietnam Memorial was dedicated in Washington, D.C. The black polished stone bears the names of those who died in Vietnam: one in every four names belongs to a United States Marine.

Operation Frequent Wind

By late April, 1975, Communist forces sat on the outskirts of the South Vietnamese capital of Saigon. The final collapse of South Vietnam had come quickly, and the North Vietnamese were prepared to march triumphantly into Saigon on May Day. Bombs and rockets had rendered Tan Son Nhut airport useless. At 22:45 hours on April 28, President Gerald R. Ford convened the National Security Council and ordered the execution of Operation Frequent Wind. The final evacuation of Saigon was about to begin. Throughout the afternoon and evening of April 29, CH-53s of Marine Heavy Helicopter Squadrons 462 and 463 brought in elements of the 2nd Battalion, 4th Marines to aid in the evacuation. Those

same Marine helicopters successfully evacuated 395 Americans and 4,475 Vietnamese from the Defense Attache Compound at Tan Son Nhut to the safety of the American fleet. The Marines set the building ablaze before being flown out.

The situation at the U.S. Embassy can only be described as chaos. Instead of the 100 people the Marines had originally planned to evacuate, more than 2,000 waited. Only two helicopters could land at a time. A CH-46 could be landed on the rooftop, the heavier CH-53 in the embassy parking lot. As an endless stream of helicopters flew in and out of the embassy compound, Marines manned the perimeter fence and beat back a frantic mob. By 02:15 hours on April 30, helicopters landed every ten minutes. At 05:00 hours U.S. Ambassador Graham A. Martin was safely evacuated. Outside, as Marines withdrew from the perimeter, the mob entered the compound. Barricading the embassy doors, the Marines moved to the roof under small-arms fire. At 07:53 hours, the final CH-46 lifted off. On board were 11 Marines. One carried the embassy flag. Operation Frequent Wind successfully evacuated 978 Americans and 1,120 foreign nationals, including Vietnamese nationals. The long war was finally over.

CHAPTER 7

SEMPER FIDELIS

On May 25, 1982, the 32nd Marine Amphibious Unit, under the command of Colonel James Mead, departed North Carolina. The MAU was to sail across the Atlantic and join the Sixth Fleet in the Mediterranean for an amphibious exercise that was scheduled in Portugal. Events in the Middle East, however, forced a change of plan.

Left: Marines of I Marine Expeditionary Force on the streets of Mogadishu, Somalia, during Operation Restore Hope in 1993.

Above: A Marine keeps watch from a sandbagged emplacement at Beirut International Airport in the Lebanon in 1982. The Marines had been deployed in the Lebanon several times in the years preceding this point and, in 1982, were there again as part of a multinational peacekeeping force.

Civil war had been raging in Lebanon since 1975. Palestinian forces in the south sought to establish a secure base, and had repeatedly attacked Israel across the border. On June 6, the Israeli Army invaded neighboring Lebanon, with instructions from the Israeli cabinet "to place all the civilian population of the Galilee beyond the range of terrorist fire from Lebanon." Initially, Israeli spokesmen declared their intention of driving forces of the Palestinian Liberation Organization 25 miles (40 km) north of the border, thus rendering PLO artillery useless. Within a few days, however, Israeli forces were approaching Beirut. The beleaguered Lebanese Government requested international assistance in evacuating foreign nationals from the war-torn country. On June 23, the 32nd MAU evacuated 580 U.S. nationals from the port city of Juniyah, 10 miles (16 km) north of Beirut.

By August, an agreement was negotiated by U.S. envoy Philip Habib. Concluded by Israel, Lebanon, and the PLO, the agreement called for a multinational force to supervise a withdrawal of Palestinian and Syrian forces from Beirut and to protect the inhabitants of west Beirut from both the Israelis and the Christian Maronite militia. The force was to remain in Beirut for no more than 30 days. On August 19, the Lebanese Government formally requested the presence of a multinational force on its shores. Six days later, 800 Marines of the 32nd MAU joined British, French, and Italian troops in Beirut. PLO leader Yasser Arafat, led by a contingent of French soldiers, walked through the cordon of Marines and departed Lebanon. By September 9, several thousand members of the PLO, as well as their Syrian supporters, had been evacuated. Although the Habib plan had envisioned the multinational force remaining in Beirut another two weeks, the MAU re-embarked on September 10 to resume its deployment schedule.

The situation in Lebanon worsened. Four days after the departure of the Marines, Lebanese President-elect Bashir Gemayel was assassinated when a bomb went off in the

Christian Phalangist Party headquarters. The Israeli Army moved into west Beirut, ignoring the Habib agreement. The following day, the Phalangist militia, aided by elements of the Israeli Army, moved into the Palestinian refugee camps of Sabra and Shatila. In the ensuing massacre, at least 800 Palestinians were killed, although other estimates place the death toll as high as 2000.

The new Lebanese President, Amin Gemayel, brother of Bashir, requested the return of the multinational force to restore order. Once again, on September 29, the 32nd MAU landed in Beirut and took up positions around Beirut International Airport. The situation into which the Marines, as well as the French and Italian forces, were thrust, was murky, at best. The MAU was given the very indistinct mission of establishing a "presence" in Lebanon "that would in turn help to establish the stability necessary for the Lebanese Government to regain control of their capital." The Marines would not, said President Reagan, engage in combat. The rules of engagement let the Marines shoot only in self-defense. They were forbidden to "chamber a round in their weapons unless they were fired upon and had a clear target." Lebanon, however, remained at war with itself. Amin Gemayel's government controlled only Beirut and a portion of Mount Lebanon. To the north, the Syrians were in control and conflict raged between pro- and anti-Syrian groups. Israeli forces had withdrawn only a few miles from Beirut and occupied much of the south. Groups of Maronite Christians and the Druze minority battled throughout the region.

On November 3, the 32nd MAU was replaced by the 24nd MAU. Two days earlier, hinting at what was to come, a 300-lb. (136-kg) car bomb exploded near the beach where the Marines unloaded supplies. Against this backdrop of violence, the Marines sought to establish a "presence." They dug in around the airport, filled sandbags, and began patrolling east Beirut. They also began training elements of the Lebanese Armed Forces.

It was a no-win situation. The U.S. role in Lebanon was increasingly questioned. Officially, U.S. Marines were in Beirut to protect civilians, but training of the Lebanese Armed Forces was seen as a guarantee of American support for the Christian government. Moreover, many Arabs felt that the American presence in Lebanon was intended not to promote stability and bring about a just peace; rather, this was seen as an American ploy to stabilize a weak Christian government, to broker a peace that would be advantageous to Israel, and to destroy the PLO. Said Marine Corps historian Alan Millett, "The Marines found themselves in a difficult position, caught between vicious and determined guerrilla armies but committed to a war zone without any mission other than to symbolize American interest and to try to help the Lebanese civil authorities preserve peace in the streets." Colonel Joseph Alexander was more succinct, calling the Marines "static, shackled, increasingly vulnerable, attractive targets."

Above: Marine Corps artist Arturo Alejandre portrays a Marine keeping watch over Beirut during the peacekeeping operation. The Marines were placed in an impossible situation in the Lebanon, with unclear rules of engagement in an increasingly hostile urban environment.

The Marines found themselves in a difficult position, caught between vicious and determined guerrilla armies but committed to a war zone without any mission other than to symbolize American interest.

Below: Entitled "Tragic Monument", this watercolor by Marine Corps artist J.T.Dyer, Jr. depicts the tragedy of the bombing of the Marine Barracks in Lebanon. A total of 241 Marines died in the suicide attack.

By mid-February, 1983, the 24th MAU was replaced by the 22nd MAU. The 22nd MAU was the redesignated 32nd MAU; this was the unit's third deployment to Lebanon. Later in the month, the Marines assumed a humanitarian role. Heavy snows in the mountains east of Beirut and flooding in the Bekaa Valley threatened many civilians. With Syrian permission, Marine amtracs and helicopters sought to rescue those in danger. In March, violence against the multinational force escalated. Gemayel's Christian government had alienated large segments of the Lebanese populace and the Marines, as well as the Italian and French soldiers, were no longer seen as peacekeepers but rather as the foreign strength behind a despised government. On March 15, an Italian patrol was ambushed. The following day, five Marines in south Beirut were wounded by a grenade; foot patrols were curtailed, and those Marines patrolling Beirut by vehicle carried loaded weapons.

The situation worsened drastically on April 18, when a pickup truck packed with explosives was driven into the lobby of the U.S. Embassy. A total of 63 people were killed in the ensuing blast; 17 of them were Americans, one a Marine Security Guard. A company of the 2nd Battalion, 6th Marines secured the area. In the aftermath of the bombing, the mission of the 22nd MAU grew to include additional embassy security. No longer were the Marines bound by their strict rules of engagement. A Marine could fire if he perceived "hostile intent." By the end of May, the 22nd MAU was replaced by the 24th MAU under the command of Colonel Timothy J. Geraghty. Security around the airport was increased. The Marines strung concertina wire, filled half a million sandbags, and dug in deeper. They also continued to patrol. On June 25, fire teams from the Lebanese Armed Forces began to accompany the Marines. A month later, on July 22, rockets and mortars fired by a Druze faction slammed into the airport. These attacks continued throughout August. On the 28th, Druze mortars killed two Marines and wounded three. The Marines began returning fire. For the first time, the fury of 6.1 in. (155 mm) howitzers was directed at a Druze position.

By early September, the Israeli Army had withdrawn to the Awwali River in southern Lebanon. Its departure created a vacuum, which the Lebanese Armed Forces could not fill.

Lebanon descended deeper into civil war. The Marines found themselves between the warring factions of Gemayel's Christian Phalangists and the Druze, who were supported by the Syrians. The Lebanese Armed Forces were pushed eastward, and the Druze controlled the high ground above Beirut airport.

On September 15, the Lebanese Armed Forces fought to hold a ridgeline against a Druze and Palestinian attack at Suk al-Gharb, south of Beirut. U.S. Special Envoy Robert McFarland argued in favor of committing the Marines to reinforce LAF positions. Instead, U.S. naval guns were fired in support of the LAF.

Colonel Geraghty opposed the order, arguing that overt support of the LAF would eliminate any question of U.S. neutrality and expose his Marines to increased hostile fire. He was correct. By late September, the Marines came under almost continuous artillery and mortar fire. A fragile ceasefire was put into place on the 26th, but snipers continued to target the Marines. A "presence" in Lebanon had escalated into an undeclared war, in which 6 Marines had been killed and more than 40 wounded.

Bomb Tragedy

Early on the morning of October 23, 1983, a single Marine sentry was on duty at the building that housed elements of the 24th Marine Amphibious Unit. A yellow five-ton Mercedes truck was observed circling the parking lot of the Beirut International Airport. At 06:22 hours, the truck crossed the parking lot at a very high speed, crashing through a barbed wire barrier and through the sentry posts. The truck continued toward the building, tearing through an iron gate and a sandbag barrier before crashing through the lobby door. The Marine sentry later said the man was smiling. In an instant, the truck, which was carrying 6 tons (6.09 tonnes) of explosives, vaporized. The building simply collapsed, killing 241 men as they slept. More Marines died in that instant than in any single action of the Vietnam War. More than 100 others were wounded.

As survivors dug through the rubble, Colonel Geraghty requested medical assistance and replacements. Both U.S. and Royal Air Force planes were used to fly the wounded to the U.S. military hospital in Wiesbaden, Germany, or the British military hospital on Cyprus. On Monday morning, General Paul X. Kelley, Commandant of the Marine Corps, visited survivors at Wiesbaden. Afterward, Kelley eloquently told the story of Lance-Corporal Jeffrey L. Nashton. The young Marine lay in intensive care, badly wounded and blinded by the explosion. Said Kelley:

Above: A Marine sniper searches for potential targets through the scope of his 0.3 in. (7.62 mm) M-40A1 rifle. He is placed in an ideal position in the Marine compound near the airport to detect any enemy activity below him. He uses a sandbag as a convenient rest for his rifle.

Above: Marines from E Company, 2nd Battalion, 8th Marines on patrol through wooded areas in Panama. In the foreground, PFC Valdez carries an M16A2 rifle. Behind him, his partner carries a M203 grenade launcher.

"When he heard who I was, he grabbed my camouflage coat, went up to the collar and counted the stars. He squeezed my hand, and then attempted to outline words on his bedsheet. When what he was trying to write was not understood, he was given a piece of paper and pencil, and then he wrote 'Semper Fi.' "

For Kelley, this was a moment of great pride amid the tragedy.

In the following months, an independent commission led by retired Admiral Robert L. Long investigated the bombing of the Marine compound. Meanwhile, as their presence in the Lebanon became the subject of debate, the Marines in Beirut were under siege behind a perimeter of dikes, concrete barriers, ditches, concertina wire, and machine guns. They continued to be wounded, and to die. In February 1984, fighting between the Lebanese Armed Forces and various Moslem factions reached a fevered pitch. The Lebanese Army collapsed and Gemayel renounced peace with Israel. On February 18, the Joint Chiefs of Staff ordered American forces to withdraw. Historian Robert Moskin later reflected,

"During the 18 months the MAUs were in Lebanon, 238 Marines were killed in combat, another 151 wounded. 'Lebanon' was inscribed on the Marine Corps Memorial as the Corps' forty-second battle honor. But on this assignment, the Marines had been stripped of their mobility and their freedom of action."

"Peacekeeping" had been a deadly assignment for the Marines.

During the 1980s, the Marines took part in two other joint operations. The first of these was Operation Urgent Fury. On October 25, 1983, two days after the bombing of the Marine Barracks in Lebanon, American forces assaulted the tiny Caribbean island of Grenada. Grenada's Prime Minister Maurice Bishop had been murdered and the Deputy

Prime Minister wished to impose a Marxist regime on the island. Various reasons were given for the intervention, which found little support from the international community. These ran the gamut from protecting American medical students enrolled at St. George's University to stopping Cuban intervention on the island. President Ronald Reagan commented,

> "Grenada, we were told, was a friendly island paradise for tourism. Well, it wasn't. It was a Soviet-Cuban colony being readied as a major military bastion to export terror and undermine democracy."

Above: Anthony Stadler depicts a Marine Light Armored Vehicle on patrol in Panama during Operation Just Cause, which was executed in December 1989.

Originally, the plans called for the Army and Marines to conduct a joint amphibious landing, a suggestion that was refused by the Marine Corps. Instead, Army Rangers and elements of the 82nd Airborne Division were to land in the southwest corner of Grenada. Marines of the 22nd Marine Amphibious Unit were to secure the airport at Pearls. In four days, the island was secured. Some 599 Americans were evacuated, as were 88 foreign nationals. Three Marine aviators lost their lives and another 15 Marines were wounded. Although portrayed as a perfect operation in which various branches of the Armed Services came together, the realities of the situation were very different. Urgent Fury suffered from bad intelligence, hasty planning, and in the words of one historian, "confusions of command, overkill in the thousands of troops involved, mistakes blamed on faulty communications, and Americans shooting Americans."

Left: A pencil drawing by Anthony Stadler portrays three Marines on duty in Panama. In the jungle's heat they are wearing forage caps instead of their helmets.

In December 1989, another joint forces operation was launched. Named Just Cause, its purpose was the capture of Panamanian dictator Manuel Noriega. Noriega had been convicted *in absentia* by a Florida court on charges of drug trafficking and racketeering. Beginning on December 20, the operation was largely conducted by the Army. A Marine Fleet Anti-Terrorist Security Team Company was the first unit to be assigned the security of the Arraijan Tank Farm, the storage facility for fuel used by U.S. forces in Panama. On April 6, Company I, 3rd Battalion, 4th Marines arrived and assumed responsibility for its security. As Marine units were rotated in and out, there were a number of firefights over the course of the next several months. Noriega eluded capture but finally surrendered to elements of the Army's Delta Force on January 3, 1990.

The total number of Marines committed to operations in Panama never exceeded 650. Corporal Garreth C. Isaak was the only Marine killed in Operation Just Cause; another three were wounded. While Noriega awaited trail in the United States, the flow of drugs through Panama into the U.S. continued. It was, however, not drugs, but the politics of oil that next called Marines to duty abroad.

Operation Desert Shield

Below: Marine AV-8B Harriers fire on Iraqi positions during Operation Desert Storm. The painting is the work of Horace Avery Chenoweth.

At 01:00 hours on August 2, 1990, three divisions of the Iraqi Republican Guards surged across the border and into the small sheikdom of Kuwait. A special-operations division was landed by helicopter into the capital, Kuwait City. By the time night fell, the city was in the hands of the Iraqis, and at this point Saddam Hussein's forces were positioned right on the border which Kuwait shared with Saudi Arabia.

The invasion had been swift—but was not unforeseen. On July 17, Hussein had threatened both Kuwait and the United Arab Emirates for exceeding the oil production quotas which had been established by OPEC. Kuwait's military seniors, Major General al-Sanii and Major General Jaber al-Khaled al-Sabah, put their forces on full alert. This decision was overruled by the Emir of Kuwait, who assumed that money would placate the volatile Hussein. American diplomats agreed, saying Hussein was simply engaging in saber-rattling. They were wrong, and Hussein's troops rolled across Kuwait.

Saudi Arabia now feared that the Iraqi Army, the world's fourth largest, would continue its advance across the border, and appealed to the United States for aid. In a meeting with Saudi Arabia's King Fahd, a series of photographs was shown of Iraqi tanks poised on the Saudi border. Some tanks, in fact, had already crossed the border. U.S. Secretary of Defense, Richard B. Cheney, delivered a message from President George Bush. "We are prepared to deploy these forces to defend the kingdom of Saudi Arabia. If you ask us, we will come. We will seek no permanent bases. And when you ask us to go home, we will leave." Fahd, the ruler of a closed and xenophobic kingdom, answered simply in English with the word, "Okay."

With Saddam's forces sitting squarely atop some of the world's largest oil reserves, the United States and the world community was swift to act. President George Bush, supported by Britain's Prime Minister Margaret Thatcher, began building a coalition of 37 nations willing to support action against Iraq. The United Nations quickly passed Resolution 660 demanding the immediate withdrawal of Iraqi forces from Kuwait. Four days later, with the passing of Resolution 661, Iraq faced international economic sanctions.

By August 7, General Colin Powell, Chairman of the Joint Chiefs of Staff, had alerted the military to prepare for possible deployment to the Persian Gulf. Operation Desert Shield, the positioning of U.S. forces in the Gulf region, had begun. Three days later, General H. Norman Schwarzkopf, the Commander in Chief, U.S. Central Command ordered three Marine Expeditionary Brigades deployed to Saudi Arabia. The 4th Marine Expeditionary Brigade (MEB) sailed out of North Carolina; the 1st and 7th MEBs flew to the Gulf. Ships of two Maritime Prepositioning Shipping Squadrons had already sailed from Guam and Diego Garcia in the Indian Ocean. They carried 30 days' worth of supplies and equipment and married up the 1st and 7th MEBs. General Schwarzkopf later recalled watching supplies unload at the port Al Jubayl in Saudi Arabia:

"Each squadron of ships was crammed with enough weapons, equipment, food, and supplies to keep 16,500 Marines fighting for thirty days ... Their deployment had been part of a controversial program after the Vietnam War. While some members of Congress had objected to the idea of letting tens of millions of dollars of military

Above: A Marine wearing desert camouflage on Sassan oil/gas separation platform during Operation Praying Mantis in 1988, when the U.S. destroyed several Iranian platforms in the Persian Gulf.

Above: A Marine of the 2nd Combat Engineers Battalion digs a hole for an explosive charge. Combat engineers were needed to breach the barriers dubbed the "Saddam Line."

gear float around unused, we were certainly glad to have it now. I watched with Lieutenant-General Walt Boomer, my Marine commander, as a procession of M-60 medium tanks rolled off one of the ships, and seeing them made me feel great."

Within four short days, the 7th MEB was combat-ready. On August 25, Major General John I. Hopkins told General Schwarzkopf that his Marines were ready to defend the approaches to Al Jubayl as well as Ju'mayah and Ras Tannurah. Hopkins had under his command a total of 15,248 Marines, supported by 124 aircraft, 425 artillery pieces, and 123 tanks. The 1st Light Infantry Battalion, as well as the reinforced 3rd Battalion, 9th Marines were forward deployed. The bulk of the 7th Marines took up positions 40 miles (64 km) north of Al Jubayl. By mid-September, there were over 155,000 Iraqi troops in Kuwait, and 1,350 tanks, 900 armored personnel carriers, and 650 artillery pieces. Another 12 Iraqi divisions were massed in neighboring Iraq. The Marines considered themselves merely a "speed bump" to slow an Iraqi invasion of Saudi Arabia.

On September 2, Lieutenant-General Walter E. Boomer, commander of I Marine Expeditionary Force (MEF), assumed command of all Marine ground forces ashore. As the buildup of U.S. strength in the Gulf continued, both Boomer and Schwarzkopf waited apprehensively for Hussein to move his massive army across the border. Colonel Joseph Alexander points out that when "asked whether his initial forces could stop an Iraqi invasion, General Boomer replied, 'I don't know how, but we will. ... We will stop them.'"

Right: Marines AAVP-7A1 amphibious assault vehicles move toward Kuwait City during Operation Desert Storm. In the background is an AH-1 Sea Cobra helicopter gunship.

By November, there were 42,000 Marines deployed in the region. With the I Marine Expeditionary Force ashore, Schwarzkopf decided to keep the 4th MEB and the 13th Marine Expeditionary Unit (MEU) at sea. A series of amphibious exercises was planned. In the first, called Sea Soldier, the Marines simulated a night amphibious landing across the beaches of Oman. Not only did such exercises provide valuable training for the Marines afloat, but they were also intended to give pause to Saddam Hussein. Did the Iraqi dictator really want to face U.S. Marines storming ashore?

In late October, General Schwarzkopf had been informed that President Bush had made the decision to go on the offensive, feeling that Hussein would respond either to diplomatic initiatives or to economic sanctions. Kuwait would have to be liberated. After meeting with King Fahd, U.S. representatives planned to address the United Nations, asking for an ultimatum for Iraq to withdraw from Kuwait. Schwarzkopf was told, "You should be prepared to build up the force and go to war." On November 8, the President announced that an additional 220,000 troops would deploy to the Persian Gulf; the number of Marines in the region was to double. General Alfred M. Gray, Commandant of the Marine Corps explained the situation. "We now have four kinds of Marines: those in the Gulf; those going to the Gulf; those who want to go to the Gulf; and those who don't want to go to the Gulf, but are going anyway!"

The number of Marines already in the Persian Gulf accounted for one-quarter of the active-duty strength of the Corps. On November 9, the 5th MEB and the II MEF, consisting of the 2nd Marine Division, the 2nd Marine Aircraft Wing, and the 2nd Force Service Support Group received orders to deploy. The last time the 2nd Marine Division had seen combat was on Okinawa. Less than a week later, 80 Marine reserve units were activated. About 1,000 Marines per day were flown into the Persian Gulf region.

The allied force amassed in the Persian Gulf region was awesome. By mid-January 1991, approximately 84,000 Marines were deployed as part of Operation Desert Shield. Two Marine divisions, as well as an airwing, operated from shore, while the 4th and 5th MEBs and the 13th MEU remained afloat. This was a larger force than that which landed at Iwo Jima. The total number of American forces in the region numbered 540,000. Across the border, Iraq fielded an army of 545,000 men, 4,300 tanks, and 3,100 pieces of artillery. General Schwarzkopf later said,

> "I imagined the enemy out there, methodically constructing formidable barriers, miles deep in places, along the border. I could almost see the minefields, tank traps, high sandbanks, razor wire, trenches, and forts. The 'Saddam Line' it was dubbed by the intelligence people, and it extended along the entire border of Kuwait and 40 miles [64 km] further along the southern border of Iraq—175 miles [282 km] in all. It had been built on the assumption that we would attack head-on."

It was with this knowledge that Lieutenant-General Walt Boomer and his staff planned for offensive action against the Iraqis. Saddam Hussein had ordered the mining of the

Below: Horace Avery Chenoweth depicts burning Iraqi tanks strewn across the desert. The largest tank battle of the war occurred near the Al Burqan oil field.

Asked whether his initial forces could stop an Iraqi invasion, General Boomer replied, "I don't know how, but we will ... We will stop them."

"I imagined the enemy out there, methodically constructing formidable barriers, miles deep in places, along the border. I could almost see the minefields, tank traps, high sandbanks, razor wire, trenches, and forts."

Persian Gulf, and any attempt to clear the Gulf for an amphibious assault would obviously take time—and cost lives. Because Hussein had three divisions of Iraqi soldiers defending the coast, Boomer decided to maintain the amphibious force as a ruse. The 1st Marine Division was to breach the Iraqi defenses near Al Wafrah; the 2nd Marine Division to pass through the lines and become the main assault force into Kuwait; and from the west, Schwarzkopf would launch his main effort—an attack on the left flank of the Iraqi forces by the U.S. Army's XVIII and VII Corps, 200,000 soldiers accompanied by thousands of tanks.

Operation Desert Storm

On January 15, the deadline given to Saddam Hussein for the withdrawal of his forces from Kuwait came and went. At 02:30 hours on January 17, Operation Desert Storm broke over Kuwait and Iraq with a fury of massive air strikes. The initial purpose of the air campaign was the destruction of Saddam Hussein's command and control network, Iraqi communication and transportation systems, and SCUD missile sites. Republican Guard reserve divisions in southern Iraq were also targeted. Air Force F-117 Stealth fighter-bombers and Navy Tomahawk missiles pounded targets inside Iraq. At 04:00 hours, the first air attacks by Marine units began when MAG-11 launched 48 F/A-18 Hornets and A-6 Intruders against Iraqi targets. MAG-13 joined the fray shortly thereafter, and AV-8B Harriers and OV-10 Broncos struck targets in Kuwait. In response, Iraq fired SCUD missiles at targets in Israel, Saudi Arabia, and Bahrain. Militarily, these adapted Soviet-built weapons were able to pack very little punch. They could, however, be used as effective weapons of terror against civilian populations.

Right: The Marines were tasked with tying down Iraqi forces in front of Kuwait City, but they made such good progress that General Schwarzkopf called their efforts "brilliant." A Marine Recon team reached the U.S. Embassy in Kuwait City only three days after the attack began.

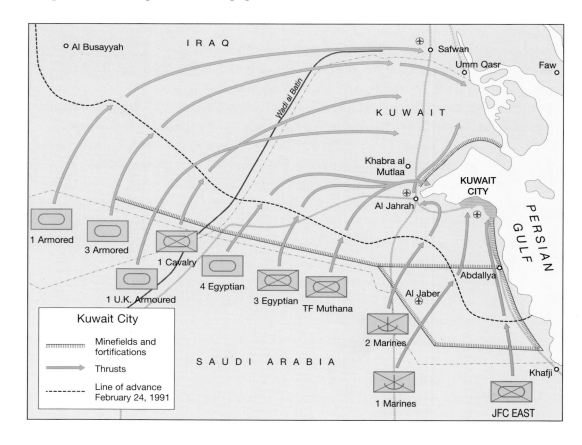

In less than two weeks, coalition forces had flown over 30,000 missions against Iraq. Initially, all air strikes were ordered by a Joint Forces Air Component Commander, but as the air war progressed, the Marine aviators, commanded by Major-General Royal Moore, were able to wean their assets and begin battlefield preparation. Said Moore, "... if a target didn't do something for the I MEF and battlefield preparation, we weren't going." For 15 days before the ground war began, Marine aircraft pounded Iraqi forward positions, reducing enemy frontline troops by more than 50 percent.

On the night of January 29, Iraqi forces moved across the Saudi border. It was unclear if this was the vanguard of a major assault or something else. Schwarzkopf later admitted that he and his staff were perplexed by an attack that seemingly "defies military logic." One probe came in front of

the 1st Marine Division lines near Al Wafrah. A column of Iraqi tanks hit an observation post manned by a platoon of Recon Marines. Artillery and air support were requested. Marine F/A-18 Hornets and Air Force A-10 Thunderbolts, the tank-killers, flew overhead. In the ensuing battle, two Marine Light Armored Vehicles were mistakenly targeted. An antitank missile struck one, the other came under fire by an A-10 and was destroyed by a Maverick missile. Tragically, 11 Marines were lost to "friendly fire." The Iraqi probe, however, was beaten back. By morning, 22 tanks were smoking ruins. A smaller probe occurred near Observation Post 2, close to the 2nd Marine Division positions, but it was quickly eliminated. The major thrust of the Iraqi assault came along the coast, as three columns of the 5th Iraqi Mechanized Division rolled southward. Two brigades were stopped by air attacks, but a third brigade quickly seized the deserted town of Al Khafji. Saudi and Qatari forces planned a counterattack, supported by Marine air and artillery, for the morning of January 31.

Two Marine Recon teams from the 1st Marine Division were already in the city. The senior NCO, Corporal Charles Ingraham, had reported the attack and had moved with his men to the top of a four-story building. The Marines set up Claymore mines in the stairwell, moved to firing positions, and watched as the Iraqi soldiers moved about in Khafji below them. From this high position, Corporal Ingraham was able to direct artillery and air support that would prove to be invaluable in the recapture of Khafji. As historian Colonel Joseph Alexander noted:

Above: FA-18C Hornets fly in formations over the barren landscape of the Iraqi desert. The aircraft shown here are armed with a mix of devices with which to pummel the Iraqis: cluster bombs and AGM-88 antiradar missiles, as well as AIM-7 Sparrow and AIM-9 Sidewinder antiaircraft missiles.

The Iraqis, for all their vaunted experience and weaponry, were unmotivated and ineffective fighters. And the Marines had junior leaders in their enlisted ranks ... who, despite their lack of combat experience, were well-trained, cool-headed, and lethal.

"The Allied recapture of Khafji revealed in advance two key aspects of the ground war that would soon follow. The Iraqis, for all their vaunted experience and weaponry, were unmotivated and ineffective fighters. And the Marines had junior leaders in their enlisted ranks, like Ingraham, who, despite their lack of combat experience, were well-trained, cool-headed, and lethal."

In the third week of January, Brigadier-General James M. Myatt, commanding the 1st Marine Division, and Major-General William M. Keys, commanding the 2nd Marine Division, ordered a series of combined arms raids targeting Iraqi artillery. The plan was simple—and very effective. An artillery battery of 6.1 in. (155 mm) guns, escorted by light armored infantry, was set up along the Kuwaiti border. In the dark of night, the Marines opened fire against suspected Iraqi artillery positions. The Iraqis fired back. The muzzle flashes were then targeted by waiting Marine Hornets and Harriers. General Myatt later said, "We convinced 'em it wasn't smart to man their artillery pieces because every time they did Marine air would come rolling in on them."

Preparations Continue

As G-Day approached, General Keys became increasingly concerned over the battle plans for the ground assault. He was certain his 2nd Marine Division could breach the Iraqi defenses, but was concerned with the prospect of passing through the 1st Division lines as Boomer's plan required. Such a passage, he felt, would simply take too much time, and render the Marines needlessly vulnerable to Iraqi firepower. Instead, Keys proposed to breach the Iraqi lines with the two divisions abreast. The attack into Kuwait would be launched on each side of Umm Hujul, the 1st Marine Division on the right, the 2nd on the left. The plan was tactically sound but, Brigadier-General Charles C. Krulak was asked, could Marine logistics support such a plan? He wasted no time: in two weeks, Direct Support Command built a new 11,280 acre (4,565 hectare) base, Al Khanjar. Within sight of the Iraqi-held territory, it was mostly underground. To support the ground assault, Krulak amassed a million gallons of water, five million gallons of fuel, and enough ammunition to cover 780 acres (316 hectares). Al Khanjar also boasted two airstrips long enough to land C-130 transport planes, a helicopter landing site, and a Naval hospital.

Final approval for the plan was given on February 14. Four days later, the two divisions began moving into position. On February 22, elements of both the 3rd Battalion, 7th Marines and Company C, 2nd Light Armored Infantry Battalion crossed the border into enemy-held Kuwait, clearing obstacles and directing air and artillery strikes. Enemy tanks, artillery, and troops were targeted, and the Marine units succeeded in convincing Iraqi leaders in Baghdad that the ground war had begun. After two days of combat, the Marines withdrew, rejoining their units for the official start of the ground war. Boomer requested that ground elements of the 5th MEB, still afloat, be landed to serve as division reserve.

By the night of February 23, allied elements were in place.

"Thousands of tanks and armored vehicles ... were now pressed against the border in battle formation, the men catching whatever sleep they could in their vehicles or on the sand outside, and eating MREs if they had any appetite. In places where we needed to breach barriers, combat engineers had moved all the way forward with their armored excavators and bulldozer tanks. Behind the battle formation, convoys

Opposite: A Marine AV8B Harrier takes off from LHA-4 Nassau during support operations for Operation Desert Storm. The helicopters shown on deck in this photograph include the CH-46 Sea Knight and the UH-1 Huey.

Right: A Marine corporal
in the turret of an
AAVP-7A1 amphibious
assault vehicle. Visible on
the sides of the turret are
smoke launchers which
are capable of generating
an instant smokescreen.
The AAVP-7A1 can carry
up to 21 fullly combat-
equipped troops.

of fuel and ammunition trucks had pulled up, ready to follow the columns into battle. Our artillery had moved forward—thousands of howitzers and guns with millions of pounds of stockpiled ammunition—ready for a massive preparatory barrage that would pound Iraqi positions throughout the night. … All along the Iraqi lines, coalition air strikes reached their maximum fury. …The weather in the battle zone was clear, except in eastern Kuwait, where Iraqi troops had begun pillaging the city and setting fire to the oil fields. There a hellish black cloud darkened the sky and obscured the crescent moon, as though Saddam were stroking the fires of war."

Thoughts of Iraq's biological and chemical weapons capabilities weighed heavily on their minds, as did estimates of heavy casualties.

At 01:00 hours on February 24, the battleships *Wisconsin* and *Missouri*, positioned off the Kuwaiti coast, commenced firing. It was part of the continuing ruse that the Marines were to make an amphibious assault. Three hours later, the 1st Marine Division initiated the ground war, hitting the strength of the Iraqi defenses. The Marines moved through wind and rain to cross "The Berm," a 15 ft. (4.5 m) earthen barrier that marked the border. Attacking between the Al Wafrah and Umm Gudair oil fields, the Division moved toward its first objective, the Al Jaber Airfield. Task Forces Taro and Grizzly, built around the 3rd and 4th Marines, secured the division's flanks. Task Force Ripper, based on the 7th Marines and fully mechanized, led the way into the Iraqi obstacle belts. At 06:15 hours, the Marines hit the first line of Iraqi defenses and easily cleared them. As Iraqi soldiers fled, Marine amtracs poured across the cleared lines. By 11:25 hours, the 3rd Tank Battalion hit the second obstacle belt and encountered Iraqi tanks dug into the sand. As the Marines began to fire, the Iraqi soldiers began to surrender.

The 2nd Marine Division hit the Iraqi lines west of the 1st Division, between the Umm Gudair and Al Manaqish oil fields. As the 2nd Combat Engineers cut through The Berm, and the Marines began to move forward, the "Marine Hymn" could be heard at full volume. It was an "added extra," courtesy of an Army psychological warfare unit. The 6th

Marines and the 2nd Light Armored Infantry Battalion moved through the Iraqi obstacles using mine rakes and mine plows. On the right flank, the 1st Battalion, 8th Marines was slowed by Italian nonmetallic mines. The Iraqis fired some 300 artillery rounds, but it was largely ineffective. Within six hours, narrow lanes were cleared through two obstacle belts, and the Marines continued their advance. Attached to the 2nd Marine Division was the U.S. Army's Tiger Brigade of the 2nd Armored Division. With 118 M1-A1 Abrams tanks, the brigade swept northward, destroying Iraqi tanks from a distance of 2 miles (3 km).

On the Kuwaiti coast, the 4th Marine Expeditionary Brigade occupied the Iraqi divisions defending against an amphibious assault. Later, the 13th MEU continued the deception. By afternoon, the 5th MEB was flown by helicopter to Mishab, where it formed the reserve for the I MEF, as per Boomer's earlier request. There were now 84,515 Marines ashore. By evening, the 1st Marine Division was poised to take the Al Jaber Airfield and push toward the oil field at Al Burqan. The 2nd Marine Division, after soundly defeating a column of Iraqi tanks, consolidated its position north of Umm Gudair. Over the course of the day, thousands of Iraqi troops surrendered. General Schwarzkopf later recalled,

> "Boomer's units were inundated with prisoners of war. The rules of warfare required us to keep the prisoners safe by speeding them to the rear. The Marines filled all the available trucks, but finally had to resort to taking the Iraqi's weapons, pointing south and saying 'Walk that way!' "

For the Marine aviators, the timing of the ground war could not have been worse. Flying conditions were terrible, some of the worst of the year. Rain fell and winds whipped across the desert. Fountains of flame and plumes of black smoke from the burning oil fields made the situation worse. Yet, on that first day of the war, aircraft of the 3rd Marine Aircraft Wing flew 671 sorties in support of the Marines on the ground. Elements of six different Iraqi divisions were struck, as well as enemy vehicles, tanks, missile, and artillery sites. Said Major General Myatt, of the 1st Marine Division, "I will never take the air-

Boomer's units were inundated with prisoners of war ... The Marines filled all the available trucks, but finally had to resort to taking the Iraqi's weapons, pointing south and saying "Walk that way!"

Left: Marine Corps CH-46 Sea Knight helicopters bring humanitarian relief to Kurdish refugees near the Iraqi-Turkish border during Operation Provide Comfort. This painting is by Marine Corps artist P.M. Gish.

Above: Marines on patrol move through a cornfield during Operation Provide Comfort in northern Iraq after the Gulf War. These men are all armed with M249 Squad Automatic Weapons (SAWs).

ground team for granted ... the result is a marvelous marriage, more powerful than the sum of its parts, where a Marine's most sought after privilege is to be able to fight for another Marine."

No one thought the Marines' progress on the first day of the war was less than breathtaking. Schwarzkopf's staff had assumed that the Marines could keep the Iraqis occupied only until they were hit by the enveloping Army forces. It quickly became clear, however, that the Marines were on their way to routing the vaunted Iraqi Army. Schwarzkopf ordered the main assault to begin 24 hours ahead of schedule. Later, the General would praise the two Marine divisions with much enthusiasm and admiration, "If I use words like brilliant, it would really be an underdescription of the absolutely superb job that they did in breaching the so-called impenetrable barrier."

On February 25, as the second day of the war dawned, the skies above the battlefield were filled with the thick, black smoke of the oil fires. By evening, the desert would be dotted with the smoking hulks of hundreds of Iraqi tanks. The first major engagement occurred early on the morning of the 25th. Tanks of the Iraqi 83rd Brigade moved along the left flank of the 1st Marine Division lines. They were met by the 1st Light Armored Infantry Battalion as well as the 3rd Tank Battalion. Within minutes, the Iraqi forces were destroyed. Three-and-a-half hours later, at 08:05 hours, the right side of the 1st Marine Division came under attack. Some 250 Iraqi tanks and armored personnel carriers, elements of the Iraqi 22nd Brigade, 5th Mechanized Division and the 501st Brigade, 8th

Infantry Division emerged from the heavy fog and blanket of smoke that covered the burning Al Burqan oil field. The ensuing battle was the largest tank battle in Marine Corps history. Marine aircraft flew overhead, but were rendered largely ineffective. The smoke was too heavy, the battlefield too confused, the U.S. and Iraqi forces too intermixed. The notable exception were the AH-1W Sea Cobra helicopter gunships. Flying at altitudes of barely 50 ft. (15 m) and vulnerable to enemy fire, the Cobras destroyed Iraqi tanks and missile launchers with TOW and Hellfire missiles.

Earlier, the 1st Battalion, 1st Marines had moved into the Al Burqan oil field, and encountered elements of the Iraqi 3rd Armored Division moving across the division's front. The Iraqis turned and moved south. By 09:30 hours, enemy forces had advanced to within 400 yards (437 m) of the 1st Marine Division forward command post, located in a grove of trees known as "The Emir's Farm." Shrouded by heavy, black smoke, elements of Company C, 1st Marines and Company B, 1st Light Armored Infantry Battalion, battled the approaching Iraqis. Battery H, 14th Marines, a reserve artillery unit, observed two enemy multiple rocket launchers nearby. At a distance of 800 yards (875 m), the 6.1 in. (155mm) guns of the Marines fired on the enemy target, eliminating it from the battle. Once again, the Sea Cobras proved invaluable, firing TOW missiles and turning the Iraqi tanks into burning wrecks. Some 90 minutes later, surviving elements of the Iraqi 501st Brigade attacked the command post of Task Force Papa Bear. A fierce attack had been repulsed earlier in the day. In this engagement, the 1st Tank Battalion and the Cobra gunships accounted for the destruction of 50 Iraqi tanks and 25 armored personnel carriers. By midday, the battle was over. Later, as the second day of the ground war drew to a close, elements of the 1st Marine Division secured the airfield at Al Jaber, destroying another 80 Iraqi tanks and taking 2,000 enemy soldiers prisoner.

Marines of the 2nd Division met equal success on February 25. In the early morning hours, the 6th Marines and the Army's Tiger Brigade were positioned south of Al Abdaliyah. Then at 06:55 hours, the Iraqi "Reveille Counterattack" hit the 1st Battalion, 8th Marines on the division's right flank. The force consisted of a large number of tanks and armored personnel carriers. In a superb example of combined arms fire, Marine units reduced a total of 39 enemy vehicles to smoking ruins. The 6th Marines came under both tank and mortar fire, but still advanced through Iraqi-held positions in the area known as "The Ice Tray." The 8th Marines secured the smaller "Ice Cube." On the division's left flank, the M1-A1 Abrams tanks of the Tiger Brigade accounted for the destruction of 50 enemy tanks; this was achieved within just two hours of battle. By the close of the day, 248 Iraqi tanks had been totally destroyed, and another 4,500 enemy soldiers had been taken prisoner.

Below: A Marine stands guard as relief supplies are delivered in Somalia during Operation Provide Relief in 1992. The painting is the work of Marine Corps artist Donna Neary.

News reports were airing footage of the burned-out wreckage of more than 1,000 Iraqi vehicles lying twisted along the highway. Elements of the press referred to it as "the Highway to Hell."

In the predawn hours of February 26, fire from the battleships *Wisconsin* and *Missouri* thundered toward the Kuwaiti coast. Marines of the 4th MEB conducted helicopter landing exercises on the islands of Bubiyan and Faylaka, north of Kuwait City. The Iraqi command, still expecting an amphibious assault, deployed a fourth division along the coast.

Throughout the night of the 25th and the following morning, aerial reconnaissance indicated that Iraqi forces were fleeing northward. More than 1,000 enemy vehicles jammed the highway that ran north to the Iraqi city of Basra. Marine aircraft from MAG-11 and MAG-33 pounded the area for more than six hours. A-6E Intruders, Hornets, and Harriers struck the enemy column again and again. Lieutenant-General Boomer called it "absolute carnage." By evening, news reports were airing footage of the burned-out wreckage of more than 1,000 Iraqi vehicles lying twisted along the highway. Elements of the press referred to it as "the Highway to Hell."

Elsewhere, the 1st Marine Division assaulted the Kuwait International Airport. They were met by tanks of the Iraqi 3rd Armored Division, including the Soviet-built T-72s. The Marines unleashed a firestorm from artillery, tanks, and airstrikes, destroying 320 tanks by nightfall. Included in the destruction were 70 of the T-72s. The long-pondered question of tank superiority had finally been answered, the Marine M60A1 having gone head-to-head with the Soviet-built vehicle. The 2nd Marine Division, which had thrown back an attack from armored personnel carriers early in the morning, now moved to cut off any Iraqis attempting to flee. The Marines and the Tiger Brigade secured the city of

Right: Gunnery Sergeant Charles Restifo gives a sack of grain to an elderly Somali man during Operation Restore Hope. More than half a million Somalis died of starvation before the massive relief operation was mounted.

Al Jahra and seized the high ground of Mutla Ridge. Another 166 Iraqi tanks were knocked out of action. Early on the morning of February 27, the 1st Marine Division secured Kuwait International Airport and prepared for a passage of lines. The Arab Joint Forces Command would enter Kuwait City. A Marine Recon unit, however, dirty and unshaven from extended time in the field, returned to the U.S. Embassy. The American flag still flew proudly. The following day, that flag was replaced by a larger one, which had flown in Vietnam. For Marines, past and present, it was a day to remember.

As the Iraqi war effort disintegrated before the Allied forces, President Bush ordered a cease-fire. The war had lasted for 100 hours. It had cost the lives of 24 Marines, and another 92 had been wounded. For the Iraqis, the price was much, much higher. The Marines had destroyed 1,040 enemy tanks, 608 armored personnel carriers, 432 artillery pieces, and 5 missile sites. Some 1,500 Iraqi troops had been killed and well over 20,000 taken prisoner by Marines of the I MEF. Said historian Robert Moskin,

> "The Marines' assault had originally been labeled a 'supporting attack.' It became the heart of the ground war. … Desert Storm was an enormous exercise that tested the Marines' newest technologies, prepositioning logistics and warmaking esprit (which used to be called fighting spirit). The Corps had no opportunity to prove it was different, but with overwhelming mobility and firepower, it proved once more in battle that it is as good as they come."

A few short months later, Marines were again called to duty abroad. This time they went not to do battle, but to provide humanitarian assistance. On April 30, a cyclone struck the

Above: Three Marines from the 3rd Battalion of the 11th Marines escort a Somali man from the scene of a riot in Mogadishu during Operation Restore Hope.

The Marines' assault had originally been labeled a "supporting attack." It became the heart of the ground war... The Corps ... proved once more in battle that it is as good as they come.

Below: Marines take cover from sniper fire in Mogadishu. The Marine in front carries an M16A2 rifle with an M203 grenade launcher attached.

southern coast of Bangladesh, ravaging the country. Winds reached 145 mph. (233 km/h). A wall of water 20 ft. (6 m) high crashed into the coast, killing 100,000 people. It was estimated that as many as one million Bangladeshi were homeless. While relief came pouring into the country, the infrastructure was so badly damaged that the government of Bangladesh was unable to distribute the desperately needed supplies. On May 11, plans for a humanitarian relief mission, originally codenamed Operation Productive Effort, were approved. The 5th Marine Expeditionary Brigade, on its way home from the Persian Gulf, was diverted to the Bay of Bengal. Other units assigned to Productive Effort included a Special Forces team, Army Blackhawk helicopters, Naval vessels, a detachment of Seabees, and Air Force transport planes.

Relief Operations

On May 14, 1991, full-scale relief operations began. The Bangladeshi referred to those involved in the effort as "angels from the sea." Three days later, Operation Productive Effort became Operation Sea Angel. Over the course of the next two weeks, thousands of tons of supplies were distributed. Much-needed water purification units arrived, and teams attached to the 5th MEB Medical Civic Action Program treated thousands. An estimated 38 tons (38.6 tonnes) of medical supplies were delivered to those in need. In all, more than a million Bangladeshi were helped through Operation Sea Angel. The relief effort officially ended on June 15.

While Marines of the 5th MEB provided humanitarian assistance in Bangladesh, other Marines returned to Iraq in Operation Provide Comfort. After the resounding defeat of his forces by the Allied coalition, Saddam Hussein focused his power against dissident groups within the borders of Iraq. In the mountainous northern regions of the country, the Kurds were driven from their homes by Iraqi tanks, artillery, and helicopter gunships. Hundreds of thousands of Kurds fled into the mountains or across the border into Turkey. Disease and starvation proved as deadly as Hussein's strong-arm tactics. More than 1,000 Kurds died each day.

An international relief effort was launched under the command of Army Lieutenant-General John M. Shalikashvili. The relief force was to consist of 21,000 troops from the U.S., as well as France, Italy, the Netherlands, Spain, and Great Britain. On April 14, the 24th Marine Expeditionary Unit was ordered to the border between Iraq and Turkey. After landing in Iskenderun, Turkey, the Marines established a forward support base in Silopi. On April 20, Company G, 8th Marines moved across the Iraqi border to secure an area near the town of Zakhu, where they were to erect a tent city to house the Kurds. Iraqi forces pulled back south of the city.

Within days, the international force erected thousands of tents, repaired an airfield to handle C-130 transports, and reopened a local hospital. The Kurds, however, remained terrified of Iraqi forces. It took several days for the refugees to move out of the mountains and into the tent city. Once this was accomplished, the Marines moved east to the city of Dahuk. The 24th MEU, reinforced with Army paratroopers, were ordered to clear the city of Iraqi forces. The Iraqis prudently withdrew and a second tent city was established. CH-46 Sea Knight helicopters of HMM-264 flew 150 sorties a day and delivered over one million pounds of supplies, including much food and water to the Kurdish refugees. By early June, the Kurds were encouraged to return to their homes and the relief effort was turned over to the United Nations High Commission on Refugees. On July 15, elements of the 2nd Battalion, 8th Marines became the last Allied troops to depart northern Iraq.

The next deployment, and the one that involved the largest number of Marines, was to the African nation of Somalia. In early 1991, as the ground war in the Persian Gulf was about to begin, Somalia descended into civil war. Three separate factions of Somali rebels fought government troops. On the morning of January 3, 1991, the U.S. Ambassador to Somalia alerted Washington that rebels had entered the compound of the U.S. embassy. He requested immediate evacuation. By 02:45 hours the following day, two CH-53E Super Stallion helicopters of Marine Heavy Helicopter Squadron 461 took off from the amphibious transport *Trenton*. Aboard were 51 men of the 1st Battalion, 2nd Marines and

Above: Marine Corps artist Burton Moore depicts Marines fighting in the streets of Mogadishu on February 24. Three Marines were wounded in an outbreak of violence that began with the holy month of Ramadan.

a SEAL team. Upon landing, part of the force secured the perimeter of the embassy, while the rest went into the streets of Mogadishu to rescue stranded Americans and other foreign nationals. The helicopters departed with 62 evacuees aboard. On January 5, ten CH-46 Sea Knights helicopters off the *Guam* continued the operation. As armed rebels scaled the walls of the U.S. compound, the helicopters lifted off, leaving Somalia having rescued a total of 281 people. By 1992, however, the Marines were ordered to return to the embattled African nation. The Somali President had fled and the country descended into chaos.

Famine plagued the population, and more than 500,000 Somalis starved to death before an international relief effort was organized. On August 18, 1992, President Bush announced that U.S. forces would take part in Operation Provide Relief. Under the command of Brigadier-General Frank Libutti, a joint task force commenced an emergency airlift of food supplies into Somalia.

Unfortunately, the people of Somalia continued to starve. With the country in such a state of political turmoil, the relief supplies were not distributed. In early December, Bush announced that U.S. troops would enter Somalia to oversee the distribution of food and supplies. On December 9, 1992, in the opening of Operation Restore Hope, Marines of the 15th MEU came ashore in Mogadishu. Port facilities and the airport were secured and the U.S. embassy reoccupied. Relief convoys were sent to the cities of Baidao, Kismayo, and Bardera. These convoys moved under heavy combined arms support. Once in the cities, Marines conducted patrols, confiscated weapons, even raided suspected guerrillas, often coming under fire from snipers or "technicals"—trucks mounted with automatic weapons, manned by various rebel groups. Said Brigadier-General Edwin Simmons, "Marine veterans of Haiti, Santo Domingo, Nicaragua, even Viet Nam, would have found it all quite familiar."

Above: Sergeant Brian R. Vig is awarded the Bronze Star for valor in Somalia by General Carl Mundy, then Commandant of the Marine Corps.

In early January 1994, the systematic withdrawal of Marine forces began. A United Nations force, including U.S. Army elements, was scheduled to assume the relief operation. There was, however, increased fighting in the city of Mogadishu. The Marines began searching for caches of arms. Their role, to be neutral and provide humanitarian assistance, was, once again, changing. A patrol from the 3rd Battalion, 11th Marines was ambushed. As the withdrawal continued, more Marines were killed or wounded by sniper fire. In February, the Islamic holy month of Ramadan brought increased violence in Mogadishu. Six Marines were wounded in the fighting. Finally, on May 4, the last Marines departed Somalia. The troubles, however, continued for those American forces who were remaining in the war-torn country. In early October, 18 U.S.

soldiers were killed and another 75 wounded in a fierce street battle that raged for two days. By March 24, all American forces were withdrawn from Somalia.

A year later, the United Nations requested U.S. aid in evacuating its besieged troops from the volatile African nation. Marine Lieutenant-General Anthony Zinni assumed command of forces for Operation United Shield. Marines of the 13th MEU proceeded to relieve Italian, Pakistani, and Bangladeshi forces in Somalia. There were 27 firefights before the operation was concluded, but the Marines sustained no casualties. With guns leveled at a mob of Somalis, they boarded transports and departed.

Operation Uphold/Support Democracy

Closer to home, events in Haiti were also a cause for concern. Since 1993, the U.S. had considered intervening to oust Lieutenant-General Raoul Cedras, commander of the Haitian Army and virtual dictator of the Caribbean nation. Cedras had overthrown the elected government of Jean-Bertrand Aristide two years earlier. Thousands of Haitians attempted to flee the country and the heavy-handed tactics of the military regime. Operation Uphold/Support Democracy was planned, with the intention of returning Aristide to the presidency. It was to be a joint mission. Landings by both Army and Marine units were scheduled for September 19, 1994. A peace commission consisting of former

Above: Marines of Fox Company, 2nd Battalion, 2nd Marines take aim at police headquarters in Grand Riviere, Haiti. Civilians gather in support of the Marines during Operation Uphold Democracy in 1994.

Above: Crowds cheer as Marines patrol during Operation Uphold Democracy. This pen and ink drawing is the work of Marine Corps artist Charles Grow.

president Jimmy Carter, retired General Colin Powell, and Senator Sam Nunn successfully convinced Cedras not to oppose the American landing and to leave Haiti.

The Army's XVIII Airborne Corps moved into the capital city of Port-au-Prince on the morning of the 19th. The following day, Marines of the Special Purpose Marine Air-Ground Task Force Caribbean, compromised of the 2nd Battalion, 2nd Marines and the reinforced Marine Medium Helicopter Squadron 264, landed on the northern shore of Haiti. Colonel Thomas S. Jones ordered his Marines to sweep the town of Cap Haitien. On the night of September 24, a squad of Marines encountered a group of Haitian military police, long known for their strong-arm tactics. One of the MPs aimed his weapon at the Marines and was promptly shot. The remaining Haitians opened fire. In the ensuing, very brief firefight, ten of the MPs were killed. General Cedras was enraged and demanded the court-martial of the Marines. His demands were ignored and any remaining organization within the Haitian military disintegrated. By October 1, Army elements had arrived in Cap Haitien and the Marines re-embarked aboard the *Wasp* and *Nashville*. They remained stationed off the northern coast of Haiti until Aristide resumed the presidency in mid-October.

Throughout the remainder of the 1990s, analysts debated the future of the Marine Corps. Were battles likely to be global conflicts or small, localized wars? In 1995, General Charles C. Krulak became Commandant of the Marine Corps. He brought with him a solid belief that the approaching century would be a "century of chaos. It would present new threats; ethnic and religious conflicts, the availability and use of biological and chemical weapons as well as weapons of mass destruction." To prepare his Marines for meeting these threats, Krulak undertook new methods of training. The Warfighting Laboratory was established at Marine Base Quantico to explore new technologies. Whatever the new century held, Krulak was determined the Marine Corps would be ready to meet the challenge.

Throughout the remainder of the 1990s, analysts debated the future of the Marine Corps. Were battles likely to be global conflicts or small, localized wars?

September 11

That challenge came on the morning of September 11, 2001. The United States came under attack, and terror was the weapon of choice. Four airliners were hijacked by members of the Al-Qaeda terrorist network led by Saudi-born Osama bin Laden. Two of the planes smashed into the twin towers of the World Trade Center. They collapsed soon afterward. The third plane was flown into the Pentagon. A fourth was brought down in a field near Pittsburgh, Pennsylvania. Casualties numbered in the thousands. A shaken but resolute President George W. Bush announced that the United States was at war with terror. In Operation Enduring Freedom, the first target was the Al-Qaeda network and the Taliban government of Afghanistan, which supported the terrorist operation.

On September 28, the 15th MEU arrived in the Arabian Sea. Nine days later, after the Taliban refused to surrender Osama bin Laden, British and American warplanes struck targets in the Afghan cities of Kabul, Kandahar, and Jalalbad. As the airstrikes continued, 100 U.S. Special Forces mounted the first ground attack in the Afghan campaign. On October 19, a U.S. Army Blackhawk helicopter crashed on operations near the Afghan–Pakistani border. Elements of the 15th MEU came under enemy fire while attempting to recover the downed aircraft. Recovery of the Blackhawk was finally completed on the 24th. The following day, aircraft from Marine Fighter Attack Squadron-251 began strike missions from the USS *Roosevelt*.

By early November, Harriers from the 15th MEU completed their first strikes against Taliban command and control targets in southern Afghanistan. As forces of the Northern Alliance (a coalition of Afghans opposed to Taliban rule) captured the city of Mazar-i-Sharif, the presence of a second Marine Expeditionary Unit was requested. On November 11, the 26th MEU was ordered to the Arabian Sea. Within a few short days, its Harriers began flying support missions off the Bataan. On November 25, Marines of the 15th MEU seized Forward Operating Base Camp Rhino in southern Afghanistan, near Kandahar. Company C, 1st Battalion, 1st Marines was inserted into the area by helicopter, followed by Alpha Company in KC-130 aircraft. There were no shots fired. Their mission was to interdict enemy movement, and by early December, the Marines had substantially increased their air and land patrols across southern Afghanistan.

On December 11, Kilo Battery, 11th Marines re-entered the compound of the long-deserted U.S. Embassy in Kabul. Two days later, Marines entered Kandahar and secured the airfield. American officials declared that Al-Qaeda had been rendered ineffective, while

Below: Marines wearing flak vests and M85 helmets move through a crowd of Haitians. In the background an American flag is being waved by a member of the crowd.

The 4th Marine Expeditionary Brigade

In late September, 2001, General James L. Jones, Commandant of the Marine Corps, ordered the reactivation of the 4th Marine Expeditionary Brigade as an anti-terrorism unit. Under the command of Brigadier General Douglas V. O'Dell, the mission of the 4th MEB(AT) is to "deter, detect and defend" and to combat the threat of worldwide terrorism. In a ceremony held at Camp Lejeune, North Carolina, on October 29, the brigade was officially reactivated. The 4th MEB merges the existing anti-terrorism capabilities of the U.S. Marine Corps. It includes the Marine Security Force Battalion, the Marine Security Guard Battalion, and the Chemical and Biological Incident Response Force, which was formed in 1996 following the sarin gas attack in Tokyo. It also includes a newly created anti-terrorism battalion. That battalion has been formed from elements of the 1st Battalion, 8th Marines, the unit which lost 241 men in the suicide bombing of the Marine Barracks in Lebanon. During the reactivation ceremony, General Jones spoke of the remarkable history of the 4th Marine Expeditionary Brigade. Men of the brigade fought on the battlefields of World War I, in the jungles of Vietnam, on the sands of Desert Storm. Said General Jones,

"Now the 4th MEB is standing up again, this time to take on a new challenge in a new conflict, in a new reality. ... Our expeditionary culture, our warrior ethos, our espirit de corps and our unique teamwork capabilities define both the 4th MEB and the Marine Corps, and I guarantee that those characteristics will be highlighted and considered an invaluable resource for our nation as it fights and wins this war against those who hate America and its freedoms and its prosperity."

commanders of the Northern Alliance declared victory. While the Taliban had fallen, and a new Afghan provisional government—which was led by Hamid Karzai—had been formed, neither Al-Qaeda nor Taliban forces were completely destroyed.

Heavy fighting occurred in the Tora Bora region, a mountainous area pockmarked by caves, where Afghans had hidden successfully from Soviet invaders in the 1980s. Afghan soldiers, aided by U.S. air strikes, sought to rid the area of Taliban and Al-Qaeda fighters. By December 19, American commanders proposed using both Marines and Army forces to aid in the search. A week later, however, Pentagon officials announced that Marines would not be part of operations in Tora Bora. Instead, on December 31, U.S. Marines departed Kandahar to search for Taliban leader Mullah Mohammed Omar in the Baghran region of Afghanistan. He was not found. As the year 2001 drew to a close, the Marines prepared to turn Kandahar airport over to the Army's 101st Airborne Division. In the early months of 2002, Marine air continued to provide support for those American forces still on the ground in Afghanistan. In early March, Operation Anaconda was launched; it was the largest ground offensive of the war to date. An estimated 1,000 Taliban and Al-Qaeda fighters had attempted to regroup in the mountains near Gardez. American forces of the 101st Airborne Division and the 10th Mountain Division battled the enemy throughout several days. Marine Sea Cobras flew in support of that mission.

As the war in Afghanistan continues, and military experts and pundits alike debate where the war on terror will take American forces in the future, one certainty remains. The battlegrounds upon which Marines fight will be remembered just as are those of the past. Belleau Wood; the Argonne Forest; the jungles of Guadalcanal; the black sands of Iwo Jima; Seoul; the frozen hell of the Chosin Reservoir; Hue; Khe Sanh; The Rockpile; Lebanon; Panama; the Persian Gulf; Somalia—like a tolling bell, the names evoke memories of Marines who have served, and fought, and bled and died. Their sacrifices will not be forgotten. The real glory of the Marine Corps is to be found in the dedication, in the courage, in the actions of those Marines, and in the Marines who serve today. Said historian Alan Millett,

> "Ultimately, the once and future Corps depends ... on the labor and dedication of those obscure Americans who choose to serve their turn in the Fleet Marine Forces. The real Marine Corps is far removed from the Corps [that] tourists in Washington see when they attend the sunset parades on Tuesday in front of the Iwo Jima monument or on Friday at the Marine Barracks on '8th and Eye.' ... On any parade evening, as the rifles spin and the trumpets blare, other Marines prowl the piney woods of Camp Lejeune or the dusty ridges of Camp Pendleton as sweat pours into their camouflage utilities."

On any parade evening, still others might be engaging an enemy in a distant land, far from home, their service never taken for granted, and never forgotten.

Below: A map showing the many locations around the world the Marines have been called to during operations since the end of the Vietnam War in 1975.

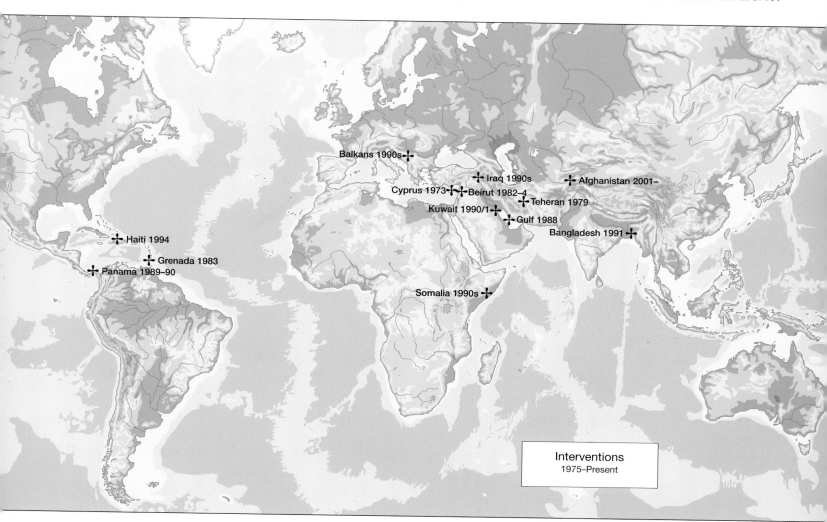

COMMANDANTS OF THE MARINE CORPS

1. SAMUEL NICHOLAS
28 Nov 1775—1781

2. WILLIAM WARD BURROWS
12 Jul 1798—6 Mar 1804

3. FRANKLIN WHARTON
7 Mar 1804—1 Sep 1818

4. ANTHONY GALE
3 Mar 1819—16 Oct 1820

5. ARCHIBALD HENDERSON
17 Oct 1820—6 Jan 1859

6. JOHN HARRIS
7 Jan 1859—12 May 1864*

7. JACOB ZEILIN
10 Jun 1864—31 Oct 1876

8. CHARLES McCAWLEY
1 Nov 1876—29 Jan 1891

9. CHARLES HEYWOOD
30 Jan 1891—2 Oct 1903

10. GEORGE ELLIOTT
3 Oct 1903—30 Nov 1910

11. WILLIAM BIDDLE
3 Feb 1911—24 Feb 1914

12. GEORGE BARNETT
25 Feb 1914—30 Jun 1920

13. JOHN A. LEJEUNE
1 Jul 1920—4 Mar 1929

14. WENDELL NEVILLE
5 Mar 1929—8 Jul 1930

15. BEN H. FULLER
9 Jul 1930—28 Feb 1934

16. JOHN H. RUSSELL
1 Mar 1934—30 Nov 1936

17. THOMAS HOLCOMB
1 Dec 1936—31 Dec 1943

18. ALEXANDER A. VANDEGRIFT
1 Jan 1944—31 Dec 1947

19. CLIFTON B. CATES
1 Jan 1948—31 Dec 1951

20. LEMUEL C. SHEPHERD, JR.
1 Jan 1952—31 Dec 1955

21. RANDOLPH McCALL PATE
1 Jan 1956—31 Dec 1959

22. DAVID M. SHOUP
1 Jan 1960—31 Dec 1963

23. WALLACE M. GREENE JR
1 Jan 1964—31 Dec 1967

24. LEONARD F. CHAPMAN, JR.
1 Jan 1968—31 Dec 1971

25. ROBERT E. CUSHMAN, JR
1 Jan 1972—30 Jun 1975

26. LOUIS H. WILSON
1 Jul 1975—30 Jun 1979

27. ROBERT H. BARROW
1 Jul 1979—30 Jun 1983

28. PAUL X. KELLEY
1 Jul 1983—30 Jun 1987

29. ALFRED M. GRAY, JR.
1 Jul 1987—30 Jun 1991

30. CARL E. MUNDY JR.
1 Jul 1991—30 Jun 1995

31. CHARLES C. KRULAK
1 Jul 1995—30 Jun 1999

32. JAMES L. JONES
1 Jul 1999 —

*(Major Augustus S. Nicholson, *the Adjutant and Inspector, served as Acting Commandant from 13 May—9 June 1864.*)

MARINE CORPS MEDAL OF HONOR RECIPIENTS

The Medal of Honor is the highest award for bravery that can be given to any individual in the United States.

ABRELL Charles G
ADAMS John M.
ADRIANCE Harry C.
AGERHOLM
  Harold C.
ANDERSON
  Richard A.
ANDERSON
  Richard B.
ANDERSON Jr. James
APPLETON Edwin N
AUSTIN Oscar P.
BAILEY Kenneth D.
BARBER William E.
BARKER Jedh C.
BARNUM, Jr.
  Harvey C.
BASILONE John

BAUER Harold W.
BAUGH William B.
BAUSELL Lewis K.
BEARSS Hiram I.
BERKELEY Randolph C
BERRY Charles J.
BINDER Richard
BOBO John P.
BONNYMAN, Jr.
  Alexander
BORDELON William J.
BOYDSTON Edwin J.
BOYINGTON Gregory
BROWN Charles
BRUCE Daniel D.
BUCKLEY Howard
BURKE Robert C.
BURNES James

BUSH Richard E.
BUTLER Smedley D**.
BUTLER Smedley D**.
BUTTON William R.
CADDY William R.
CAFFERATA, Jr. Hector
CAMPBELL Albert R.
CAMPBELL Daniel
CANNON George H.
CARR William L.
CARTER Bruce W.
CASAMENTO Anthony
CATLIN Albertus W.
CHAMBERS Justice M.
CHAMPAGNE David B.
CHRISTIANSON
  Stanley R.
CLAUSEN, Jr.

Raymond M.
COKER Ronald L.
COLE Darrell S.
COLEMAN John
COMMISKEY Henry A.
CONNEY James
CONNOR Peter S.
COOK Donald G.
COURTNEY, Jr. Henry
CREEK Thomas E.
CUKELA Louis
DAHLGREN John O.
DALY Daniel**
DALY Daniel**
DAMATO Anthony P.
DAVENPORT Jack A.
DAVIS Raymond G.
DAVIS Rodney M.

DAY James L.
DE LA GARZA, Jr.
  Emilio A.
DEBLANC Jefferson J.
DENIG Henry J.
DEWEY Duane E.
DIAS Ralph E.
DICKEY Douglas E.
DOUGHERTY James
DUNLAP Robert H.
DYER Jesse F.
DYESS Aquilla J.
EDSON Merritt A.
ELROD Henry T.
EPPERSON Harold G.
FARDY John P.
FIELD Oscar W.
FISHER Harry

FLEMING Richard E.
FOLEY Alexander J.
FORD, Jr. Patrick F.
FORSTERER Bruno A.
FOSS Joseph J.
FOSTER William A.
FOSTER Paul H.
FOX Wesley I.
FRANCIS Charles R.
FRANKLIN Joseph J.
FRY Isaac N.
FRYER Eli T.
GAIENNIE Louis R.
GALER Robert E.
GARCIA Fernando L.
GLOWIN Joseph A.
GOMEZ Edward
GONSALVES Harold
GONZALEZ Alfredo
GRAHAM James A.
GRAVES Terrence C.
GRAY Ross F.
GROSS Samuel
GUAGHAN Phillip
GUILLEN Ambrosio
GURKE Henry
HANNEKEN Herman H.
HANSEN Dale M.
HANSON Robert M.
HARREL William G.
HARVEY Harry
HAUGE Jr Louis J.
HAWKINS William D.
HEISCH William
HELMS John H.
HILL Frank
HILL Walter N.
HORTON William C.
HOWARD Jimmie E.
HOWE James D.
HUDSON Michael
HUGHES John A.
HULBERT Henry L .
HUNT Martin
IAMS Ross L.

JACKSON Arthur J.
JACOBSON Douglas T.
JANSON Ernest A.
JENKINS Jr Robert H.
JIMENEZ Jose F.
JOHNSON James E.
JOHNSON Ralph H.
JULIAN Joseph R.
KATES Thomas W.
KEARNEY Michael
KEITH Miguel
KELLOGG, Jr. Allan J.
KELLY John D.
KELLY John J.
KELSO Jack W.
KENNEMORE Robert S.
KINSER Elbert L.
KOCAK Matej
KRAUS Richard E.
KUCHNEISTER
   Herman W.
LA BELLE James D.
LEE Howard V.
LEIMS John H.
LEONARD Joseph
LITTLETON Herbert A.
LIVINGSTON James E.
LOPEZ Baldomero
LUCAS Jacklyn H.
LUMMUS Jack
MACKIE John F.*
MACNEAL Harry L.
MARTIN Harry L.
MARTIN James
MARTINI Gary W.
MASON Leonard F.
MATHIAS Clarence E.
MATTHEWS Daniel P.
MAUSERT III Frederick
MAXAM Larry L.
MCCARD Robert H.
MCCARTHY Joseph J.
MCGINTY III John J.
MCLAUGHLIN Alford
MCNALLY Michael L.

MCNAMARA Michael
MCTUREOUS, Jr.
   Robert M.
MILLER Andrew
MITCHELL Frank N.
MODRZEJEWSKI
   Robert J.
MONEGAN, Jr. Walter C.
MOORE Albert
MORGAN William D.
MORLAND Whitt L.
MORRIS John
MURPHY John A.
MURPHY Raymond G.
MURRAY William H.
MYERS Reginald R.
NEVILLE Wendell
   Cushing
NEW John D.
NEWLIN Melvin E.
NOONAN Jr. Thomas P.
NUGENT Christopher
O'BRIEN, Jr. George H.
O'MALLEY Robert E.
OBREGON Eugene A.
ORNDOFF Harry W.
OSTERMANN Edward
OVIATT Miles M.
OWENS Michael
OWENS Robert A.
OZBOURN Joseph W.
PAIGE Mitchell
PARKER Pomeroy
PAUL Joe C.
PERKINS, Jr. William T.
PETERS Lawrence D.
PFEIFER Louis F.
PHELPS Wesley
PHILLIPS Franklin J.
PHILLIPS George
PHILLIPS Lee H.
PHILLIPS Reuben J.
PHIPPS Jimmy W.
PITTMAN Richard A.
PLESS Stephen W.

POPE Everett P.
PORTER David D.
POWER John V.
POYNTER James I
PRENDERGAST
   Thomas F.
PRESTON Herbert I.
PROM William R.
PRUITT John Henry
PURVIS Hugh
QUICK John H.
RAMER George H.
RANNAHAN John
REASONER Frank S.
REEM Robert D.
REID George Croghan
ROAN Charles H.
ROANTREE James S.
ROBINSON Robert G.
ROUH Carlton R.
RUHL Donald J.
SCANNELL David J.
SCHILT Christian F.
SCHWAB Albert E.
SCOTT Joseph F.
SHIVERS John
SHOUP David M.
SHUCK, Jr. William E.
SIGLER Franklin E.
SILVA France
SIMANEK Robert E.
SINGLETON Walker K.
SITTER Carl L.
SKAGGS, Jr. Luther
SKINNER, Jr. Sherrod E.
SMEDLEY Larry E.
SMITH Albert J.
SMITH John L.
SMITH Willard M.
SORENSON Richard K.
SPROWLE David
STEIN Tony
STEWARD James A.
STEWART Peter
STOCKHAM Fred W.

SULLIVAN Edward
SUTTON Clarence E.
SWETT James E.
TALBOT Ralph
TAYLOR Karl G.
THOMAS Herbert J.
THOMASON Clyde
THOMPSON Henry A.
TIMMERMAN Grant F.
TOMLIN Andrew J.
TRUESDELL Donald L.
UPHAM Oscar J.
UPSHUR William P.
VANDEGRIFT
   Alexander
VANWINKLE Archie
VARGAS Jay R.
VAUGHN Pinkerston R.
VITTORI Joseph
WALKER Edward A.
WALSH Kenneth A.
WALSH William C.
WATKINS Lewis G.
WATSON Wilson D.
WEBER Lester W.
WEST Walter S.
WHEAT Roy M.
WILLIAMS Dewayne T.
WILLIAMS Ernest C.
WILLIAMS Hershel W.
WILSON Alfred M.
WILSON Harold E.
WILSON Robert L.
WILSON Jr. Louis H.
WINANS Roswell
WINDRICH William G.
WITEK Frank P.
WORLEY Kenneth L.
YOUNG Frank A.
ZION William

*   First Marine recipient of the
      Medal of Honor

**Awarded the Medal of Honor
      twice for two separate actions

INDEX

PICTURE CREDITS

Foreword image: TRH Pictures / M. Roberts

Aerospace Publishing: 96, 107. **De Agostini UK:** 108, 164 (b), 194, 201, 212 (t). **John Bachelor:** 41. **Defense Visual Information Center:** 222, 225, 226, 230 (both), 233, 236, 238, 240, 241, 242, 244, 245, 247. **General Douglas MacArthur Memorial Foundation:** 102, 118, 121, 122, 129, 130, 152. **Marine Corps Art Collection:** 10, 11, 12, 13, 14, 15, 16, 17, 18 (t), 20, 23, 26 (b), 32, 33, 34 (b), 36, 39, 48, 49 (t), 50, 51, 52, 57, 58, 60, 67, 70, 76 (t), 82, 83, 92, 98, 106 (b), 116, 125, 127, 136, 139, 143, 168, 171, 173 (t), 182, 193, 197 (t), 199, 204, 209 (b), 213, 216, 223, 224, 227 (both), 228, 231, 237, 239, 243, 246. **Marine Corps Research Center:** 22, 34 (t), 88, 93, 99, 109, 181. **Navy Art Collection:** 87, 95, 111, 113, 120, 149, 166, 209 (t). **Tim Ripley:** 248. **Sam Houston State University Library:** 40. **TRH Pictures:** 8–9, 27, 30–31, 43, 44, 47, 54–55, 59, 61, 66 (b), 74, 79, 80–81, 104–105, 110, 112, 132, 146, 147, 159, 160–161, 169 (t), 176 (b), 186, 187 (b), 219, 220–221, 229, 235. **US National Archives:** 18 (b), 21, 25, 26 (t), 28, 29, 35, 37, 38, 42, 45, 49 (b), 53, 56, 62, 63, 64, 65, 66 (t), 68, 69, 72, 73, 75, 76 (b), 77, 78, 84–85, 86, 89, 90, 94, 97, 100–101, 106 (t), 114, 115, 117, 119, 123, 124, 126, 128, 133, 134, 138, 140, 142, 144, 145, 150, 151, 153, 154, 156–157, 158, 162, 163, 164 (t), 165, 167, 169 (b), 170, 172, 173 (b), 174, 176 (t), 177, 178, 179, 180 (both), 183, 184, 185, 187 (t), 188, 189, 190–191, 192, 195, 196, 197 (b), 198, 200, 202, 203, 206, 207, 208, 210, 211, 212 (b), 214, 215, 217, 218 (both).

Maps by Patrick Mulrey